Wishing you success
in your business venture

The Honeycomb Group
020 8390 8850

June 2000

Manual of
SALES
Negotiation

By the same author
How to Recruit and Select Successful Salesmen (2nd edition)
Making Effective Presentations (audio manual)
Marketing Planning for the Pharmaceutical Industry
Motivating your Sales Force
Negotiating Profitable Sales (handbook for the Video Arts film of the same title)
The Sales Presentation (with Peter Kirby)
Training Salesmen on the Job (2nd edition)

Manual of
SALES
Negotiation

John Lidstone

Gower

First published 1977 by Teakfield Limited as *Negotiating Profitable Sales*

This edition published 1991 by Gower.

Gower Publishing Company Limited
Gower House
Croft Road
Aldershot
Hants GU11 3HR
England

Gower Publishing Company
Old Post Road
Brookfield
Vermont 05036
USA

British Library Cataloguing in Publication Data

Lidstone, John 1929–
    Manual of sales negotiation.
    1. Salesmanship
    I. Title   II. Lidstone, John 1929–. Negotiating profitable sales
    658.85

Library of Congress Cataloging-in-Publication Data

Lidstone, John, 1929–
    Manual of sales negotiation / John Lidstone.
        p.   cm.
    Rev. ed. of: Negotiating profitable sales. 1977.
    Includes bibliographical references and index.
    1. Selling.   2. Negotiation in business.   I. Title
    HF5438.25.L5   1990
    658.85—dc20   90–19860
                                                    CIP

ISBN 0–566–02788–7

Contents

List of figures · vi
List of tables · vii
Preface · ix
Acknowledgements · xiii
Introduction: Selling today · 1

Part I **Financial techniques in selling**
1 Improving business performance · 9
2 Improving customers' profits · 27
3 Costing as an aid to sales · 39
Appendix: Financial skills checklists · 49

Part II **The negotiation process**
Introduction to Part II
4 The nature of negotiation · 57
5 Preparing to negotiate · 77
6 Calculating the costs of concessions · 91
7 Buyer behaviour · 119
8 Conducting negotiations · 127
Appendix: A planning format for major customers · 141

Part III **The skills of negotiating**
Introduction to Part III · 175
9 Effective listening · 177
10 Accurate interpretation of body language · 185
11 Effective presentation · 215
12 Developing negotiating skills · 241

Part IV **Case studies**
Introduction to Part IV · 251
Case study I: A traditionally trained salesman selling to a highly skilled buyer · 253
Case study II: A salesman trained in negotiating techniques negotiating with a trained buyer · 267
Case study III: A negotiation between two skilled negotiators in the fashion industry · 283

Recommended reading and viewing · 301

Index · 303

List of Figures

1.1   The business cycle · 13
1.2   Balance sheet · 14
1.3   Balance sheet (summary): 'account' format · 14
1.4   Balance sheet (summary): 'net asset' format · 15
1.5   Profit and loss account · 16
1.6   Return on capital employed formula · 19
1.7   Return on capital employed formula for a national ware-housing and distribution company · 20
2.1a Customer financial needs analysis form · 32
2.1b Equipment required · 34/5
3.1   Model break-even chart · 41
3.2   Example A · 43
3.3   Example B · 44
3.4   Example C · 45
3.5   Example D · 47
4.1   Stepping stones in a sale · 60
4.2   Buy phases · 64
4.3   Questioning techniques · 67
4.4   Questioning and presentation · 67
4.5   Identifying the gap · 74
4.6   Selling versus negotiation call – different ingredients · 75
A.1   Strategic decision options · 153
11.1 Meeting planning and format · 219
11.2 How the human communication system operates · 220
11.3 Presentation planning chart · 238
11.4 Effective speaking plan · 239
11.5 Effective speakers dos and don'ts · 239
12.1 Negotiating skills: personal training needs analysis · 242
12.2 Negotiation observation and evaluation sheet: phase 1 · 246
12.3 Negotiation observation and evaluation sheet: phase 2 · 247

List of tables

1.1   Key profitability ratios · 18
6.1   Acquisition/disposal of pastoral property · 109
6.2   Purchase of grain/livestock · 112
6.3   Lease of abattoirs and/or boning room · 112
6.4   Sale of meat products · 114
6.5   Illustration of costing control · 115
6.6   Negotiation principles: checklist · 116
7.1   Customer organization profiles: checklist · 124
7.2   Negotiation strategy checklist · 125
7.3   Checklist for negotiation planning · 126
8.1   The contract between buyer and supplier in the plant. Soft drinks situation: supplies · 132
8.2   The contract between buyer and seller in foodchain. Typical soft drink situation · 135
8.3   Negotiation tactics: checklist · 137
8.4   Negotiation details: checklist · 138
8.5   Negotiation warnings: checklist · 139

Preface

Negotiation, or the art of bargaining, is, like selling, as old as human history. Yet in 1977, when I wrote *Negotiating Profitable Sales*, on which this present manual is based, very little published material and no training films were available to help negotiators to develop their craft. In the intervening years, negotiation has received much closer attention, reflecting its importance for every organization, whether business and industry or in government, utilities and local authorities. Negotiation is a most difficult art to master. It is also one that can make or lose more money more quickly for your organization than any other.

The nature of the selling job and the nature and scale of the transactions handled today demand that, to be effective, anyone selling has to be a good negotiator. Selling has traditionally been seen as the process through which the individual seller persuades the individual buyer to purchase products, services or ideas. The proposition presented by the seller has usually been a fixed, invariable one. In order to succeed in selling such propositions, sales personnel have, down through the years, been trained in a wide variety of persuasive communication techniques. The need for selling skills has not diminished, as I demonstrate in the manual. What needs to be understood and recognized are the circumstances in which the parallel and subtle skill of negotiation is required to ensure that the business gained is profitable business.

The environment in which selling takes place is changing very rapidly. The characteristics of the market place in which all organizations operate have been changed dramatically in the last ten years by the emergence and growth of the big buyer. More and more commercial and industrial sectors are becoming dominated by fewer companies. Takeovers and mergers bear ample testimony to this development. Our daily newspapers and television bring frequent examples of this trend from banking and insurance to the giant food and pharmaceutical manufacturers, hotel and supermarket chains, local and national newspapers and advertising agencies. These large buyers face more complex and competitive conditions in their markets. Consequently, your major customers are more complex to sell to, more demanding, more professional in their approach to buying and above all much more aware of the financial implications of each buying decision they reach.

These buyers who are larger in size but less numerous represent for many suppliers over 70 per cent of their business. So the defection of only one of them can be costly to your company in terms not just of volume but of profitability. Because such customers are the cornerstones of prosperity, of profit, and of your own selling job, you need to master much more than the basic selling skills and techniques to survive and compete successfully for worthwhile business now and in the years ahead.

The effective seller must be skilled not only in the art of selling but also in the techniques of handling these professional larger buyers. He or she must also recognize that they operate in a market place not just of national but of international competition.

Purpose of the manual

This manual is designed to help the advanced seller to develop his or her knowledge and skill in three key areas of activity:

- How to understand the financial aspects of the work in relation to major customers. On the basis of this knowledge he or she must be capable of ensuring that an order or flow of orders obtained is profitable. In far too many examples I have analysed, a company's top twenty accounts were the least profitable simply because the company did not know what the costs of doing the business were. And if they did know they failed to negotiate appropriate concessions with the buyer to offset them. This manual will show how to use financial knowledge and techniques when selling to these bigger buyers.

- How to prepare, in far more detail than is usually done, strategies for each of these major customers so that all the resources of the company can be harnessed to achieve short- and long-term customer satisfaction at a profit. New material showing you how to calculate values and costs of concessions has been included, together with a comprehensive planning format which is now used by the key account salespeople in more than 52 countries.

- How to negotiate with these major customers to the point of obtaining mutually satisfactory long-term business rather than using persuasive techniques for the occasional 'your turn this time around' type of order. Remember that many of these buyers have no option but to purchase from the supplier who can guarantee to supply on a long-term basis. But the key to success, if such business is to be worthwhile, is the terms on which the contract to trade is agreed.

Who should read the manual

This manual has been compiled for the benefit of three groups of people:

- Firstly, all important account sales personnel responsible for selling to large buyers. Their titles may range from managing director or key account executive to senior salesman. For them the manual will function as a self-teaching text and practical source of reference when planning major customer strategies.

- Secondly, sales managers, marketing managers and those sales training managers responsible for the management and development of these key account sales personnel, I hope that for them the manual will provide a practical and realistic means of developing their own and their sales colleagues' skills in planning, in finance and in sales negotiation.

- Thirdly, people working in negotiating positions in government and other organizations as well as non-sales personnel in business and industry who have to negotiate: for example, accountants and auditors, contractors and office managers, personnel managers and union officials.

Structure

The manual is in four parts:

- *Part I* examines the market place in which salespeople operate and the changes that have led to the emergence of the larger companies and more professional buyers and consequently the necessity for sellers to be fluent and knowledgeable in new areas of skill, attitudes and expertise; the need for financial awareness in selling so that sales staff can direct their efforts towards the profits of their valuable customers and those of their own companies; the effects of costs and break-even in a business.

- *Part II* concentrates on the ingredients of negotiation: understanding the differences between selling and negotiation; preparing to negotiate; buyer behaviour and motivation; the strategy and tactics of negotiation.

- *Part III* contains new material relating to the social skills involved in negotiation: effective listening, learning and communication; non-verbal communication and body language; making effective presentations. The final chapter in this part provides guidance for line managers and training managers on how to develop the negotiation skills of their key account sales personnel to the point of practical application on the job.

- *Part IV* brings together the case studies presented in the original book and also two new case studies from successful training films. Together they show, in a dramatic way, how the concepts and techniques described in the text can be applied.

Throughout this manual there are planning formats, checklists, diagrams and illustrations which I hope will enable those who do not claim to be numerate to be able to grasp the arithmetic of finance (which is a subject far too important to be left to accountants). There are also numerous 'real life' examples to help negotiators in every type of business and organization to use this book as a source of reference in planning profitable negotiating for their customers and for their own companies — and for themselves in personal negotiations such as buying a house or reviewing the terms of a new appointment.

Finally, I do hope that those who use the techniques explained in the manual will derive enjoyment as well as success from their negotiations, because business for profit alone is not much fun. But, like all successes, successful negotiations are the outcome of thorough and meticulous preparation before each meeting and the astute perception and weighing up of all the variables and how they can be adapted and refined.

JOHN LIDSTONE

Acknowledgements

It is now over 21 years since my colleagues and I at Marketing Improvements were first asked to research and develop the organization structures, systems and training programmes needed by companies and multinationals such as Corn Products, JCB, Lever Brothers, ICI, Shell International and many others, in order to equip their staff with the necessary skills for negotiating successfully with their major customers and suppliers.

Since then we have undertaken similar assignments for companies large and small in every branch of commerce and industry throughout the world, as well as for government departments, local authorities and public utilities, public and private hospitals, and charities.

To all of these organizations, too many to name, and to the MI consultants who have worked on them, I express my thanks for validating, refining and developing the techniques included in this manual.

I would like to thank especially Sir Antony Jay and his erstwhile colleagues at Video Arts for making the two-part film, *Negotiating profitable sales*, based on the first edition I wrote of this manual. As a result of this film package, many hundreds of organizations and thousands of people have been able to develop their knowledge and sharpen up their skills in negotiation.

To David Wilson and his team at Yorkshire Television, who produced the Open College negotiation series, *Reaching agreement*, and to Ric Vanes who wrote the shooting script, my thanks for allowing me to reproduce an edited version of *Own label* in this manual.

Finally I should like to thank Sir John Harvey-Jones for permission to quote from his thought-provoking book, *Making it happen*.

J.L.

Introduction: Selling today

The development of the 'marketing concept' approach to business – the creation of customers and keeping them satisfied profitably by finding out what they require and then making it, rather than by the traditional method of making things, and then trying to sell them – has produced some revolutionary changes in the market place, in the attitudes of manufacturers to their customers and suppliers and in the role of the sales force.

But this customer-facing marketing concept – a new label for a very old recipe for commercial success, as blacksmiths, portrait painters and bespoke tailors will testify – however imaginatively and vigorously pursued, no longer answers the problem of how to survive and prosper.

What one company decides to do can also be done by others since modern technology, new materials and new inventions have enabled national and international companies to adopt the marketing concept. In addition they are able to exploit the repertoire of marketing, production and distribution techniques available to all in providing custom-built products and services at prices people can afford and be persuaded to pay. The knowledge, skills and information among competing manufacturers, large and small, throughout the world today are similar. What one company spends millions of pounds, dollars or francs on over several years and invents today others can imitate tomorrow; so another fact of commercial life in this last quarter of the twentieth century which companies have to accept is that imitation is quicker and cheaper than invention and far less risky. Frequently, companies even spurn to copy and instead take over the source of competitive inventions. Similarly, the costs companies incur in producing and distributing their products and services tend to be alike, as are their ultimate selling prices to the buyer.

The marketing environment

The environment in which manufacturers, commercial and service companies operate and compete with each other is characterized by three factors.

1 Similarity of products and services

The products and services offered by competing companies tend to be similar if not identical in appearance and advantages. In many markets, such as food, paper tissues and paint, a brand leader faces

1

a similar product on an opposite shelf in supermarket, self-service and cash-and-carry outlets. Except that a twin has 'own-label' packaging, it is the same product, made by the same company. The same duplication is discernible in the basic design of mass-produced cars from Britain, Europe and Japan. In the electrical gadget field, the only difference between transistor radios, pocket calculators and tape recorders in similar price brackets is the manufacturer's name. Take the back off and all share a common origin and source of cheaply produced printed circuitry. The catalogue of identical products is endless, reflecting the age-old ability to imitate rather than to invent. Services such as banking, insurance and packaged holidays follow similar patterns.

2 Similarity in prices and discounts

The prices charged by companies for similar products and services also tend to be alike. New and/or demonstrably superior products and services are charged at a premium until a competitor enters the field and starts to encroach on sales. Then prices are reduced. The result is that with few notable exceptions the majority of products and services we buy – clothing, detergents, food, petrol, banking, insurance, estate agency – those offered by competing companies tend to be alike in product and service benefits and in the prices we pay for them or in the discounts we are allowed if we are the distributor. And this is true whether we are marketing in Lisbon or London, in Bangkok or Brussels, since multinational companies develop worldwide specifications for their products and parity of standards.

3 Presentation to the customer

The main difference between competing manufacturers, suppliers of services, supermarket chains and multiple stores is in the way they communicate with their customers. It is in this area where the greatest control and direct influence can be brought to bear. In the presentation and pricing of products; in the services and ideas offered to the customer or consumer by means of public relations, advertising and publicity, direct mail, telephone selling, exhibitions and the sales force.

However good all the other methods of persuasive communication are, in the majority of companies the bulk of the presentational effort and persuasion is carried out by the sales force. Their importance can be judged by the fact that in some markets the only difference between competing companies is the relative quality of their sales forces. In markets such as agricultural implements and construction machinery, banking and life assurance, and office equipment, the buyer's decision is more often than not determined by who calls on him, what is said to him and how it is said. Now, more than ever, a salesman's *authority* and *ability* to *make* and *take* negotiating decisions without reference back to his supervisors is increasingly evident. In many markets, a company relies on its sales force to gain advantage over competitors.

Ironically, the grouping of larger companies into competition with one another, the ease of imitation despite patent laws, the very success of companies to sell their products and services through the efforts of their sales forces, has resulted in other developments which are changing the attitude and role of buyers of products and thus the nature of the selling job.

The changing nature of the selling job

Four major changes are affecting the role and the importance of the sales force.

1 The growth of multinational companies

Since 1970 the development of multinational companies whose operations span the globe has accelerated. The products of American, British, Dutch, French, German, Japanese, Swiss, and other international companies, are manufactured in nearly every major country by their own factories or under licence. The European Economic Community has already changed the approach of many capital-goods producers, chemical manufacturers, tyre and rubber combines, and retail stores, towards their markets.

2 Companies are tending to become larger in size but less numerous

Takeovers and mergers bear ample and almost daily testimony to this development, frequently encouraged by governments. Before 1939 there were over 40 motor-car manufacturers in the United Kingdom. Today there are only four important ones and even the future of these cannot be predicted.

In brewing, in food manufacturing, in oil and petroleum, sugar refinery and supermarketing, companies are tending to become larger in size but fewer in number. Such a development means that no supplying company and, in particular, no salesman can hope to retain the business of giant organizations unless product quality and service is sustained. For the salesman and saleswoman, whose job it is to develop and maintain business with such giant organizations, the implications are stark. 'I was just passing by so I thought I would pop in to see if there was any business' is thankfully rarely heard by customers when salesmen call on them. No less dangerous is the attitude of any salesman to a call that failed in its objective, either through lack of planning, seeing the wrong buyer, discussing the wrong product to meet a particular customer requirement, or failing to understand the customer's profit or cost problems: 'Oh well you can't win them all. I will get the order next time round'. There will not be a next time round for the salesman who has not done his homework before he calls on a customer.

This is true of more and more marketing situations. For example, two independent breweries were both taken over by an important hotel group. Before that takeover there were three independent groups of buyers upon whom the salesman of products and services could call and sell, ranging from the supply of bottles, caps, hotel cutlery and crockery, food, industrial cleaning machines, bulk tankers, etc. Now there is either one buyer or one buying committee. This committee will not convene nor give a second interview to any salesman who has evidently not studied their needs. The salesman has to develop relevant plans and solutions to meet and satisfy them in terms of improving profit opportunities, reducing costs, product quality, pricing and follow-up service, and technical advice.

Manufacturing companies also have to market and to advertise their products to help sell them and so need effective, creative and, above all, efficient, advertising agents to help them wisely invest their money on promotion.

Advertising agencies have experienced a marked decline in profit margins and so every account must be profitable. If, due to mistakes, an advertising agency has to spend more time on an account worth, say, £100 000 a year, it could cost them more money to service it than it is actually worth.

3 Buyers are becoming increasingly powerful

Because of the concentration of strength, buyers in larger companies, manufacturers and retail distribution chains of products, services or ideas, whose purchases represent a major percentage of the supplying company's turnover and profits, are becoming much more powerful. Each purchasing decision they make, the size of the orders they can give, the effect they can have upon the subsequent purchases of products, can have dramatic repercussions upon every facet of the supplying business, from cash flow, production, distribution, and finally even to the levels of employment. The stock-control decisions made by Marks & Spencer demonstrated this upon some of their suppliers; Corahs is no longer trading.

Matching this increased power and influence, these buyers are becoming much more knowledgeable and well informed about the *products and manufacturing processes of their suppliers*; in *finance* and the financial effects on profitability of their buying decisions, particularly when they buy to re-sell; in *negotiating* the purchase of supplies, and above all in their own *marketing* and *selling*.

An electronics group, employing over 70 000 people, one of the world's largest car manufacturers and a Swiss chemical group have expanded the education and skills development of their purchasing officers. They are not only trained to buy but are given selling courses alongside their own company's sales force so that they have a better understanding of the selling techniques used by salesmen who call on them.

4 Competition

Competition between these giant organizations is increasing to the point that, not only are they employing many more methods of presentation and communication (including telephone selling), but they are taking over their distributors or, alternatively, developing their own powerful distribution outlets so that they can control the factors that influence buyers' decisions.

The changing role of the sales force

The role and importance of the sales force is not lessened by factors of economic life and changes occurring in the market places in which a company operates. Far from it. The sales force will have a more decisive influence upon the success of marketing strategies and plans as their work becomes more specific. Companies have come to recognize that customers create a business; only by keeping them satisfied and by meeting their requirements can a company survive and prosper. If they do not others will.

This means that in order to deal with and take advantage of these changes, companies have continually to improve their methods of marketing and selling. Above all, they need to ensure that the sales force is *organized* to deal with these larger *key* buyers and has the relevant new knowledge and skills to plan and achieve *profitable* business with major market segments and important individual customers.

Customers are becoming more knowledgeable, not only about the products and services they buy or reject but *how to buy them*, which makes them far more critical of those who supply them. The salesmen who sell to them must be more professional. Whilst all commercial organizations seek a financial objective, the margins of error are now so narrow that salesmen will be needed as never before to perform a vital but changing function. Where once the results of selling were measured and rewarded in terms of the volume, units or tonnages, now they are being judged by the amount of profit produced. Where once the salesman was a jack of all trades, selling everything to every outlet or customer, he must now specialize in directing his selling skills to carefully selected markets and to significant buyers. The sales force and each member of it must be the spearhead and apex of a triangle through which more costly and tailored company resources flow.

New skills needed

All these factors make selling a much more creative job, providing opportunities for a new and more influential role in the company, based upon three principal skills:

1 Knowledge of the financial and operational needs of his own company and of the customer's business and how to apply that knowledge in his selling to major customers.
2 Knowledge and ability to plan long-term, mutually profitable customer strategies and to implement those strategies and plans successfully.
3 Knowledge, skill and expertise to negotiate profitable business with key accounts.

The principles, knowledge, methods and techniques salesmen and saleswomen can use to develop their skills and expertise in these three areas – *finance, planning* and *sales negotiation* – are set out in the following chapters.

Part I

Financial techniques in selling

1

Improving business performance

In running a business both buyer and seller are subject to the same commercial realities and disciplines. Profit is the ultimate objective, although there may be many other goals which individual companies seek to achieve. But profit, how much is made and over what period, is the yardstick by which commercial and industrial companies are judged by those who own them – the shareholders. 'PROFIT', as William Howlett of Consolidated Foods Corporation aptly put it in 1966, stands for: 'Proper Return on Funds Invested Today and Tomorrow'. Buyers are buying profit opportunities, whilst those who sell to them do so in order to make a profit.

But until recently salesmen have not been deeply involved in or even aware of – assuming that their companies or customers allow them to be – the overall effect of their products and services upon the profitability of a customer's business. Today, the need to understand the principles of finance and how to apply and use them in selling is essential for a number of reasons:

1 Customers buy products as a part of their management task of helping them to achieve their profit objectives. Buyers are becoming more efficient in running their companies and more astute in their buying as competition for their business and competition in the markets to which they sell increase.

2 As companies, through takeovers and mergers, grow larger in size but fewer in number, so the orders that are placed become larger; but the buying points are becoming fewer in most industries.

3 Because of the speed with which even newly launched and successful products can be copied, resulting in profit opportunities being slashed overnight by competition, companies have had to become expert in financial controls and management accounting.

4 For this reason, buyers need far more objective proof of financial gain, as a result of their major buying decisions, from those who sell to them.

5 The application of financial techniques in marketing and the routine use of common standards and controls by which companies can measure their performance week by week, month by month and year by year.

6 The increasingly complex decisions customers have to make

about products and their relative value and benefits when so often superficially they look alike.

A sound knowledge of finance applied to selling will enable you to understand the changing needs of your customers' business. This will put you in a much better position to help make the best possible contribution to achieving both volume and profit goals for your main customers and for your own company.

Finance affects everyone in a business and should therefore be understood by everyone and not left solely to accountants. Too often in recent years non-financial people, particularly in marketing and in selling, have regarded finance as a mystical subject. In reality, as you shall see, it is relatively easy to acquire a practical and working knowledge and develop it as a selling skill on the job.

There are three main aspects of finance that you need to grasp:

1 The operation of finance in a business.
2 The measurement of business performance in financial terms.
3 The role of the sales force in achieving business results expressed in financial terms.

Let us examine these three aspects in detail and, through simple examples, familiarize ourselves with how money works.

The operation of finance in a business

All businesses, from the corner shop to the vast industrial corporations, supermarketing chains and financial institutions are governed by their ability to attract and use money and people to make profits.

The ingredients of commercial success thus depend upon the ability of the management of a business to use the resources they have obtained with the money they have attracted, in the most effective and efficient way. This can be in one or a combination of methods, for example by:

1 Making more sales.
2 Increasing the margin between costs and selling prices.
3 Increasing output in relation to costs (remember how, to their surprise, many British companies during the three-day week in the winter of 1973 produced as much as during a normal five-day working week).
4 Using less money to run the business (reducing the amount of reserve stocks and the amount of interest paid on money borrowed from the bank to finance such stocks).
5 Reducing production costs by replacing old, slow-working ma-

chinery by new plant able to produce twice as much in the same time as the old, etc.

So money provides the wherewithal to obtain the resources of people, machinery, raw materials and all the other requirements upon which profits are based. But it is not just creating resources that builds a business. The lubricant that makes a business run smoothly and profitably is the *flow of funds*. The salesman needs to understand the source of this flow, the nature and kinds of business activities which influence it and how the behaviour of these funds are recorded on paper.

Indeed it is by understanding such records and what they tell him that the salesman can make any plans to contribute to a customer's profit improvement. Figure 1.1 illustrates, in very simple terms, the process of attracting and using resources to generate profits.

Recording business performance

Money invested in a business exists in many forms: as plant and machinery; as raw materials; as work-in-progress and finished goods in warehouses; as goods and services sold to customers but not yet paid for.

In order to measure how successful the management of a business is in making the most effective use of these resources, it is essential to be able to record, in commonly understood financial terms, how a company is performing. The success or otherwise of management performance is usually expressed by means of financial accounts, of which the two most important are: the balance sheet and the profit and loss account. The law requires all limited companies to publish these accounts in a prescribed form at least annually. By this means, the proprietors of the company can see how their funds have been used and the profits (or losses) that have been made. The company's creditors or intending creditors can then judge the soundness of the business. What do these two financial statements tell you about a company?

1 A *balance sheet* is a statement showing the financial position of a company at a specific date. It summarizes what a company *owns* (its *assets*) and what it *owes* (its *liabilities*). See Figure 1.2.

2 A *profit and loss account* is a statement of a company's trading performance, *over a stated period of time*, showing how revenues were made, the costs incurred, and finally the profit made. See Figure 2.5.

Comparing these two statutory documents, the profit and loss account gives you a picture, in monetary terms, of the buying, making and selling of a company's products *over a period* (usually twelve months); the balance sheet is a still-life picture, in monetary terms, summarizing what the position was on the last day of that 12-month period in terms of the sources of money and how it has been used.

Now let us examine these two documents in more detail so that you understand the principles upon which they are constructed, their form and content.

Balance sheet

A balance sheet is designed to communicate two pieces of information: what a particular company *owns* at a stated date; and what that company *owes* at a stated date.

Assets The assets in a balance sheet are what a company owns. If necessary they can all *in time* be converted into cash, but those which can readily and quickly be realized are known as *current assets*, whilst those unlikely to be converted are known as *fixed assets*.

Fixed assets consist of items likely to be used over a longer period of time than one year by a company and may include:

(a) land;
(b) buildings;
(c) plant and machinery;
(d) transport;
(e) furniture and fixtures, etc.

Current assets consist of items for short-term use during the operating 12 months' cycle of a company and may include:

(a) raw materials;
(b) stocks;
(c) work in progress;
(d) finished stocks;
(e) debtors (money owed by customers who have bought goods but not yet paid for them);
(f) cash, etc.

Liabilities The balancing factor in a balance sheet is the liabilities which represent what a company *owes*. Liabilities may be divided into three groups.

Shareholders' funds for the company's long-term use are not normally liable to be repaid quickly. They include:

(a) share capital (the money put into a business by the owners);
(b) capital surplus (profits realized from the sale of assets);

(c) reserves (accumulated profit available for distribution but retained as provision against unforeseen possibilities).

Long-term liabilities for the company's long-term use are not normally liable to be repaid quickly. They include:

(a) long-term bank loans;

(b) mortgages;

(c) bonds, etc.

Current liabilities. These consist of monies owed and likely to be due for payment within the company's current operating business cycle (normally 12 months or less). They include:

(a) creditors (money owed to other people);

(b) bank overdraft;

(c) taxes;

(d) dividends to shareholders;

(e) interest due on loans.

Why is a balance sheet so called? Traditionally, balance sheets have been drawn up showing the total liabilities on the left-hand side and the total assets on the right-hand side. When the values given to each section on either side are added up they must balance. How does this happen? Money subscribed by shareholders to start a company is used to buy assets, such as buildings, plant machinery, raw materials, and all the other necessities to enable products or services to be produced. So £100 000 of

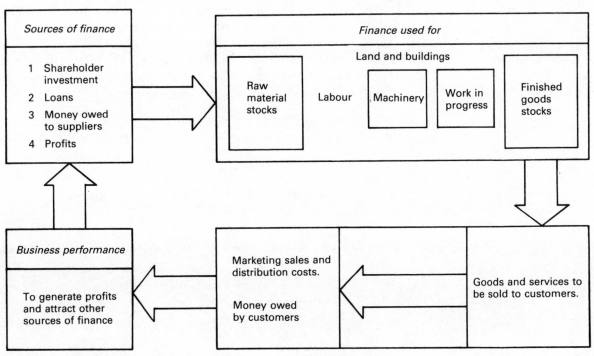

Figure 1.1 **The business cycle**

FARR & WYDE PLC
Balance sheet, 31 March 1990

	£			£
Share capital		Fixed assets		
100 000 Ordinary shares	100 000	Freehold property		50 000
		Fixtures and equipment at cost *less* depreciation		30 000
Reserves				80 000
Profit and loss account (unappropriated balance	20 000			
Shareholders' funds	120 000			
Long-term liabilities		Current assets		
Loans	20 000	Stock	40 000	
		Debtors	35 000	
Current liabilities		Cash	15 000	
Corporation tax	7 000			
Creditors	18 000			90 000
Ordinary dividend	5 000			
	30 000			
	£170 000			£170 000

Figure 1.2 **Balance sheet**

shareholders' funds – a liability in a company balance sheet – is balanced by the value of the assets that money, or a proportion of it, is used to purchase. This is shown in the specimen balance sheet in Figure 1.2.

A balance sheet will normally show not only the financial position of a company at a particular date, but also the figures for the previous year or period, thus providing a comparison.

You can also assess the *solvency* and *liquidity* of a company from the figures presented in a balance sheet. Solvency is the ability to

Liabilities (sources of funds)		Assets (uses of funds)	
	£		£
Share capital and reserves	120 000	Fixed assets	80 000
Long-term liabilities	20 000	Current assets	90 000
Current liabilities	30 000		
	£170 000		£170 000

Figure 1.3 **Balance sheet (summary): 'account' format**

14

meet outside liabilities from total assets. Liquidity is a company's ability to meet its current liabilities (pay its creditors, bank interest, etc., on due dates) from its current assets – notably from cash.

Presentation of accounts The traditional 'account' format for balance sheets, as shown in Figure 1.3, has now almost universally given way to the 'net asset' format which highlights capital employed and working capital, as in Figure 1.4. This narrative form of presentation is laid out as a businessman thinks when analysing the costs of setting up and running a business.

Share capital and reserves		120 000
Long-term liabilities		20 000
Capital employed		£140 000
Fixed assets		80 000
Current assets	90 000	
Less: Current liabilities	30 000	
Net current assets ('working capital')		60 000
Net assets		£140 000

Figure 1.4 **Balance sheet (summary): 'net asset' format**

Limitations of the balance sheet The picture given by the balance sheet of a company is an incomplete one for a number of reasons:

1 It cannot show the market or competitive situations in which a company traded to produce the results.

2 The figures shown cannot in all cases be exact or accurate. The valuation of stock is just one example. Decisions on value which are either very conservative or very optimistic can markedly influence the apparent strength of a company's position.

3 The ability of a company's management team cannot figure, yet it may be a company's principle asset.

4 It can only concern itself with those factors which can be expressed in monetary terms.

Profit and loss account

The profit and loss account will show the results of a company's trading performance over the period stated in the document – usually 12 months. It will indicate revenue, costs and profits. See Figure 1.5.

FARR & WYDE PLC
Profit and loss account
for the year ending 31 March 1990

	£
Sales	240 000
Trading profit for the year	17 000
Less: Debenture interest	1 000
Profit before tax	16 000
Corporation tax	7 000
Net profit for the year after tax	9 000
Less: Ordinary dividend	5 000
Retained out of the year's profit	4 000
Add: Unappropriated balance brought forward	16 000
Unappropriated balance carried forward	£ 20 000

Figure 1.5 **Profit and loss account**

The items identified will vary in type and detail, but normally a profit and loss account has three separate parts.

Trading account, showing:

(a) sales revenue;

(b) cost of sales;

(c) trading profit (or loss).

Profit and loss account, showing:

(a) trading profit (or loss);

(b) other income (e.g. interest received);

(c) expenses (e.g. depreciation, interest paid, directors' fees, auditors' fees, bank and legal charges);

(d) taxes payable;

(e) net profit before tax for the year.

Appropriation account, showing how the profit has been 'distributed', e.g. paid as dividends to shareholders, transferred to reserves, accumulated as unappropriated profits carried forward to the balance sheet.

The profit and loss account provides a detailed picture of how well or badly a company is trading and how profitable or otherwise the various sections of the business are. As a salesman you have a major influence on the figures that appear in the trading account section, in terms of sales revenue and the costs of sales, e.g. sales revenue results from:

(a) number of units/services sold;
(b) prices obtained;
(c) mix of sales.

Cost of sales include:

(a) selling costs;
(b) marketing costs;
(c) administrative costs;
(d) distribution costs;
(e) production costs.

But in order to draw conclusions from such financial statements it is necessary to understand the relationships between a number of items which are in different forms, such as:

(a) the capital originally invested in a business;
(b) the plant and machinery, and the extent to which it is fully utilized in producing finished products;
(c) the relationship between sales being made and availability of finished stocks;
(d) the balance between sales being made and money owed to customers, etc.

All these business relationships help to make up a picture of a company's business performance. These relationships between various activities and the financial results they produce in the balance sheet and profit and loss account are of the utmost importance in understanding *why* a business is doing well or badly and, above all, *where* adjustments or corrections need to be made.

Measuring business performance

The successful business managers you sell to and negotiate with measure and assess their purchasing, trading and financial operations on a continuous basis. This enables them to take advantage of favourable marketing conditions or avoid risks, such as building up stocks of raw materials when prices are rising, or having to borrow money at high rates of interest to keep customers supplied because credit control is out of hand and customers are delaying paying their accounts.

By looking at the relationships between key factors in a business, management can assess not only the effects of those decisions and business activities but also the causes.

The figures in a company's accounts can be made much more understandable if they are related to each other in a series of ratios. Such ratios can then be used to analyse past performance and to plan future performance. (See Table 1.1 Key profitability ratios.)

The most widely used *overall* measurement of performance is the amount of profit made in relation to the capital employed in a business. Capital employed is a company's total assets minus its current liabilities. Profitability is usually expressed in the financial ratios we will now examine as the Return (R) on Capital employed (CE). So the primary financial ratio which expresses the return on capital employed is shown as:

$$\frac{\text{Return}}{\text{Capital employed}} \text{ or } \frac{R}{CE}$$

It is the financial expression of the effectiveness of a company's management and can be used to compare one business with another or to other alternative forms of investment. It makes us ask the question: 'Would we have done better to use our money in some other way?'

The Return on Capital employed in a business results from two other financial measurements. They are:

Return on Sales, which is the net profit before tax, expressed as a percentage of sales and is shown as:

Table 1.1 **Key profitability ratios**

Ratio	How to calculate	What it means
1 Return on Capital employed $\frac{R}{CE}$	$\dfrac{\text{Net profit before tax \%}}{\text{Total assets employed minus current liabilities}}$	It measures the effectiveness of management. It measures the earning of a sufficient return on investment in assets to ensure per-petuation of investment/profit/ investment cycle
Example: What is the $\frac{R}{CE}$ of Farr & Wyde Plc?	$\dfrac{16\,000}{(170\,000-30\,000)140\,000} = 12\%*$	
2 Return on Sales $\frac{R}{S}$	$\dfrac{\text{Net profit before tax\%}}{\text{Net sales}}$	Measures the success any company has achieved in meeting the objec-tive of realizing profit from each pound's worth of products or services it sells
Example: What is the $\frac{R}{S}$ of Farr & Wyde Plc?	$\dfrac{16\,000}{240\,000} = 7\%*$	
3 Turnover of Capital employed $\frac{S}{CE}$	$\dfrac{\text{Sales}}{\text{Total assets minus current liabilities}}$	This ratio also measures the effectiveness of management – whether it is doing an adequate job with regard to sales in relation to assets employed
Example: What is the $\frac{S}{CE}$ of Farr & Wyde Plc?	$\dfrac{240\,000}{(170\,000-30\,000)140\,000} = 1.7*$	

* Figures rounded for simplicity

$$\frac{\text{Return}}{\text{Sales}} \text{ or } \frac{R}{S}$$

Sales on Capital employed, which is the number of times capital is turned over in relation to sales made and is shown as

$$\frac{\text{Sales}}{\text{Capital employed}} \text{ or } \frac{S}{CE}$$

These three important ratios can be combined to present a financial picture of actual or planned performance.

Figure 1.6 illustrates a 'hierarchy' of management ratios used by operating managers in a business to analyse profitability. It is called a 'hierarchy' because at one end can be seen how these ratios influence the total profit of a business, and at the other end how they can be related to individual performance.

Figure 1.7 shows a hierarchy of management ratios in a company that markets warehousing and national distribution services to manufacturing companies producing dry goods.

The number and type of ratios used and their relative importance is individual to every business. The interpretation of the ratios is also individual to every business. Here is a comparison made possible by using the financial ratios of two widely differing business enterprises.

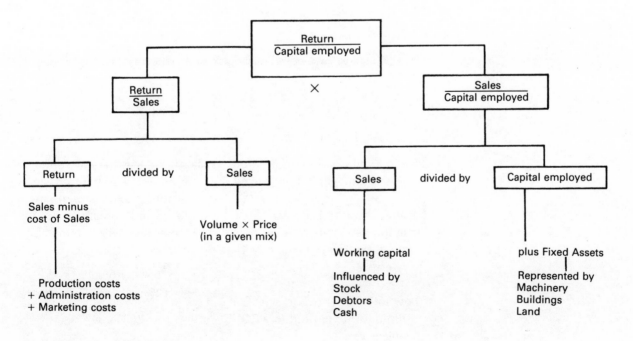

Figure 1.6 **Return on Capital employed formula**

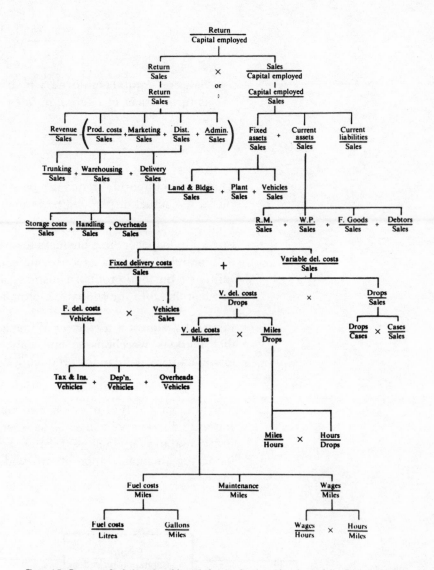

Figure 1.7 **Return on Capital employed formula for a national warehousing and distribution company**

A distributive business

Fixed capital is low in relation to working capital employed.

Therefore Sales : Capital employed – the number of times capital is turned over – is crucial.

Low ratio of return on sales but rapid turnover produces ROCE objective:

A heavy engineering business

Margin on sales is much more important. The high proportion of fixed capital employed in the business means capital turnover is inevitably slower:

$$\frac{R}{S} = 12\%$$

ROCE 24%

$$\frac{S}{CE} = 2.0\times$$

$$\frac{R}{S} = 4\%$$

ROCE 24%

$$\frac{S}{CE} = 6\times$$

Therefore key management activity:

(a) achieve rapid stock turn;
(b) fine control of buying and selling prices;
(c) make optimum use of ware-house space and transport.

Therefore important manage-activity:

(a) control manufacturing costs;
(b) maintain output;
(c) control capital employed;
(d) maintain margins.

Manufacturers normally have a higher return on sales than distributors and a lower sales on capital employed. Distributors tend to operate on lower margins, but have a higher ratio of sales on Capital Employed, as these two examples illustrate.

Now the figures from these same two businesses, and those already given for Farr & Wyde Plc, are brought together to show how different types of business can achieve the same Return on Capital Employed from very different return on sales (i.e. margins) and Sales on Capital Employed. The influences of the sales force are listed.

Return	equals	Return	multiplied by	Sales
Capital employed	=	Sales	×	Capital employed
Engineering 12%	=	8%	×	1.5
Consumer 12%	=	4%	×	3
Farr & Wyde				
Plc 12%	=	7%	×	1.7

Influenced by:
(a) volume;
(b) price;
(c) costs;
(d) mix of products sold.

Influenced by:
(a) volume;
(b) price;
(c) stock control;
(d) control of debtors;
(e) use of fixed assets.

These financial ratios can be broken down further to reveal other important ratios which measure business performance, e.g.

1 Is profitability falling: $\dfrac{\text{Return}}{\text{Capital employed}}$?

2 To what is this due: $\dfrac{\text{Return}}{\text{Sales}}$ or $\dfrac{\text{Sales}}{\text{Capital employed}}$?

3 If it is $\dfrac{\text{Return}}{\text{Sales}}$ what changes have occurred?

4 How can we identify these changes:

   (a) price changes?
   (b) product mix changes?
   (c) cost changes?
   (d) volume changes?

5 If falling profitability is due to $\dfrac{\text{Sales}}{\text{Capital employed}}$

   is this due to $\dfrac{\text{Sales}}{\text{Fixed assets}}$ or $\dfrac{\text{Sales}}{\text{Working capital}}$?

6 If due to $\dfrac{\text{Sales}}{\text{Fixed assets}}$ is this *either* under-utilization of plant and machinery *or* because new assets are not yet producing a return?

7 If due to $\dfrac{\text{Sales}}{\text{Working capital}}$ is this:

   either a stock turnover problem: $\dfrac{\text{Stock} \times 365 \text{ days}}{\text{Sales revenue}}$

   or a debtor turnover problem: $\dfrac{\text{Debtors} \times 365 \text{ days}}{\text{Sales revenue}}$

Ratios can be extended to the point where perhaps a works manager looks at the output per hour on his machines, or a transport manager examines cost per mile or delivery cost per pack. Meanwhile, your customers are analysing profit on capital turnover in relation to feet of facings, or the cost of assembly per order. (See Table 1.1.)

The financial effects of the sales negotiator

The main account negotiator can have a major impact on his company's profitability through the effective use of his selling and negotiating skills, influenced by such financial ratios as those illustrated in the distributive and heavy engineering examples on pp. 20–21.

You can 'read' your effect on your business by examining the two ratios:

$$\frac{\text{Return}}{\text{Sales}} \quad \text{and} \quad \frac{\text{Sales}}{\text{Capital employed}}$$

Whilst, as salesmen, you probably do not set the standards in these areas of financial performance, it is nevertheless your responsibility to achieve them. This is because the standards set in each of these areas add up to the returns from the sales target set for the company in relation to the amount of capital we tie up in doing it.

Cash flow

Sales and marketing people are most often concerned with sales volume and turnover, not with the actual receipt and payment of cash. As soon as an order is taken, the sale for the salesman is complete. *When* the money is paid is generally outside his control.

However, for the company the important measure is *cashflow*, i.e. the flow of funds in and out of the company. Only cash pays bills, and lack of it, even for a short period, is a common cause of bankruptcy. Cash-flow forecasting is essential for management to plan its use of resources and to recognize cash needs in the future. Cash flow is forecast by:

1 Producing a detailed sales forecast, related to cash generated.
2 Relating cost of sales to cash outgoings.
3 Including all capital expenditure when it occurs.
4 Establishing cash requirements for the business.

The main points for sales and marketing people to note about cash flow are:

1 The importance of accurate sales forecasting.
2 The need to speed up payment of invoices.
3 The need to hold low stocks relative to sales volume.
4 The drain on cash caused by sudden sales volume increases (because the goods or component materials have to be paid for before sales revenue is received).
5 The need to improve sales margins.
6 The need to curb interest costs incurred by funding rapid sales increases, or sales shortfalls on budget.

The following example illustrates how profit shown on a profit and loss account bears no relation to cash actually generated and used by the business.

Cash budgeting

Problem Company A manufactures and sells a product which retails for £1 000. Manufacturing costs are £500 per unit, other costs total £10 000 per month. The company gets paid on average one month after invoicing, invoices being sent when the product is dispatched; raw materials and labour costs are incurred on average one month before sale. There is a seasonal sales pattern which rises during the first half of the year to a summer peak, falling during the second half to the lowest figure in December and January.

The company's cash situation is tight and therefore the managing director has asked the sales manager to prepare a forecast for the first six months of next year. This is:

Revenue, Cost and Profit forecast
6 months January–June inclusive

Revenue 210 units at £1 000		£210 000
Cost Manufacturing costs 210 at £500	£105 000	
Other costs at £10 000 per month	£60 000	£165 000
	Profit	£45 000

The managing director is very pleased with this but decides to analyse it in a little more detail to see the cash-flow situation.

Assumptions

1 Assume sales pattern:

D	J	F	M	A	M	J	J
10	10	20	30	40	50	60	60

2 Assume no cash brought forward at beginning of period. See page 25.

Some key financial terms

Return: Net profit (usually before tax and sometimes before interest charges where levied by a parent company or a subsidiary).

Capital employed: Fixed assets plus working capital.

Fixed assets: Money tied up in land, buildings, plant and machinery, etc.

Current assets: Money tied up in stock, work in progress, debtors, cash, etc.

Current liabilities: Money owed in the short term, e.g. creditors, overdraft, tax, dividends.

Working capital: Current assets minus current liabilities.

Fixed liabilities: The long-term money in the company, i.e. shareholders, equity, long-term loans, retained profits.

Margin: Sales revenue minus cost of goods sold.

Balance sheet: Statement of a company's position at one moment in time, usually at the end of the financial year, showing the sources of the money in the company (fixed liabilities plus current liabilities) and how it is deployed (fixed assets plus current assets).

Profit and loss account: Statement showing the results of a company trading in the period indicating revenue, expenditure, and thus profit.

Answer to problem

	D	J	F	M	A	M	J	J
Sales forecast	10	10	20	30	40	50	60	60
Revenue		10 000	10 000	20 000	30 000	40 000	50 000	
Manufacturing costs		10 000	15 000	20 000	25 000	30 000	30 000	
Other costs		10 000	10 000	10 000	10 000	10 000	10 000	
Total costs		20 000	25 000	30 000	35 000	40 000	40 000	
Surplus		−10 000	−15 000	−10 000	− 5 000	−	+10 000	
Brought forward		−	−10 000	−25 000	−35 000	40 000	−40 000	
Carried forward		−10 000	−25 000	−35 000	−40 000	−40 000	−30 000	

2

Improving customers' profits

The skilled application of financial knowledge gives you a very powerful tool which can be used to influence the profitability not only of your own but also your customer's business. By analysing the customer's business needs in financial terms you can develop and present benefits in financial terms.

Analysing customers' accounts

A close examination of the Return on Sales and the Sales on the Capital employed will identify opportunities to make the customer's operations more profitable.

Return on sales This figure is the result of sales revenue minus the cost of generating it. You may be able to improve it by reducing the customer's costs in certain areas, for example:

Operational costs

(a) better delivery arrangements?

(b) easier, more economic processes?

(c) less damage or waste?

(d) easier handling?

(e) more economic use of labour or raw materials?

(f) more economic use of space?

Sales and distribution costs Can you offer:

(a) more economic selling methods? (through sales aids);

(b) better use of salesmen's time? (through stimulation of demand);

(c) lower transport costs?

(d) fewer complaints?

Administration costs Can you offer:

(a) streamlined paper work systems?

(b) less time spent on administration?

(c) fewer administrative tasks?

(d) better payment terms?

(e) simpler stock control and order system?

Alternatively, you may not be able to reduce his costs but you can increase his Return on Sales by helping him to:

(a) achieve a higher margin;

(b) get a better product mix;

(c) sell more effectively;

(d) increase his sale of complementary lines.

Sales to Capital employed This figure represents the volume or value of sales compared with assets required to generate it. You may be able to improve this figure either by helping the customer increase the volume or value of his sales, or by reducing the value of assets involved.

Sales volume or value Can you offer:

(a) greater acceptance of your products by his markets?

(b) greater market penetration for his products or services?

(c) help with advertising, selling, etc?

(d) better sales results from salesmen, transport, etc?

(e) more effective promotions?

(f) merchandising support?

(g) reduced out-of-stock?

Asset reduction Can you offer:

(a) less capital tied up in stocks?

(b) less space required to stock?

(c) faster through-put?

(d) fewer debtors?

(e) better use of spare cash?

(f) better use of existing fitments and space?

An example Consider the following key ratios taken from the annual accounts of two comparable grocery firms:

	Superstores		Prestwicks	
	1989	1988	1989	1988
Return on Capital employed	26.2%	35.9%	30.7%	35.0%
Return on Sales	4.6%	5.8%	2.0%	2.1%
Sales to capital employed	5.6%	6.2%	15.2%	16.6%

	Superstores		Prestwicks	
	1989	1988	1989	1988
Sales to Fixed assets	6.6%	6.3%	14.1%	10.9%
Sales to Working capital	36.0%	67.8%	–	–
Stock turnover	42 days	41 days	24 days	27 days
Debtor turnover	3 days	4 days	–	–
Creditor turnover	43 days	48 days	26 days	31 days

The main points to note are:

1 The very high Return on Capital employed of Prestwicks, made up of a low margin but very high asset turnover.

2 The decline in profit margins on sales, a result of cost inflation and government controls.

3 The dependence of wholesalers and retailers on credit from manufacturers to fund the business. Prestwicks has, in fact, a *negative* working capital, i.e. current liabilities exceed current assets.

4 The improved Stock turnover of Prestwicks, which leads to a higher asset/turnover ratio.

The implications of this analysis for negotiations are:

1 Retailers and wholesalers need a very high return from any capital invested. Can your ideas help?

2 Retailers and wholesalers are under pressure on margins on sales, which implies more pressure on terms from suppliers, especially overriders.

3 Retailers will be very interested in a higher rate of stock-turn to improve the Sales to Capital employed ratio when sales margins are falling. Can you demonstrate this in negotiations? (*Note:* Superstores' slower rate of Stock turnover is caused mainly by non-food sales.)

In practice, you will be able to obtain much more information on your accounts' business than that contained in annual reports, e.g. gross margins, Stock turnover by line, cash margins. Use of this data can form the basis of very effective negotiations by showing how well you understand the customer, his problems and his objectives.

Analysing customer business needs

You can look at the use of financial knowledge in analysing customer business needs by considering some further examples.

Selling to multiple grocery outlets

This requires skilled negotiation. The major national outlets have prospered through their ability to manage financial resources in large-scale distribution.

The salesman, in this situation, needs to discuss not only his product and its appeal to the housewife, but also its potential profitability to the distributor. He also needs to assess not just its profitability per unit, but its profitability in terms of turnover of stock relative to the volume and location of the space occupied, in comparison with a vast range of alternatives open to the store.

The salesman must therefore be able to discuss, for example, with the buyer:

1 The sales of his product per foot of space occupied.

2 The stock-turn ratio – how many times the stock will turnover and make use of the space allocated to it.

3 The margin per unit × stock-turn to give margin per foot of space.

4 The relationship between promotional costs, discounts, volume, stock-turn and margin.

5 The relationship between site in store and the achievement of target sales and margins.

Selling to the agricultural industry

This is one of the most competitive for any salesman. Many of the products sold to agriculture have become commodities as technical differences have narrowed or disappeared.

Some of the most successful agricultural salesmen succeed in this situation by selling from a financial base. They sell not products, but management systems which enable the customer to make most profitable use of the product. The salesman is trained to discuss and analyse business ratios with his customers and to help the customer to improve his business performance.

As just one case, an agricultural salesman selling to a bacon-pig production unit is in a much stronger selling position if he can discuss, for example, with his businessman customer:

Costs of production per lb of liveweight gained:

(a) how his products can reduce that cost;

(b) the implications in terms of profitability;

(c) the implications in terms of return on capital invested.

Capital costs related to the efficiency of alternative production systems:

(a) matching system to capital available;

(b) sources of finance and supportive enterprise budgets;

(c) cash-flow implications.

Cost of production to return per unit of sales:

(a) relationship between cost and return;

(b) implications of increasing unit costs in return for greater increase in unit returns;

(c) margin as a percentage of output;

(d) how his products can improve the ratio.

Selling capital equipment and industrial machinery

The salesman can no longer depend on easily identified product advantages to win a sale. He can sell more easily if he is able, for example, to identify:

1 Whether the customer should buy, rent or lease?

2 What form of finance is most appropriate to the customer's business?

3 What capital allowances are available?

4 In what ways do purchase costs, running costs, maintenance costs and output performance affect the profitability to the customer?

The salesman should therefore be able to use 'financial merchandising' techniques. He may therefore need to discuss, for example, with the buyer:

1 The best use of capital in the business, relating availability of capital to the efficiency of the business at present and as projected.

2 The tax implications of purchasing equipment outright, leasing it, or using loading facilities. Sources of finance.

3 The output of equipment relative to its capital costs and running costs. (The most expensive equipment to buy might well produce the most economic output.)

4 The needs of the business in financial terms and how these affect the purchase decision: e.g., the buyer who is purchasing equipment for rehire has different financial needs to the user purchasing for his own use.

5 The cost of equipment relative to savings in labour costs or increase in output.

In all three examples of selling, financial knowledge enables value to be added to the product and is a major aid to making sales.

Developing and presenting financial benefits

Development

You all know that a 'benefit' is what your product or service offers to the buyer, and that the most effective benefits are those which do something for him which he wants done and can recognize. It is one thing to use financial knowledge to identify customer needs – but sales success depends on your skill in developing and presenting financial benefits persuasively.

Financial benefits should be *understandable, accurate* and *attractive,* and need careful presentation. In developing them you need to ask:

1 What does the buyer want done? For example:

   (a) savings in costs?

   (b) increase in output?

   (c) improvement in cash flow?

   (d) more efficiency?

   (e) easier administration?

   (f) increase in sales?

   (g) improvement in profit?

   (h) increase in value of his product?

   (i) improved labour relations?

   (j) financial security?

   (k) convenience?

2 What is the value of the benefit to his business – at what cost?

3 What financial and management measurements are important to his business?

4 How do the benefits offered by your product or service affect these measurements?

5 How can these effects be explained and presented attractively in financial terms?

Financial merchandising Presentation of financial benefits can be described as 'financial merchandising'. Done well it can add value to the offering which is disproportionate to the real value.

For example, one company operating in a high-volume commodity market no longer 'sells' its products to major customers. What it does is to provide a management accounting service to these customers to help them to make the most profitable use of the products in their business. The service is self-help, with some assistance from technical representatives. At relatively low cost the company maintains high-volume customers by helping them to run their business more effectively.

A commodity has derived added value from financial merchandising. In more immediate and practical terms, you can produce financial benefits during sales interviews by developing aids designed to link your offering with the customer's business. For example, a company selling process equipment and materials uses the format in Figures 2.1a and 2.1b very effectively to progress from the identification of financial needs to purchase order during the interview.

Prepared for: Name: ....

                       Title: ....

            Company: ....

            Location: ....

SAVINGS FOLLOWING INSTALLATION   Annual
savings

1 *Material savings*   Used/yr   Price

   Present material   .... × .... = ...
   Proposed material   .... × .... = ...
   Net savings

2 *Labour savings*

   Machine clean-up   .... hrs/yr × £ ....per hr =
   Material handling time   .... hrs/yr × £ ....per hr =
   Reduction in direct labour hours to produce same
      yearly requirements   .... × £ ....per hr =

3 *Increased machine productivity*
   Added capacity
   Reduced floor space   .... sq ft × £ ....per sq ft =
   Elimination of bottlenecks

4 *Reduced rework or scrap*
   Labour savings   .... hrs × ....per hr
   Savings on packs
   Product saving

5 *Other benefits*
   Eliminated process failures
   Standardized materials
   Other – specify

Total savings ....

Total equipment investment ....

Figure 2.1a **Customer financial needs analysis form**

Details of installation: ....

EQUIPMENT REQUIRED   ....

Description	Part no.	Quantity	Price	
			Unit	Total
Pumping unit				
Working heads				
Injectors				
Hoses				
Couplings				
Controls				
Thermostats				

Figure 2.1b

	Description	Part no.	Quantity	Price	
				Unit	Total

Solenoids
Solvent fluid
Oiler
Oil
Others
Total equipment
  investment

Signature: ....Title: ....Date: ....19 ....

Figure 2.1b **concluded**

The use of financial knowledge as an aid to both buyer and seller

Similar objectives

Buyer and seller work in the same commercial environment. Both buyer and seller are, in the long term, dependent on achieving similar business objectives.

Balancing the sales and purchase of 'profit'

Whether he is a professional buyer or just a hard-headed business-man, the customer always aims to make the 'best' decision for his business. He tries to balance his use of resources with the objective of maximizing his returns, and in doing so must compare what is being offered to him.

The negotiator with financial knowledge benefits in most circumstances

With the professional buyer you can plan your presentation to meet the buyer's needs. You can identify more clearly what those needs are and how your offering can satisfy them. You can talk the same language as the buyer and gain both orders and respect. With the hard-headed businessman you can demonstrate the business advantages being offered. You can identify, with the buyer, business opportunities which the buyer may have overlooked.

Financial knowledge can enable you to:

1 Identify the commercial needs of the business with the buyer.

2 Show how your products or services can meet those needs.

3 Justify and obtain higher prices.

4 Avoid the pitfall of professionally 'selling in' a product which may sell out badly, or prove unsatisfactory in use.

5 Consolidate and obtain more repeat business.

6 Deal better with irrational objections by using demonstrable facts.

7 Predict, show and use post-sale proof of your commercial claims.

8 Be more convincing, confident and authoritative as a negotiator.

9 Identify your sales potential through the eyes of the customer's business.

In exchanging profit opportunities through the proper use of financial knowledge, both buyer and seller benefit, for example:

Benefits to buyer	*Benefits to seller*
Better and more profitable decisions.	Opportunity to influence those decisions.
Is helped to identify business opportunity.	Trust and repeat business from the buyer.
Looks at all alternatives objectively with you.	You become part of the buyer's business.
Makes the profitable purchases.	Profitable sales.
Is given an objective approach to complex problems.	Convincing sales based on objective information.
Confidence in decisions produces success in use or re-sale.	Success by the buyer produces repeat business.
Greater confidence in supplier and your products or services.	Adds value to the product or service in the face of competition.
Business objectives achieved.	Business objectives achieved.

What do you know? What do you need to know?

Successful business development and negotiation rest upon making products or services that people will need and then being able to get *in* to supply them to the customers you want to supply and *stay in* there. You will have a bank of information about your key customers, which may range from the manufacture of sub-assembly parts for their machines or 'own label' products for them to sell; through what they have purchased from you, how often, what they use your products for, how much they buy from competitors, their financial relationships with you, how often your sales force, or delivery vans, call etc.

The bulk of what you need to know about your important customers' business, in order to help improve their profitability, you can only find out from your major customers, usually by exploring the following sources of information.

Customers' markets

1 What changes are taking place in their markets that are the basis of their demand for your products or services?

2 Will these changes happen overnight or gradually?

3 What new product research, conception, testing or development are they investing in to meet market changes?

4 What information do they collect about the market they serve?

Customers' competition

1 Who are their competitors?

2 How strong are they?

3 What share of the markets do they have?

4 If competitors take business from your main customers what will that do to your business overall?

The economy of the country

1 Are your principal customers likely to be affected by current economic changes?

2 Favourably or unfavourably?

3 If the economy improves, what pressures will this put on your main customers?

4 If it deteriorates how soon will your important customers be affected?

5 What percentage of your key customers' business is done outside the home country? What percentage is home trade?

Government legislation

1 What effect will legislation have on your important customers' products, prices, freedom to advertise, profit margins, etc?

2 What effect will foreign government legislation have on your customers' overseas business?

New technology

1 How vulnerable are your principal customers' products to new developments, new materials?

2 How can your new technology/new developments help them?

3 How soon will new technology threaten your customers' products unless they change?

Conclusion

It has not been the habit of most companies up to now to educate salesmen in areas such as costs, break-even analysis, and the behaviour of markets. But a negotiating salesman must have a working knowledge of all these and their implications if he is to be able to affect the business of key customers where it matters most – in the amount of profit they make. Only by knowing about these things can he then find answers to the question: What can you do to help me? The answers to that question then enable him to construct a customer plan for the small number of key customer or market segments that contribute the bulk of the profitable sales for which he is held accountable. (See Figure 2.2.)

Item	Information	Action required

Objectives to be achieved by:

1 Profit improvement objectives
2 Return on capital employed
3 Return on sales
4 Sales revenue
5 Cost reductions

Plans:

1 Profit improvement activities
2 Sales volume projects
3 Market support
4 Cost reduction projects

Timing of activities to achieve objectives

Controls:

1 To measure profit target
2 To measure volume target
3 To measure cost reduction target
4 Contingéncies

Figure 2.2 **Customer profit plan checklist**

3

Costing as an aid to sales

In the development of business with customers a salesman must always keep two considerations in mind when planning the details of his approach and negotiation. First, how to *minimize* the costs customers invest in their products and services upon which their budgeted profits are based. Second, how to *maximize* the profit his company receives from the sales of its products and services. These two objectives are vital in business dealings with the valuable accounts which contribute the bulk of a company's profits.

To be in a position to influence these two objectives, a salesman must have an accurate and comprehensive knowledge and understanding of costs and profit levels, and how these costs and profit levels move in relation to sales volumes produced and to price changes.

The *prices* a company charges for its products or services, the *volume* of sales achieved and the *costs* incurred to produce and sell them are the three principal elements which influence profitable marketing. The relationship between *prices, volume* and *costs* is not direct and simple, but will conform to certain standards. Prices and sales volume interact with one another to give sales revenue. Obviously the extent to which sales revenue either *exceeds* or falls *below* total costs produces a profit or a loss.

If a salesman is to be in a position to ensure that the products, engineering, processes or services he sells do not result in his customer's costs, and therefore market prices, being adversely affected, he must understand his customer's markets, pricing and costings.

Definition of costs

In simple terms, the costs a company incurs to develop products or services are of two kinds: *fixed* and *variable*. Fixed costs are sometimes referred to as 'overheads'; and over a defined period, usually of a year or more and within specified ranges or limits, do not vary with changes or variations in volume output. Fixed costs will usually include:

1 Management salaries and related expenses.
2 Rents, rates, heating, lighting, telephone, telex, etc.
3 Office expenses.
4 Fixed costs of sales force salaries, cars, equipment.

Variable costs are those which literally vary according to the volume of products produced or services held available and sold. They include:

1 Raw materials and consumable supplies.

2 Direct labour costs.

3 Fuel and power related to specified production processes.

4 Packaging.

5 Commission to agents, distributors, salesmen.

6 Royalties on sales, etc.

The distinction between fixed and variable costs is not absolute and clear-cut and for this reason operating management (and not the accountant) needs to decide how such costs are to be treated. Management approaches the problem of defining what are fixed and what are variable by bearing in mind a number of factors.

If a cost is deemed variable, such as direct labour hired for a specific process, it may need a more complicated and costly control system to measure it so that a true cost is finally reflected in the selling price.

When in doubt in such a situation, optimistic managers will call a cost variable, whereas a pessimist confronted by the same question will call such a cost fixed. In a well-run business the way costs have moved in the past in relation to volume are analysed in order to predict whether the pattern will continue as before or change. Then a decision can be made which reflects as nearly as possible the truth as it is measured.

Allocation of costs

Having defined costs as either fixed or variable, the next task is to allocate such costs to the various products or services marketed by a company. In the rare event of a company only having one product or service this task is unnecessary! Variable costs are usually not difficult to allocate to individual products. Indeed they may well have been calculated by product originally.

Fixed costs represent more of a problem. Some companies allocate fixed costs in the production area on a physical basis. Rents, rates, lighting, heating, power, are calculated as a cost per square foot. A calculation is then made of the total area taken up by each product, and the costs allocated on this basis. Other fixed costs are allocated on either a value or a unit basis.

Whatever the basis for the allocation of fixed costs to individual products, that allocation can be arbitrary and inaccurate, and give a misleading picture of the true profitability of individual products, and of individual management performance. Indeed, in many companies the allocation of fixed costs is seen to be so inaccurate and time-consuming, that it is not done at all. Instead all fixed costs are put together, and set off against the money that results from sales revenue exceeding variable costs.

The allocation of all costs, both fixed and variable, to individual products is called the *full absorption system*. That is to say, all costs are fully absorbed by all products.

Where only variable costs are allocated to individual products and fixed costs are expressed as a total, this is called the *contribution system*. That is to say, each product contributes the amount by which its revenue exceeds its variable costs to a pool, out of which fixed costs are paid and net profit before tax remains. The contribution system of cost allocation is now widely accepted as the more realistic system and, importantly, the system which gives the best information on which to base marketing decisions.

Break-even charts

The break-even chart is simply a series of 'photographs' of the business at various levels of activity. It shows the relationship between sales revenue and profits, when profit starts and how it grows. In particular, it enables an assessment to be made of risk by illustrating the relationship between the point of break-even and the total projected performance. (See Figure 3.1.)

Such break-even 'photographs' of various levels of activity and alternatives in a business are not only invaluable internally but, more important, they forewarn the salesman. They provide him with an insight into the value or cost impact of a proposition he may put forward to an important account customer and the likely favourable or unfavourable reaction to it.

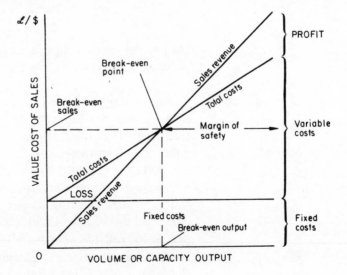

Figure 3.1 **Model break-even chart**

Examples of the need for advanced knowledge

Let us examine three entirely different business situations:

1 A salesman selling a range of chemicals to a company which is considering the possibilities of launching a new product within certain defined cost and price brackets. Unless he can plot the effect on such a customer's fixed and variable costs he cannot even tell whether his price will be acceptable or otherwise.

2 Suppose you are a salesman selling warehousing and distribution services to a food manufacturer. Here again your proposition will stand or fall, not upon the crude price of such a service, but the effect such a service would have upon the food company's existing fixed costs of its present warehousing and the variable costs it incurs in distributing its products to its retail outlets.

3 A salesman selling a service-type system – liquid-beverage vending machines on annual rental – to small shops and offices. His proposition may involve a potential customer spending over £1 000 per year to install such a service for his staff of 40 people. The price may or may not appear as a significant stumbling block. But the chances of his proposition being favourably considered will be greater if he has, at his fingertips, the knowledge of what costs are incurred by such a company at present to provide liquid refreshment for its staff. He can then compare them with the costs of his proposition and hopefully demonstrate a saving.

How to plot break-even charts

Break-even charts, plotted on graph paper, can provide a salesman with useful information; the management in the company to which he hopes to sell can use this as the basis for making decisions. It is worth the time and effort spent in constructing them. Furthermore, for many people, a graph or picture composed by themselves often enables a situation to be understood much more clearly than a mass of figures.

Let us take four examples, based upon an imaginary company, and working with some simple figures.

Example A

The most simple starting-point is to plot a situation where cost and revenue relationships do not change over the period of a total manufacturing project. In Example A (Figure 3.2), predicted sales of 1 000 manufactured units at £10 each produce a total revenue of £10 000 (£10 × 1 000). There are fixed costs of £2 500 which remain unchanged throughout the period of producing from 0 to 1 000 units. Variable costs totalling £5 per unit are shown in addition to fixed costs and total (£5 × 1 000) £5 000. The break-even point occurs at 500 units and the profit upon 1 000 units sold is £2 500. In this commercial situation the margin of safety – the difference between the break-even point and the total sales forecast of 1 000 units – is 500 units.

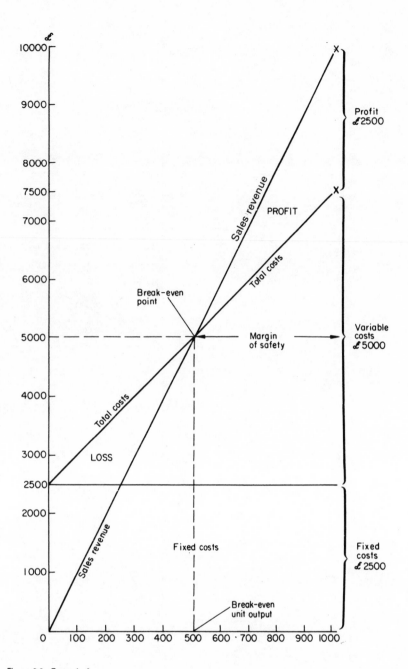

Figure 3.2 **Example A**

Example B   In Example B (Figure 3.3) precisely the same figures are used except that the fixed and variable cost amounts have been revised. Although the total costs and the total revenues remain the same at £7 500 and £10 000 respectively, the break-even point has been increased from 500 units to 675. Such a revision will be all too familiar to a manufacturer who has contracted to supply a given number of units to a customer at an initial fixed price, but between agreeing the price and supplying the units, variable and sometimes fixed costs have risen. The commercial risk in Example B is higher than A despite exactly similar profitability. Why? Because more sales have to be made to reach the break-even point.

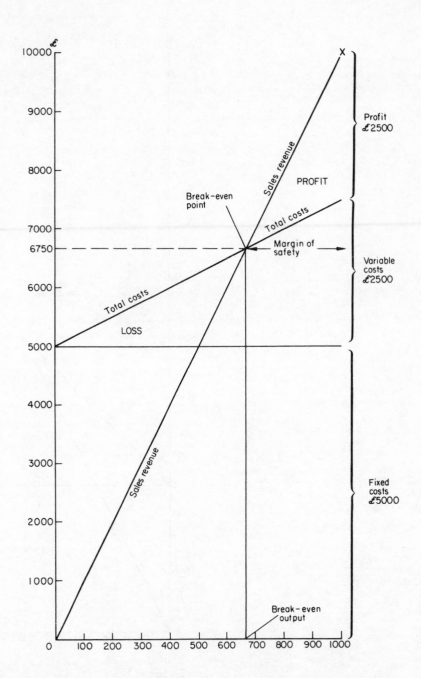

Figure 3.3 **Example B**

Example C Historically many companies based (and some still do) the price of their products on a 'cost plus' approach. This is arrived at simply and mathematically by adding up all the costs involved in making a product and then dividing this figure by the quantity of products actually produced or planned to be produced. To the resulting figure management then adds a marginal figure, hence the term 'cost plus'; but this approach does not help a company to answer the question of whether to accept or reject additional orders, over and above those they have planned to produce. So it is necessary to have a 'market' approach to pricing products and services which enables a company to judge, once fixed costs have been covered, whether marginal business, which can make a contribution to the company's sales turnover, is worth accepting or rejecting.

Some businesses prefer to plot variable costs before fixed costs on a break-even chart. This is so that the contribution can be graphically

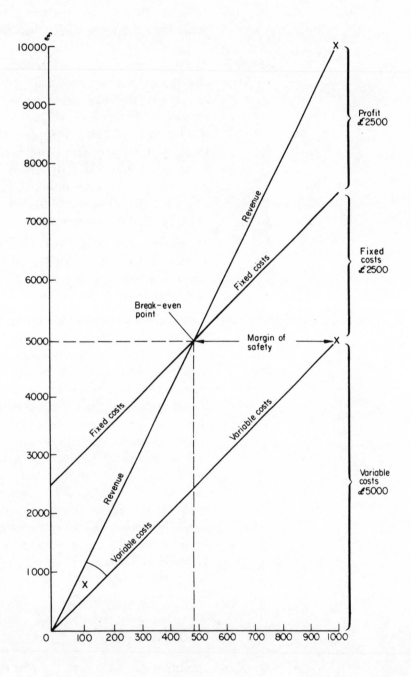

Figure 3.4 **Example C**

shown and illustrates what is known as the 'marginal costing' approach. In Example C (Figure 3.4) the same figures as in A have been used.

The gap marked 'X' between the revenue and variable cost lines is in fact 'contribution': it is therefore possible to see, for example, that when 250 units have been sold, although no profit has been made, all the variable costs thus far have been covered and 50 per cent of the fixed costs have been paid off. Such a cross reference between sales and their contribution to meeting fixed costs cannot easily be made from the more traditional form of break-even graph.

Example D The break-even chart is flexible enough to cope not only with changes in revenue and costs but to feed back the impact of such changes in terms of profit and loss positions of a manufacturing project. In Example D (Figure 3.5) fixed costs starting at £2 500 remain so until 750 units when they increase, perhaps because a larger delivery van was bought. But variable costs from 750 units have been reduced slightly which could be due to being able to bulk more orders into each delivery, giving a saving in transport costs. There is a flattening out of the revenue line from 1 050 units, which indicates that the final few sales have been made at reduced prices.

There are now, as a result of changes during production in the amount of fixed and variable costs, two break-even points, one at about 525 units the other at 900 units, and thus two profit areas, indicated as shaded sections.

Such a chart indicates the various volumes at which profit is made. For example, at 749 units the profit is about £1 200 but a comparable amount does not recur until sales have reached 1 050 units and, even then, the profit is likely to be a little over £1 100. Such a break-even graph indicates that if the company sells between 749 and 900 units it will make less than if it only sold 749 units. This example also shows, as is common in more and more manufacturing companies, where revenue and cost patterns change over the span of projected unit sales, against which production targets and output have been based. Ever since the dramatic and frequent rises in the price of crude oil, the majority of companies throughout the world have had to check changes in fixed and variable costs sometimes daily and certainly weekly. By keeping break-even targets in sight constant adjustments (always upwards!) in their prices can be made, as we all know to our cost.

Conclusion

The break-even chart is a useful device for presenting a picture of cost/volume/profit relationships, to show the effects of changes in various factors such as *volume sales, price* and *costs*.

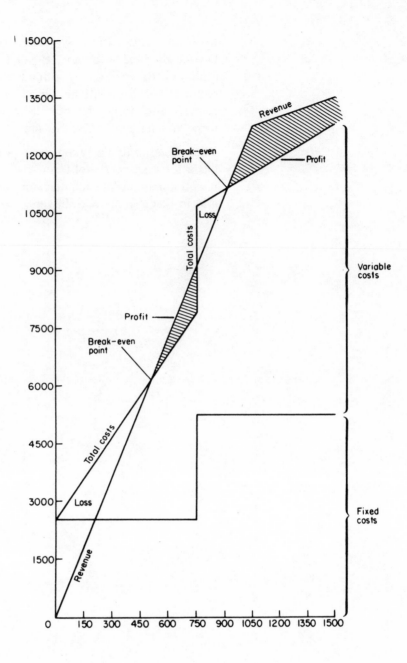

Figure 3.5 **Example D**

One of the main problems of the break-even chart is that the revenue
line assumes a constant product mix, i.e. that ten units of sales are
always worth the same amount of revenue. In single-product companies, and even those producing a range of different products
where the mix is easily controlled and assumptions about revenue
line can be made, care must be exercised otherwise the chart
becomes unrealistic.

In negotiating with large buyers where pricing can be flexible beyond the break-even area, the chart provides key account salesmen and marketing colleagues with a basis for assessing tactical marketing situations on propositions. These cover various forms of promotional activity and different methods of sales compensation to the sales force, to agents, distributors, etc.

When used in this way the break-even chart can provide a graphical basis for assessing profit and risk and so help important account negotiators to make such decisions on behalf of their own companies and in discussions with buyers.

Appendix: Financial skills checklists

All businesses face increasing commercial pressures. One of your prime responsibilities must be to assist your customers in creating and using profit opportunities through the use of your products or services.

Financial knowledge is an important selling tool to help you in achieving your objectives. It will be essential in the future for all business negotiators to understand the nature of profit and the factors affecting the commercial success of both their own and their customers' businesses.

The following checklists will help you to assess your own financial knowledge and awareness and enable you to identify how best you can develop financial selling skills as an aid to profitable long-term sales. By asking these questions and by quantifying the answers you can establish how you can improve your customers' financial returns, how you can translate the improvements into benefits which he will understand and accept, and how you can communicate them to him effectively – more effectively than your competitors.

Financial knowledge checklist

	Yes	No	Action
Do I have a basic knowledge of finance in business?			
Do I understand the nature of the following and the influence of my activities on them?			
The balance sheet			
The profit and loss account			
Sources of capital			
Uses of capital			
Fixed assets			
Current assets			
Long-term liabilities			
Short-term liabilities			
Capital employed			
Sales revenue			
Profit			
Return on Sales ratio			
Sales to Capital employed ratio			
Return on Capital employed ratio			

	Yes	No	Action
Cash flow			
Fixed costs			
Variable costs			
Contribution			

Internal financial needs checklist

In evaluating your own selling activity you can apply the same criteria as for checking your own financial knowledge. The results of your selling activity have considerable implications both for Return on Sales and sales: Capital employed.

	Yes	No	Action

Return on Sales

(a) Are we selling our targeted volume?

(b) Are we achieving target prices?

(c) Are we giving away excessive or unnecessary concessions?

(d) Are we achieving the targeted mix?

(e) Are we looking at our selling costs relative to volume?

(f) Do we make full creative use of expenditure on sales support activities?

(g) Are we being cost-effective as salesmen?

(h) Can we quantify our activities in terms of costs and opportunities?

	Yes	No	Action

Sales:Capital employed

(a) Are we selling our targeted volume?

(b) Do our forecasts accurately reflect future sales?

(c) What effect do wrong forecasts have on capital tied up in stocks and the cost of stocks?

(d) Are we keeping debtors to targeted levels?

(e) Are we using our time and expenditure to achieve effective new sales?

(f) Can we quantify our activity in terms of the relationship between sales and capital employed?

(g) Are we keeping stock levels too high to make selling 'easier' (but no more effective)?

(h) Are we selling factory capacity?

Customer financial needs checklist

	Know	Don't know	Action

How is the customer's business structured in
financial terms?
What financial ratios are crucial to his
business?
How can our products or services improve
his results?
How can these be quantified?

1 Improve return:sales ratio
   (a) reduce production, marketing,
       administrative or distribution costs;
   (b) make functions more cost effective;
   (c) increase sales volume;
   (d) increase sales revenue;
   (e) improve margins;
   (f) add value to his products;
   (g) achieve larger unit sales/better
       sales mix.

2 Improve sales: capital employed ratio
   (a) increase production sales;
   (b) reduce stocks of finished goods or
       raw materials;
   (c) reduce debtors?
   (d) speed through-put/stock turnover?
   (e) reduce need for cash?
   (f) make better use of fixed assets?
   (g) reduce machinery costs?
   (h) reduce labour costs?
   (i) make better use of space?
   (j) reduce distribution costs?

Part II

The negotiation process

Introduction to Part II

'The main task of business is a long-term one. A fly-by-night approach to commerce is quite hopeless . . . Our aim has to be to try to develop a sense of mutual interdependence.

We all know that in private life such relationships can only be built on trust, and a very full understanding and tolerance of individual motives and behaviour. The same is true in business. Under pressure for short-term performance there is an increasing tendency to forget this simple fact. But businesses are not disembodied entities, they consist of people. The individual banker who has lost money on a deal which you made too keen will learn from that experience, and will seek to recoup on a later occasion. Good business should contain something for both parties and people who seek continuously to disadvantage the other partner soon run out of potential partners, in just the same way as the pyramid seller never achieves the nirvana promised by his theory. I am always worried when we do a deal which is too favourable to us at the expense of our business partner because I know that the day will inevitably come when the position will be reversed.

People do not always look far enough ahead to see the consequences of a particular course of commercial action. It requires understanding, sensitivity and perception to know what the long-term consequences of one's actions may be'.

John Harvey-Jones, *Making It Happen*: reflections on leadership
William Collins Sons & Co Ltd. 1988 pp. 118–19

4

The nature of negotiation

What do we mean by the term *negotiation* and how does it relate to or differ from *selling*? We need to answer these questions before we can look in greater depth at the principles of negotiation.

Many buyer-supplier relationships which salesmen have traditionally regarded as 'selling' situations have changed considerably over the last ten to 15 years. These changes and their effect on the role and relationships between buyer and seller need to be understood if salesmen are to operate successfully in the market place described in the Introduction.

In recent years the distributive trades and important industrial, service and financial customers have developed their own marketing and business expertise, and with it, their own commercial strategies and plans. Among the major distributors in the grocery and food markets are many groups whose marketing skills are equal to, if not more advanced than, some of the major food manufacturers who supply them. In the opening chapter reference was made to other factors that have changed, the most important of which is the considerable concentration of buying power into fewer but larger purchasing units.

Greater buying expertise and greater buyer power have led to an increased amount of interdependence between manufacturers or suppliers and distributor or users. Although the two sides still occasionally make independent warlike noises there is a growing amount of tacit recognition that they need each other if they are to achieve their respective commercial objectives. This relationship and interdependence calls for a subtle understanding by the salesman of the skills he needs and when he should use them.

In terms of 'selling' activity this means that there is a greater balance of needs on both sides. The need to buy and the need to supply, viewed over a period of time, are more or less equal.

'Negotiation' is the term generally applied to the more complex situations involving buyers and sellers, in which both make a number of proposals and counter proposals before an agreement is reached. 'Persuasive selling' is still needed, particularly with new customers, in the more competitive industries (e.g. food groups) or when presenting a new product or idea. But given commonality of needs in the majority of cases between buyer and seller, it is the parallel subtle skill of negotiation that is required to ensure that the business gained by you is profitable.

How does negotiation relate to selling?

Traditionally 'selling' is seen as the art of persuading someone, who at the outset of a sales interview is reluctant to buy, that he should do so. You are familiar with the selling process involved. You have a product or service to offer to a customer and attached to your offer is a price and standard terms of trade. You have either existing or prospective customers whom you need to persuade to buy your product or service at the best prices. *Selling* is being able to persuade the customer to buy from you rather than to say 'no' at the prices and on the terms of business you have quoted and go elsewhere.

In many everyday transactions in retail shops and supermarkets, this selling process is simple and straightforward. On the other hand in commercial and industrial purchases, the selling process can often be quite complicated, spanning several sales interviews over many months. A high level of skill is required not only to persuade the customer to buy what you are offering but to do so in quantities that are profitable and within pre-determined product ranges and price bands.

Within the buyer-seller relationships I have just described, the challenge is a basic one that has not changed down through the years: *If you want to sell to a customer what, in the end, is good for you, you have to start by thinking about what is good for the customer.* By that approach you stand the best chance of the customer buying from you rather than from someone else. The art of persuading someone to buy because it is in his or her interest to do so is *selling*.

Where does negotiation fit in?

Repeated and successful sales, applying the selling technique, produce the basis for negotiation. You will be familiar with many selling situations in which the customer says in effect, 'I like the idea of buying from you, *but* I am not happy with the terms you are suggesting'. Equally, from your point of view, as the seller, you have probably felt or even expressed the thought, 'I would be happy to supply the product range and in the quantities he is wanting but *not* on the terms that he is suggesting.

You have a mutual desire to trade together but you still have a *gap between you that must be bridged*. By sales technique, the customer is moved to a position where, in order to satisfy his *now heightened perception of his needs*, he considers the purchase decision. His attention is turned from saying 'yes', or 'no' to the terms and conditions of the sales purchase.

Repeated application of the selling process has created the mutual desire to trade and now it is the process of *negotiation* that will close the gap. Having been satisfied during the selling phase that the product or service has benefits which meet his needs, as well as or better than those offered by competitors, the customer then focuses more closely upon the many detailed factors surrounding the buying decision. This is the most marked difference between selling and negotiation – *the nature of the end result for both sides*. In selling we are concerned with *benefits related to products or services*. In negotiation we are motivated by *the effect on the profitability or reduction in costs to both sides* of the outcome of our discussions.

Some definitions

What is selling?

Selling is the means used by the seller to persuade someone to buy from you where initially your *desire* to supply *exceeds* the buyer's need to buy.

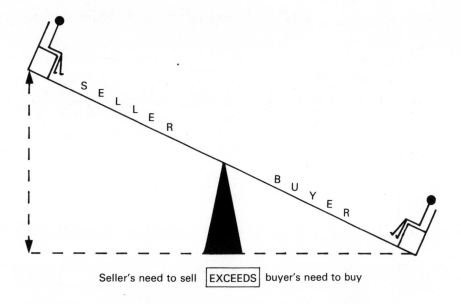

Seller's need to sell EXCEEDS buyer's need to buy

What is negotiation?

Negotiation occurs in the relationship between supplier and buyer where the desire to supply and buy is more or less equal but there is a *gap* to be closed covering the terms on which both sides will agree to trade with one another.

How can the gap that separates buyer and seller be closed? What types of negotiation are there that can cause one side or the other, or both, to move towards each other to close the gap? Let us take an example, an original equipment manufacturer (usually shortened to an OEM) who is willing to buy 20 000 of component A. Your price,

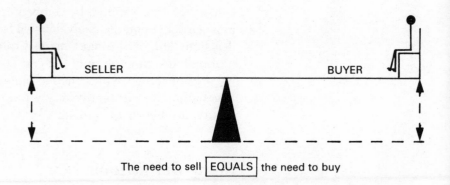

The need to sell │EQUALS│ the need to buy

as a supplier, is $1.50 per unit, based on the buyer spending a minimum of $30 000 over a defined contract period. But the potential OEM buyer says that he will only pay $1.35 per unit which will cost $27 000 over the contract period. Here is a situation that will be familiar to many of my readers. How can the gap of $3 000 be closed?

By Selling? You might persuade the buyer to pay your price of $1.50 for 20 000;

Figure 4.1 **Stepping stones in a sale.**

this would be *selling*. No negotiation will have taken place *because you have not moved*. You have persuaded him to accept your proposition as it stands – on this occasion. You have used selling as a means of inducing or motivating the buyer to move towards you (see Figure 4.1 Stepping Stones in a sale).

By Capitulation? The buyer, on the other hand, might persuade you to supply at $1.35. This would be *Capitulation* by you. No negotiation has taken place because *the buyer has not moved*. You have accepted the buyer's proposition as it stands and it could be said that you capitulated because you needed the business, or as does happen, the buyer sold to you.

For *negotiation* to take place, *both sides* must be willing to move together. However, you will be more successful if you can draw the buyer nearer to your price of $1.50 than his of $1.35. The middle price between the two is $1.425.

If you agree anything higher than $1.425 you have achieved a better deal than the buyer. But if you do, how will the buyer feel? What if you settled for $1.40? The buyer will be happy – but will you be?

By Distributive or Divisive Agreement? This suggests two other ways of closing a gap: close the gap with a distributive or divisive agreement. The gap is closed and the agreement to supply and buy is made, but one side is unhappy. During the lifetime of that particular contract, it is likely that the side that is unhappy will try and *claw back* the advantages it lost at the negotiation. Remember what John Harvey-Jones said: 'The individual banker who has lost money on a deal which you made too keen will learn from that experience, and will seek to recoup on a later occasion'.

It will be an agreement that will *divide* the two sides, tending to keep them apart, and making the next contractual negotiation unnecessarily difficult. The basic fault lies in seeing – in our simple example – the $3 000 as a sum that has to be *distributed* between the two sides, with what one side gains being seen as a loss for the other side. There is another way!

By Integrative or Collaborative Agreement Agreeing to close the gap but with an *integrative* or *collaborative* agreement. That is, the gap is closed, the agreement to supply and buy is made, and both sides are happy. How can this happen if both sides have to move from their favoured position? By the application of two factors.

The gap is seen by both sides as having something of value in it for both of them. Both sides will work at closing it for mutual benefit. The solution will be based on *collaboration*, *integrating* the principal desires of both sides.

This can only happen if you recognize that, as *you* move (i.e. give up or *concede* something) what you offer has a *cost to you and a value to the buyer*. Similarly, if the *buyer* concedes something to you, it will have a *cost for him*, but a *value to you*. If the buyer adds up all the values he has obtained from you, deducts the cost of what he has conceded to you, and has a positive value at the end, he will feel he has done a good deal.

As the supplier, you can make a similar calculation. So, in our simple example, you could perhaps agree at the mid-point of $1.42½. Apparently you are in balance. However, if in foregoing $0.07½ ($1.50 less $1.42½) you have conceded elements which *to the buyer* are worth more than $0.07½ per unit, or $1 500 overall, he will feel he has gained well, and left you in a reasonably happy position. Similarly, if in foregoing $0.07½ per unit, the buyer concedes elements that overall are worth more than $1 500 to you, you will feel that you have obtained a satisfactory agreement.

If both sides can genuinely feel they have got a deal that is good for them, then they have an agreement that will be of advantage to both sides and relatively trouble-free.

From all this comes a fundamental principle of negotiation:

'IT IS SUCCESSFUL WHEN BOTH SIDES HAVE WON AND BOTH FEEL THE OTHER SIDE IS CONTENT WITH THE OUTCOME'.

Clearly, the ability to close the gap is vitally important. But equally important is '*where is the Gap?*' To revert to our example, the gap may not have occurred at $1.50–$1.35. It might have occurred at $1.40–$1.25 (bad for you) or $1.60–$1.45 (good for you). The same gap, but the total outlay differs considerably. *How to close the gap is negotiation. Where the gap occurs is selling.* The art is to use your selling skills so well that when the gap is identified, it is already well on your side of what would be advantageous *and* by the successful use of selling skills the buyer is happy as well.

From this, a second principle arises:

'THE SKILLS OF SELLING PROVIDE THE BASIS OF SUCCESSFUL NEGOTIATION AND PREPARE THE WAY (THROUGH IDENTIFYING WHAT IS VALUABLE TO THE BUYER) FOR SUCCESSFUL NEGO- TIATION, I.E. A GOOD NEGOTIATOR NEVER STOPS SELLING'

'SELL WELL AND YOU WILL HAVE TO NEGOTIATE LESS'

What do you require? Answer:An integrative, collaborative type of agreement, which is profitable to you and to the customer.

In that way you can build longer-term loyalty and security of outlets for your production capacity. Divisive or distributive agreements are troublesome, of doubtful profitability at the end, and provide no satisfactory basis for a significant presence in the market.

Against this background we will now go on to look more carefully at the stages involved in a negotiation before considering in some detail each stage and how to be successful in it.

The stages in a negotiation

Negotiation is a continuing process. But to understand it we need to look at it in stages.

1 Selling to the customer.
2 Identifying the gap:
    – where is it?
    – what is in it?
    – how big is it?
3 Preparing to negotiate:
    – analysing both the customer's needs and our own;
    – deciding what we want from the deal and how we are going to achieve it;
    – adopting starting positions, or *stances*;
    – exchanging *concessions* and trading to bridge the gap.

Selling to the customer

Successful negotiating requires a high level of selling skill:

– to create a desire to buy;
– to position 'the gap' more favourably;
– to identify what will be of real value to the buyer;
– to present your case attractively;
– to answer objections that might be raised;
– to ensure you close on an agreement.

Remember – you do not always have to negotiate

Your aim should be to sell and close the sale on your standard terms and conditions of sale, with no gap to be bridged by negotiation.

However, we are assuming that is not the case and you will have to enter the process of negotiation.

Basic training in selling is contained in any effective industrial selling course. Here we only highlight the main points. But we shall consider additional aids, that are often overlooked, on questioning techniques and need identification, both of which are essential if you are to position 'the gap' favourably to you and identify what is of real value to the buyer.

The structure we shall follow is:

1 Understanding the industrial buyer and the process by which he buys.

2 The framework of a sales call and the opening techniques.

3 Questioning techniques to identify the real needs of the buyer.

4 Presenting to him, and selling to him the benefits he is seeking.

5 Dealing with objections.

6 Closing techniques.

Understanding the industrial buyer and the process by which he buys

There is a typical industrial-buying process, involving different people of different levels. Effective selling means matching this buying process with your selling process. Typically, the 'buy phases' start from a broad position and gradually filter to a refined, detailed purchasing order. Within the process, the number and seniority of the persons involved declines as the filtering progresses. (See Figure 4.2.)

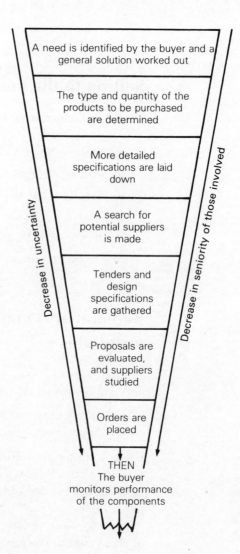

Figure 4.2 **Buy phases**

The salesman needs to be aware of the 'buy classes' into which his customers fit. Are they:

—   NEW BUY?
—   STRAIGHT RE-BUY?
—   MODIFIED RE-BUY?

The buyer could have a variety of pressures on him:

—   PRESSURES FROM OUTSIDE THE COMPANY;
—   PRESSURES FROM WITHIN THE COMPANY;
—   INDIVIDUAL/PERSONAL PRESSURES.

The BUY PHASES, BUY CLASSES and BUY PRESSURES on a buyer must be recognized by the salesman if he is to be able to offer a personal service to the buyer. He will then have control over three vital elements to successful selling:

—   *where* is he in the buying and decision-making process?
—   *what* type of process is it?
—   *who* is he dealing with?

In responding to such a variety of situations the salesman will need to adopt a variety of roles:

—   the consultant,
—   the salesman,
—   the negotiator,
and understand the persons in the process:
—   decision-makers,
—   influencers,
—   processors.

These points in selling techniques are essential to effective negotiations. You need to know:

—   *Where* am I in the buying and decision-making process?
—   *What* sort of process am I in?
—   *Who* am I dealing with?
—   *What* motivates him?

The Framework of a Sales Call and

The Opening Techniques

A sales call has a framework that corresponds to the buying process.

Attention	
Interest	Attention
Desire	Benefits
Action	Close

In any sales call there is:

  (i) An *OPENING* period, during which you need to gain the $\boxed{\text{attention}}$ and $\boxed{\text{interest}}$ of the buyer.

 (ii) A *MIDDLE* period, where interest leads to $\boxed{\text{desire}}$, as the buyer sees the $\boxed{\text{benefits}}$ of trading with you.

(iii) An *END* period, where the sale is $\boxed{\text{closed}}$ and $\boxed{\text{action}}$ agreed.

Each sales call requires preparation. The framework is:

— set the call objectives;

— decide how to achieve the objectives;

— prepare the support materials, visual aids etc.

The three main techniques for an effective opening are:

  (i) Think about what you look like and your behaviour.

 (ii) Think about what you say to gain the attention of the buyer.

(iii) Think yourself into the buyer's shoes and his NEEDS.

These simple points become vitally important in the process of negotiation. In the process, there could be two, three or more interviews, each one a sales call in its own right:

— each with an opening, middle and end;

— each with its set of objectives;

— each requiring pre-call preparation.

But they will be inter-linked within the process of the *total sale*, *which will have its own overall opening, middle and end.*

Diagrammatically, the typical process is shown in Figure 4.3.

Questioning techniques to identify the real needs of the buyer

When selling there are two types of questioning techniques:

— asking 'open' questions;

— asking 'closed' questions.

'Open' questions are those that begin with words like, 'what', 'why', 'which', 'where', 'when', 'how', 'who'. They can only be answered with a flow of information. They are therefore most useful in the earlier stages of an interview or where the conversation is about extracting information from the other side.

'Closed', or, 'dead-end' questions are those which are capable of being answered with 'yes' or 'no', or a flow of conversation that says, in fact, little more than 'yes' or 'no'! They are most useful in the later

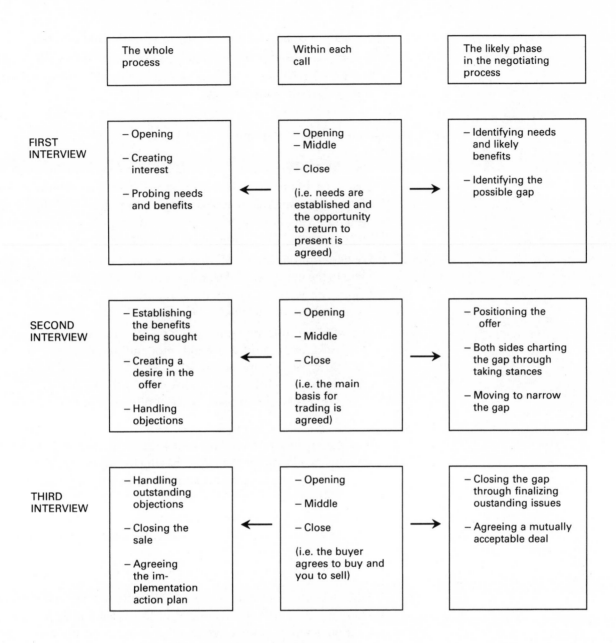

Figure 4.3 **Questioning techniques**

stages of an interview, when the salesman needs to control the conversation on the closing details and avoid opening up wider issues. They are also useful as questions where the buyer does not need to be encouraged to give information but the salesman needs to control the direction and progress of the conversation.

Essential to successful negotiation is a more sophisticated questioning technique. Its purpose is to identify the real needs of the buyer and position you as the supplier who best understands his requirements and can therefore improve its chances of winning the order on attractive terms. The advantages in negotiation are:

- the 'gap' will be positioned near to your desired position;
- the assessment of that which will be of value to the customer and that which will not be, will be more accurate and strengthen your ability to trade concessions.

The questioning technique is as follows:

(i) You ask *background* or *situational* questions, to understand the customer, his trading details, etc. Poor salesmen ask these sorts of questions and then make a big assumption – 'if that is the situation you are in, what you need is . . .'. Frequently, the customer says, 'No, I don't'. There is a better way.

(ii) Background or situational questions need to be asked, but limit them to the main items of clarification you have already researched before you went into the call. Then move the questioning on to the *priorities and problems* being faced by the buyer:

i.e., give an interim summary of your understanding of the background situation and then continue, e.g.
'So what you are saying is . . .'
'So what will be your priorities over the next year?'
'What then do you see as the problems you will face?'
etc.

It is the answer to these questions that will cause the buyer to *state* his needs, rather than your having to assume or guess them, i.e., having given an interim summary of your understanding of the implications, continuing with, e.g.

'So what you are saying is . . .'
'In order to avoid these implications happening, you need to . . .'
'What do you need to do to avoid these implications?'

The answer will be stated needs, not implied or assumed needs. There are two further advantages in this questioning process.
- a buyer may not always be clear himself on his real needs. This process will help him clarify his needs for himself.
- if, at the end of the process you have still not understood his needs correctly, you can go back up the process to seek clarification, and then come down again to a re-statement of needs, e.g.

Buyer – 'No!' That is not what I need'.
Salesman – 'I'm sorry if I misunderstood you. What are your priorities?'
Buyer – 'What I wanted to say was . . .'.

And the conversation can progress to a re-statement and agreement on the real needs.

Throughout this questioning process, 'open' and 'closed' questions will be used as appropriate.

Replying to the buyer and selling to him the benefits he is seeking

Two points need to be emphasized here:

1 Customers do not buy products as such, but *the benefits they can derive from them*.

2 Explaining the benefits of your products can be helped by the use of *benefit analysis sheets* and the use of your communication skills.

The use of the questioning technique described will give you many further advantages:
- you will be much more confident that you know which benefits the buyer is really needing;
- you will know how your product/service package can uniquely provide them.

In short, you will be replying with rifle-shot accuracy rather than throwing your product features at the buyer like shrapnel, hoping one bit of the grenade lands on target. (See Figure 4.4.)

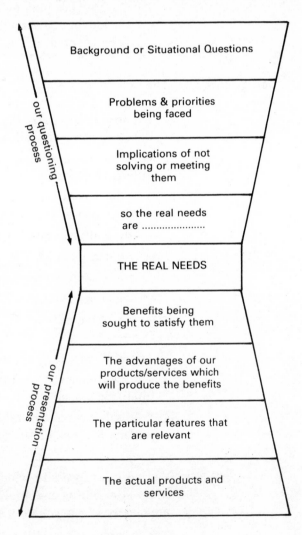

Figure 4.4 **Question/Presentation process**

If the questioning and presenting (or replying) processes are done well, you will greatly strengthen your negotiation position by:

– locating any gap nearer to your favoured position;

– providing a much greater understanding of what in the deal will be a real value to the buyer and what will not.

Dealing with objections   The key points are:

1   Objections are an important form of feedback on how close we are to meeting the buyer's requirements.

2   The types of objections met and how to handle them. The skills of handling objections are vital in negotiation in at least two areas:

(a) As an objection could well be the buyer taking a stance or position in the negotiation, you need to ensure you have really understood what the objection is before trying to reply.

(b) Within your plan for conducting a negotiation, you may well decide the answer must be postponed until further ground has been covered.

Closing techniques   The main points are:

1   We need to recognize the opportunities given by a buyer to close the sale. These are called *buying signals*.

2   We need to understand and be able to use as appropriate the different techniques of closing. The ones covered are:

– Trial closes (i.e. accumulating increasing commitment from the buyer at each stage of the sale)

– alternative closes;

– summary closes;

– concession closes;   See pages 32–4 for explanations and examples of each of these closing techniques.

– quotation closes;

– direct request closes.

You will need to apply the same skills in negotiation:

3   You will need to recognize and test when you are near to finalizing a deal.

4   You will have to close the agreement, and you will see that it is preferable if *you* close, rather than the buyer.

Summary   Selling is a process in which the need to negotiate may recur. But never stop selling and applying selling techniques even where you are clearly in a negotiating situation.

The techniques of selling apply directly to the application of the techniques of negotiation.

The most important selling skills you need to master in order to be good negotiators are questioning and need identification.

Types of TRIAL CLOSING Techniques

Technique	Example
1 Alternative Close Offering more than one option, either of which is acceptable to you:–	'We can supply you in container loads, or pallets. Which suits your needs better?'
2 Summary Close Summarize the customer's needs as a complete package of requirements and then conclude that your package of recommendations provides the best solution:–	'You want a heating system that can cope with occasional peak demands, that is easy to maintain with semi-skilled labour and that is economical in its use of fuel. The best fit to meet all these requirements of yours is our Titan Powerpack. When would be the best time to install it?'
3 Concession Close Offering a concession as a means of reaching an agreement:–	'The final item is delivery. If we agree to split this between two locations rather than to one site with no additional cost to you, when can we programme our tanker to complete this order?'
4 Quotation Close Offering to commit to a specific quotation in return for an order:–	'If we incorporate this redesign feature for the factory extension on the lines you now want, when can you give us your written go-ahead to start building?'
5 Direct Request Close Used in situations where the customer likes to make his own decisions. * Beware. It runs the risk, that whilst he may say 'yes', he may say 'no' and then you have to re-trace your steps to find out where you went wrong:–	'Shall we go ahead then and install these improvements?'

Applied well, selling skills can mean:

1 You succeed without having to negotiate.

2 You need to negotiate but the gap starts nearer your favoured position.

3 Your ability to trade across the gap towards a profitable outcome is greatly increased.

The principles of negotiation

As a result of the selling process you will have identified a gap, to be filled by negotiation. But in order to do that you need to know where the gap is, what it consists of and how big it is.

The most common description of a gap is *price*. But very rarely will price be the only factor. There could be many. They separate into:

— operational items,
— financial items,

and depending on what you know about the customer they can be:

— quantified,
— not quantified but capable of subjective weighting.

Typical elements include:

— operational items:
  — volumes/shares/mix;
  — range supplied;
  — stock holding·
  — delivery;
  — application engineering support;
— financial items:
  — price levels and changes;
  — timing of price changes;
  — stability of price changes;
  — credit period.

All of these are capable of quantification. But, in addition there are other elements that are not easily quantified but are important in the balance of a negotiation, e.g.:

— The benefit of trading with a national, a local, or an international supplier.
— The sort of human relationships that exist.
— Geographical convenience etc.

Some principles:

(i) You need to understand and be able to quantify financial items.
(ii) You need to look much further than mere price levels when trying to understand the gap between you, and your customer. You need to search for all the elements and find which ones can be treated as a variable in the negotiation.

(iii) You need to put yourself in the place of the buyer and see *his* side, objectively and unemotionally.

(iv) You need to have all the important facts in order to be able to quantify as many of the elements, and their variations, as possible.

(v) Very little is *not negotiable* in a deal.

With the gap analysed, *you need to prepare to negotiate*. This will be looked at in more detail later. For the moment, here are some basic principles.

You need to analyse both the customer's needs and your own. How well you can do this depends on how well you have sold. It is relatively simple to do it in two stages:

(i) Consider what your overall objective is for the customer and what are likely to be the customer's objectives.

(ii) List and analyse all the variables, which ones are essential, and which are not.

Try to make the same calculation for the customer:

- Those which are of great importance to one side or another will have a value, which may well exceed the actual cost of supplying them.

- Those which are of less importance have a much lower value, even though there will be a financial cost involved.

- By this process you will identify what will be valuable to one side or the other in trading, and what the cost will be.

Some principles:

(i) The art of negotiation is trading values, not costs.

(ii) You need to enhance the value to the customer of the concessions you are offering and minimize the value to you of the concessions you are receiving.

(iii) But *concessions do* have a cost so as you enhance the value of your concessions to the customer you need to minimize the cost he will believe he is paying. Similarly, as you minimize the value to you of the concessions you are receiving you need to enhance the cost you have to pay.

You should consider the person(s) you are going to see.

Some principles:

(i) Negotiation ought to take place between people who see each other as equals.

(ii) Try to keep numbers to a minimum. The fewer the participants, the sooner agreement can usually be reached.

(iii) Try to keep negotiating teams even. Do not be over-powered, and do not over-power.

Consider where the meeting will take place and the situation you will face.

Some principles:

(i) Respect the buyer and his ways of behaving. 'When in Rome, do as the Romans do'.

(ii) Meet on your own ground, if you can.

(iii) Sit where you can look at, see and hear everyone else.

(iv) Avoid agreeing to long sessions – they can be very tiring.

(v) Be careful of negotiation related to lunch and drinks. Few of us are good at negotiating on a full stomach.

Consider how you will conduct the negotiation meeting. You know the gap; you know what you want from the deal (i.e., where you want to finish within the gap). You should also decide what is the worst position you will accept (your minimum or 'fall-back' position), less than which would be unacceptable. Diagrammatically using the previous example:

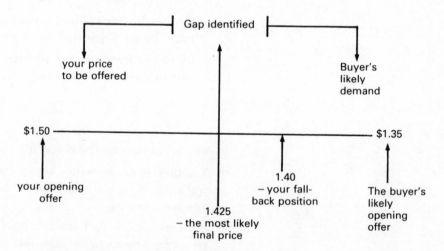

Figure 4.5 **Identifying the gap**

Within these limits you can plan how you will conduct the negotiation. This will be looked at in more detail later, but first some principles:

(i) Be willing to communicate in advance of the meeting your interest and openness. It can help prepare for an integrative collaborative agreement.

(ii) Negotiation is like a game. It has ritual and rules. Keep to them to maintain the fabric of negotiation.

(iii) Be yourself. Do not act or over-react, you will be mistrusted.

(iv) Be reasonable. Do not pursue what the buyer cannot be expected to agree to. Do not be greedy – you want long-term collaborative relationships.

(v) Start your trading high, i.e. your opening stance ($1.50 in our example or a small concession to $1.48), and trade-down. It is virtually impossible to trade-up.

(vi) Do not go below your fall-back position.

In preparing for a difficult negotiation recognize that the gap may be only partially closed at the first meeting. This raises principles about the use of time.

(i) Make use of time. Be prepared to break off or use some delaying tactics if things are not going your way.

(ii) Do not be pressurized or rushed – into a poor deal. Better to break off and meet again later.

Consider how you will record the final agreement.

Objectives of	Selling Call	Negotiation call
The Call	To persuade the buyer to buy your product(s) at your quoted prices.	To persuade the buyer to accept a price rise or a delivery schedule by showing benefits/concessions; dealing with questions and reaching agreement
The Opening	To explore and identify customer's needs	To identify and meet the initial stances of the buyer; maintain the fabric of the negotiation and establish buyer's NEEDS
The Sales Presentation	To select and present relevant customer benefits which will meet and satisfy the customer's specific needs	To establish the gap in actual stances between buyer and seller; To concede high-value/low-cost concessions To obtain high-value concessions from buyer
Handling Objections	To prevent by anticipating snags likely to arise or to handle objections raised so that the customer is satisfied with the answers	To keep the initiative by not giving a concession unless one of equal or greater value to the salesman is obtained from the buyer. To maintain the buyer's motivation to negotiate by making him feel he is doing a good deal
Getting a Buying Decision	To obtain a buying decision from the customer or a commitment to the sales proposition presented to him	To reach an agreement on the basis of the planned point of need balance by the salesman. To ensure that the agreement reached is seen to be valuable and fair to the buyer.

Figure 4.6 **Selling versus negotiation call – different ingredients**

Some principles:

(i) Take notes.

(ii) Summarize at the end.

(iii) Be willing to write to confirm the details – it gives you a lot of power.

Conclusion

At the beginning of this chapter, I described negotiation as a parallel skill to selling. Figure 4.6 summarizes the differences between a selling and a negotiation call on a customer or prospective customer.

5

Preparing to negotiate

This chapter sets out the seven steps in planning negotiation that should be followed when preparing for the first meeting. They should be re-checked when preparing for subsequent meetings that might be necessary before a conclusion is reached.

Throughout your planning keep in mind two abiding principles which provide the foundation of effective and successful negotiations.

1 Have a total negotiating plan – a plan that covers the whole process. How to put it together is the subject of this chapter.
2 Start your side of the negotiation early, by collecting relevant information, talking to appropriate people, taking every opportunity to understand the customer and the decision-makers. Know before you start the negotiation meeting exactly what you want and how you intend getting it.

The seven-step negotiation planning process

STEP 1. Set the objectives for the negotiation.

STEP 2. Identify the customer's requirements.

STEP 3. Identify the elements that are likely to arise in the negotiations.

STEP 4. Decide the concessions to be exchanged and calculate their costs and values.

STEP 5. Calculate the overall effect of these concessions on both you and the customer.

With this information;

STEP 6. Prepare your stances.

STEP 7. Prepare how you will conduct and complete the process of negotiation.

The following pages explain how these seven steps apply on the job.

STEP ONE

Set the objectives for the negotiation

You should be clear what you want to achieve and have a firm opinion of what the customer will want. How accurate that opinion will be will much depend on how well you have already applied your selling skills, and especially those of Needs Identification.

Principles to follow in setting objectives:

1 State them in terms of the *customer's* needs.
2 They should be commercially profitable to you.
3 They should fit into your overall sales and marketing strategy.
4 They should be achievable within the resources available to you, and the market conditions in which you are working.
5 They should be specific.
6 They should be clear.
7 They should specify a time-limit.

For example, in a renewal of the annual contract with a manufacturer who is experiencing small growth in a market which is:

(i) over-supplied;
(ii) expected to be flat and depressed for the next 12 months;
(iii) should then pick up again.

Objectives:

(i) To increase our sales over the contract period by x per cent to y per cent itemized as . . . with types . . . added to the range of . . . volumes
(ii) Net contribution will be . . .
(iii) To provide service back-up of . . .
(iv) To increase stock support by . . . to . . .
(v) Overall, to support the client's objective of sustaining a growing presence in his market, for our longer-term objective of being a favoured supplier.
(vi) To be willing to offer cash-flow support to the client equivalent to our foregoing invoice settlement by . . . days. ($. . .).

Likely client objectives:

(i) To require . . . volume of products, an increase of . . . per cent over the 12 months.
(ii) To buy at net prices that exceed last year by only . . . per cent.
(iii) To have supply reliability.
(iv) To need service support – possibly free of charge.
(v) To protect cash-flow position.
(vi) Overall, to obtain help from suppliers over the depressed year.

Objectives of this kind are difficult to establish; but unless you do, you are not preparing your case as well as you should. You *must* know what you are aiming to do.

Contrast the following alternative, and relatively useless, 'objectives': they do not deserve to be called objectives – they are nothing better than wishful thinking.

Objectives: (i) We shall look for significant increases in volumes and financial contributions from this large customer.

(ii) To meet our own internal economies, we shall need to tighten our credit control and watch carefully how much service back-up we provide.

Relate these objectives to the principles we have stated. On how many counts do they fail? Add the following on – they are too vague for either the salesman to know what he is meant to achieve, or for the client to know what he is reasonably expected to do.

STEP TWO

Identify the customer's requirement

This step encapsulates the findings of our selling to the customer.

(i) Can you identify the key items in the customer's commercial and financial situation?

(ii) Against that background, what problems is he facing? What do you know of his priorities? What alternatives are open to him?

(iii) What is your relationship with him? What competition is he known to favour or dislike? Can you say why?

(iv) What do you know of the people you will meet? – their subjective/personal needs? What is the decision-making structure?

(v) How do the 'rational/objective' needs of the customer's company relate to the 'subjective/personal' needs of the decision-makers?

(vi) What therefore appear to be the needs of the customer's company and the benefits sought? How can you help to satisfy those needs?

A simple example from the client mentioned at Step One. In practice, you should be able to complete the needs analysis in much more detail:

(i) Depressed market, over-supply. Price-conscious customers. A main supplier in its markets (possibly 15–20 per cent market share). Achieving small growth through competitive pricing, reputation for reliability of supply, and high personal service to customers.

(ii) Like its other important competitors, known to be struggling to maintain share, let alone achieve small growth. Has earlier made large investments in improved warehousing and stock-control and distribution facilities to its customers. Now fairly highly geared. Known to need to achieve growth to finance the investment, but cannot afford to reduce prices too much. Needs to continue to offer good customer service, but believed to be concerned by the high overheads involved.

(iii) Has good relations with suppliers . . . They are similar to us in price, range and service. The OEM reduced its purchases from supplier . . . when a strike made them unable to supply. We are liked because we have in addition had the flexibility to cater for some sudden changes in demand.

(iv) The chief buyer has to meet financial budgets that are believed to give him scope for balancing the buying in price with supply and service support. His staff member, who you increasingly meet, is more price-conscious, though his attitude eased at the time of . . .'s strike. This suggested the buyer's priorities are regular supply to manufacturing. Both people easy to meet. Chief buyer has about four years to retirement. The staff member will probably move on in two years. He reports to the chief buyer, who reports to the finance director, with a dotted-line relationship to the manufacturing director.

(v) There is no clash in the relationships.

(vi) The priority needs:
   – a totally reliable supply of . . . products and quantities.

STEP THREE

Identify the elements that are likely to arise in the negotiation

1 List them

Typical areas have already been covered in the chapter 'Financial techniques in selling'.

A simple method is to list them in a column, separating those that can be quantified from those which in your company may not be quantifiable e.g.

Quantifiable Elements	e.g. List price
	Quantity discount
	Volume mix
	Range additions
	etc.
Unquantifiable elements	e.g. Technical Support
	Advertising support
	etc.

Do not assume that certain areas will be excluded. Remember the principle that you need to seek for variables. Start by identifying all possible variables now, before you meet the customer.

2 Identifying the competitor position

Very often in negotiations a competitive offer will be quoted to you, and it can appear that over many areas there is always a competitor better/cheaper, etc., than you! Be careful. You must distinguish between the best/cheapest position of *ALL* competitors combined and the best/cheapest position that any *ONE* competitor can offer. The buying negotiator will normally quote the former, not the latter.

Add this information to your analysis sheet, viz:

Elements	*Competitive Position*
Quantifiable	
Unquantifiable	

Where facts are not available, use your best judgement. Remember the objective: to anticipate the most likely competitive case that *in fact* you will face so that, when the buyer quotes competitive offers to you, you are well armed to distinguish *theory* (possible lowest positions) from *fact* (what anyone competitively can really supply).

3 Having listed the elements and the competitive position the next task is to assess their relative importance.

(i) Which elements are *essential* (E) for one side or the other?

(ii) Which elements are *attractive extras* (A) for one side or the other?

(iii) Which elements are *relatively unimportant* (U) to one side or the other? It is here that you need to use your imagination to search for variables. What you may consider to be your normal policy may be *not* so normal to the customer. As we shall shortly see, you need to consider how you can confer value to the customer with some item which, for you, is *relatively unimportant* because we always do it that way.

4 Having decided the level of importance, take *each* element and again establish three categories (i.e. for each element):

(i) What is your best estimate of the likely point of agreement (judgemental comments only will be possible for those items you cannot quantify).

(ii) Given your objectives and profitability criteria, what is the lowest/worst position you can accept (less than which makes the deal unprofitable)? You may well need to clear this with your senior management. (We shall call this the fall back position.)

(iii) Try to estimate what the same position will be for the customer, given what you know of his business objectives and profitability criteria.

See Appendix Planning Format for major customers pp.141–171.

STEP FOUR

Decide the concessions to be exchanged and calculate their costs and values

1 In each of the areas that you believe will be negotiated, you have to consider the concessions you are prepared to *give* and the concessions you want from the customer in *exchange*.

2 To do this effectively you have to work out the *costs* and *values* involved.

3 For example, price and volume are often negotiated together.

Assume you have submitted a written quotation for 1 000 units @ $10.50 each and your gross margin is 40 per cent.

If accepted, you will achieve $4 200 gross profit. In order to maintain the $4 200 gross profit you might prepare the following list of concessions:

Negotiating item PRICE/VOLUME

Concessions from you:	Concessions from customer:
1. Reduce our price to $10.00	1. Increase the volume to 1 150 units
2. Reduce our price to $9.50	2. Increase the volume to 1 320 units
3. Reduce our price to $9.00	3. Increase the volume to 1 560 units

4 Similarly, in the other areas that may be negotiated consider:
   – what you are prepared to concede;
   – what it will cost you;
   – what value it will give to the customer;
   – what you want in return.

See Appendix Planning Format for major customers pp.141–171 and pp.91–109.

For examples of how to calculate the figures, refer to the chapter 'Financial Techniques in Selling'.

5 You will want to remember two other points when considering the concessions to be exchanged:

5.1 Flexibility
   Although, on paper, you will list the concessions in each negotiable area, in practice you may need to be more flexible.

   For example, instead of insisting on yet another increase in volume to compensate you for a further reduction in price, you may ask for concessions in other areas, e.g.
   – additional items
   – faster payment
   – price increase on another type
   – central delivery

5.2 Selling Skills

When preparing your concessions to the customer, consider:
- the high value to him;
- the high cost to you.

When preparing the list of concessions you want from the customer, consider:
- the low value to you;
- the low cost to him.

This will help you to achieve a better deal in the face-to-face situation.

STEP FIVE

Calculate the overall effect of these concessions on both you and the customer

1 Although we have so far considered your negotiation by individual items, it will be the *total* deal or package you will be negotiating. You now therefore need to do two things:

(i) Calculate the total effect of all the concessions.

(ii) If the total position does not meet your criteria, reconsider the *individual* concessions to ensure the *totals* are acceptable.

2 The objective is to calculate the total financial outcome of the quantifiable elements, to ascertain:

(i) The overall financial value of the likely point of agreement – Is it acceptable to us? Is it likely to be acceptable to the customer?

(ii) The overall financial value of fall-back positions for you – is it acceptable?

(iii) The likely overall financial value of your estimate of the customer's fall-back position. From what you know of his interests etc., is it sufficiently attractive?

3 These financial results will need qualification in so far as the unquantifiable elements have importance. Obviously, the more the negotiating items can be quantified, the more accurate your preparation will be.

4 With the completion of this step, you have gathered and considered all the information you need to help you with the next two steps. In these you will plan how you will *move* from the *static* position we have so far calculated to close the gap at a point of agreement that is acceptable to both sides.

STEP SIX

Prepare your stances

1 This step is never easy. However, your success will be greatly helped by having completed your initial selling meetings well and understood the needs of your customer, the benefits he is seeking, and the sort of person he is.

2 The principles you should use are as follows:

2.1 In simple picture form, the process of negotiation is like a see-saw, or old-fashioned weighing scales. I illustrate in Part II 'The negotiation process'.

 – the likely point of agreement is the point of balance;

 – on either side of the point of balance is the gap you have to close;

 – you need to try to start *your* side of the negotiation so that you are approximately in balance with where your customer starts, i.e.:

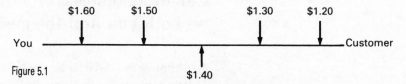

Figure 5.1

In very simple terms, assume the only element you have to worry about is price. Assume you have calculated that the most likely point of agreement is $1.40. If the customer intimates he will only pay $1.30, you should aim for a starting position of $1.50. You have taken a reasonable stance in relationship to the customer and given yourself the same room for movement as the customer has taken.

If you had replied with $1.60, you would be indicating you thought $1.45 was the more likely point of balance. If competitive offers were in the range of $1.37–$1.40 your opening stance would appear unreasonable and would set the scene for a divisive negotiation.

On the other hand, if the customer had opened with $1.20 and you replied not with the 'balancing' $1.60, but $1.50, you are not giving yourself enough room for moving and trading to reach $1.40. Obviously, negotiations will usually be more complicated and the 'likely point of agreement' will not always be so easily identified. But the same principles apply – having identified there is a gap:

(i) Where is the likely point of agreement?

(ii) Where does the customer appear to be standing for *his* opening stances on *his* side of the gap?

(iii) Where therefore should *you* start to offer an opening stance that is reasonably in balance with the customer?

2.2 Be very careful not to make too many assumptions before you begin your negotiation. It could limit the area of movement and your opportunities later, when the discussions may be difficult, to search for variables.

2.3 In determining your opening position, keep the *total* deal or package in mind. But prepare how you will negotiate *each* element. Here you need to distinguish between those that are essential to you and those that are not. You need to try to do the same for the customer. Your aim will be to move to a point of agreement on the *total* package, but moving *less* on those items that are essential to you, and more on those which are not. Again taking a simple example:

- assume only total volume and unit price are the elements
- volume matters most to the customer.
- the likely point of balance is a total spend by the customer of $1 500, comprising 1 000 units at $1.50 each.
- the customer could start at 950 units at $1.40 each (total spend $1 330)
- you could start with 1 100 units at $1.52 each (total spend $1 672, balancing the $1 330)
- very simply, in this example, the opening stances have established
    - the gap;
    - the individual interest of each side, and,
    - a declared willingness to move to a mutually satisfactory agreement.

By moving to a point of balance, you will achieve 1 025 units at $1.46 each, a total spent of $1 500. Both sides then win what is really important to them and let go what is relatively unimportant. That is a perfect integrative negotiation – an agreement where both sides win.

3 The stages of preparation are therefore:

3.1 Over the total package, try to estimate where you believe the customer will start.

3.2 Make the opposite point of balance your overall starting position.

3.3 Consider each individual element in turn:
- estimate where the customer might start;
- determine where you will start, paying attention to:
    - the individual points of balance;
    - the overall package, and,
    - the different emphases to give to each element, depending on its importance to each side;
    - the fall-back positions.

3.4 Use common commercial sense when it comes to the unquantifiable elements.

Having considered all these points summarize them on the Appendix Planning Format for major customers pp.158–159 in the sections headed your STANCES and CUSTOMER STANCES.

The calculations will not necessarily come right first time: this part of your preparation takes time, and trial and error as you try to find the right balance of all the elements. You will find, too, that when the implications of the next step are considered they will also affect how you evaluate your starting positions.

STEP SEVEN

Prepare how you will conduct and complete the process of negotiation

In Chapter 8 on the conduct of a negotiation, we shall consider how to carry out an actual negotiation meeting in detail. However, even before you begin such meetings you should have prepared a plan for how you *will* conduct the negotiations. In this step we cover the principles you should follow.

1 Principles of trading:

1.1 To reach a mutually acceptable, integrative solution, both sides need an open mind. Precondition the other side to be receptive from the very beginning. One method is to plan to offer a concession at the outset, in an area where you know the customer has firm, entrenched views.

1.2 You are preparing to trade. You have calculated the *cost* of the elements and you have decided which are important, etc. However, the skill in negotiation is to trade *values*, not *costs*, i.e.

(i) how to attribute to the customer *value* on items that are not valuable to you and,

(ii) how to minimize the value to you of items offered by the customer.

Therefore never give a concession; trade it, reluctantly!

– Prepare what you can *give*:

(i) how can you add value to it for the customer?

(ii) can you suggest how costly it is to you? If you can, he will feel he has gained value.

– Prepare what you are *likely to be offered*

(i) how can you reduce its apparent value to you?

(ii) can you suggest how little it will have cost the customer to give it?

(iii) or how costly it will be for you to accept it?

- Prepare where you can *devalue*
  (i) the cost to the customer and
  (ii) the value to you of the customer's concessions
- Prepare where you can *increase the value* of
  (i) concessions offered to the customer and
  (ii) the cost of your giving it

Get your customer to work hard for his deal. He will value it all the more.

Anticipate how you can neutralize value or cost offered by the customer.

Be prepared for negative reactions to your trading offers. Your customer will understand negotiating tactics too!

Your aim will be not to believe everything he says but rather to understand *why* he is saying what he is saying.

1.3 Before beginning your meetings, think through what you will say and what the customer can be expected to say.

- Unless you have specifically planned an opening concession, aim to preserve your own neutrality early on:
  (i) get him talking;
  (ii) listen to what he says;
  (iii) avoid taking hard stances too early that can lead to deadlock;
  (iv) prepare to maintain flexibility of movement in the early stages.

- Before you begin to trade item for item you should aim to understand the whole of the customer's package. If you do not you may find you have traded all your items and he has still one or two more demands left. Of course, he may not want to tell you everything he has in mind. (He will expect to have the same problems with you!) But the foundation of an integrative, collaborative agreement is a mutual willingness to understand each other's 'shopping list'.

- Be prepared to start your trading at your opening position and trade down. It will be virtually impossible to trade-up from a lower position.

- When trading, expect to give a bit at a time:
  (i) each time, get something in return;
  (ii) do not let go of a concession completely until you are sure of the total situation. (e.g., be prepared with phrases like 'Yes, that is something I think we can consider'; meaning, you are prepared to consider conceding, but for the moment you have not committed yourself!)

- Whilst preparing to handle the detail of each item, do keep in mind the likely *overall* aim of your customer. You could otherwise find you are winning too many details and the customer will lose hope of a satisfactory overall deal.

– Remember negotiation is a serious game with its own rules. An underlying rule is honesty and integrity if you are to achieve an integrative solution. So:

   (i) be yourself: do not promise what neither you nor your company can do;

   (ii) keep control of your emotions.

1.4 Your objective in preparing for your negotiation is to reach agreement.

– Be on your guard for signs of deadlock.

   (i) Avoid taking entrenched positions.

   (ii) Do not aim to achieve more than can be reasonably hoped for.

   (iii) Expect to have to disagree – but aim to do so from a neutral, objective, third-party, or devil's advocate point of view and in that way the customer will not feel got at, or attacked.

   (iv) Be prepared to help your customer if he seems to be in a position from which you will not achieve a mutually satisfactory agreement.

– Be prepared to make use of time:

   (i) Be patient.

   (ii) Remember negotiation requires stamina. So avoid long sessions and avoid negotiating on a full stomach.

   (iii) Do not expect to reach agreement at the first meeting. Be prepared to postpone with some of the gap still to be closed at a later time. Do not be rushed into an unsatisfactory deal.

1.5 Always rehearse your negotiation. Tell yourself what you are going to say, how you are going to say it, and when. This is especially important where you have a colleague with you.

– What are your respective roles?

– Who will lead?

– Who will take the subordinate role and observe? (Seniority does not matter.)

– When will the second person come into the conversation? The 'observer' can be very useful in:

   (i) noticing when the negotiation is not progressing well;

   (ii) changing the way a conversation is progressing.

Practise, and role-play your arguments.

1.6 Decide how you will control your part of the negotiation.

– Be specific on points of agreement, so there can be no confusion.

- Remember your fall-back position: do not settle for a deal that is below or worse than that position.
- Try to ensure that all communications between the customer and your company are channelled through you. Only then can you have full control.
- Be on your guard *before* or after a negotiation meeting. Apparently small points raised at these times might be part of the customer's total package.
- Be ready to record what is being agreed, and to summarize from *your* notes.
- Prepare your own agenda for each meeting. As far as possible, follow your agenda – it will give you more initiative in the actual meeting.
- Be prepared to maintain the fabric of negotiation. Remember you are involved in a ritual game, with its own rules and played for stakes of hard financial reality.
- Remember your selling skills, especially the use of:
  (i) interim summaries to clarify complicated conversations and
  (ii) trial closes to check progress towards agreement.
1.7 As far as possible, try to negotiate in your native language.
1.8 Beware of post-negotiation celebrations! They might be the prelude to re-opening the negotiation, or catching you off-guard.

You should now be able to tackle preparing for an actual negotiation. After that, we will consider how you should conduct the actual meeting. It will draw on the principles covered here, but will also look in more detail at the art of trading and the ways you should (and should not!) behave.

Calculating the costs of concessions

1 Introduction

Negotiation implies concessions from both sides. Every concession has a cost to the giver and a value to the receiver. Therefore, any concession you are prepared to give *must* be financially calculated, because you need to recover that cost in the concessions you receive.

2 What areas of a customer relationship can be negotiated?

There are many negotiable areas. Some are very common; others are occasional. Since they all have an impact on your profit you must be able to calculate the financial implications of any concessions you make.

Typical negotiable areas include:

- Price
- Volume
- Timing
- Range
- Mix
- Stocks
- Credit Periods
- Delivery
- Support

Each of these areas is covered in detail on the following pages. As you will see, they are often interrelated, for example, price concessions from you in return for volume concessions from the customer.

The areas of negotiation examined here are those most often met by sellers in industrial and commercial markets. Some readers working in, for example, the financial sectors may not have to contend with items such as buffer stocks. But if you are selling through brokers you would certainly be concerned with support services. So for those of you for whom some do not apply, either adapt the principles described or develop specific models for your industry or organization.

Price

Introduction   1 Price × Volume sold = Sales Revenue

The only way to affect sales revenue is to change the price or the volume sold in a given mix.

2 Assuming volume remains constant, a change in price will directly affect profits, for example:

		5% Price Increase	5% Price Reduction
Sales	100 000	105 000	95 000
Variable Costs	60 000	60 000	60 000
Gross Profit	40 000	45 000	35 000
Fixed Costs	25 000	25 000	25 000
Net Profit	15 000	20 000	10 000

Small changes in price have a dramatic effect on profit.

3 To be able to negotiate successfully on price you must:

- Be able to justify your prices.
- Know the margins of the various products you sell.
- Be able to calculate the implications of price changes, for example:
  - Small reductions in price require disproportionately large increases in volume to compensate. (See Table 6.1.)
- Small increases in price can offset quite large reductions in volume.

Justifying your prices

1 Sell the benefits to the customer of buying from you, for example:

- Less maintenance
- Continuity of operation
- Customer satisfaction
- Continuity of supply

2 Do not negotiate on price when you can prove better value for money from you.

Knowing the margins

1 Different products have different costs and prices; therefore, margins can vary.

2 If you know you will have to negotiate on price, find out what the normal margin is.

This is particularly important if price and volume will be negotiated together.

Calculating the effects of price changes

1 Remember, if you are forced to concede a price reduction, there are many ways in which you can get your money back:

- Increased volume.
- Faster payment.
- Additional types.
- Change of mix to the more profitable items.
- Reduction in support.
- Less frequent delivery.

The most common method is to seek increased volume – but only if it is part of your overall objective.

2 Make sure you can calculate the changes in volume you need to compensate for a price reduction. (See Exercise 1.)

Remember that where price changes lead to volume changes there will be some effect on overheads. Usually these effects are minimal.

Conclusion 1 Buyers are paid to negotiate lower buying prices.

2 Always try to cost-justify your prices.

3 If you have to concede a reduction in price:

Table 6.1 **Implications of price reductions on volume**

If you cut your price	If your present gross profit margin is						
	5%	10%	15%	20%	25%	30%	40%
	you need an increase in unit sales of . . .						
1%	25.0%	11.1%	7.1%	5.3%	4.2%	3.4%	2.6%
2	66.7	25.0	15.4	11.1	8.7	7.1	5.3
3	150.0	42.9	25.0	17.6	13.6	11.1	8.1
4		66.7	36.4	25.0	19.0	15.4	11.1
5		100.0	50.0	33.3	25.0	20.0	14.3
6		150.0	66.7	42.9	31.6	25.0	17.6
7		233.3	87.5	53.8	38.9	30.4	21.2
8			114.3	66.7	47.1	36.4	25.0
9			150.0	81.8	56.3	42.9	29.0
10			200.0	100.0	66.7	50.0	33.3
11			275.0	122.2	78.6	57.9	37.9
12			400.0	150.0	92.3	66.7	42.9
13				185.7	108.3	76.5	48.1
14				233.3	127.3	87.5	53.8
15				300.0	150.0	100.0	60.0
16				400.0	177.8	114.3	66.7
17				566.7	212.5	130.8	73.9
18					275.1	150.0	81.8
19					316.7	172.7	90.5
20					400.0	200.0	100.0
21					525.0	233.3	110.5
22					733.3	275.0	122.2
23						328.6	135.3
24						400.0	150.0
25						500.0	166.7

– Be aware of the effect on profit.

– Make sure you get back from the buyer a concession whose value to your company is equal to, or better than, the cost of your price concession.

Exercise 1 Price and volume relationships

Work out the answers to the following questions:

1 You have quoted a distributor $10 for an item against a potential quantity of 100 units. The gross margin at this price is 40 per cent ($4 per unit). The distributor wants you to reduce your price to $9 per unit. Your objective is to make $400 gross profit on the deal. How many must you sell @ $9 per unit to make $400 gross profit?

2 The same distributor is also interested in buying 100 units of a different item, where the price per unit is $50 and the gross margin at that price is 20 per cent. What size of order would you need to compensate for a price reduction to $45?

3 A direct customer tells you he can increase his order by 10 per cent if you can reduce your price by 5 per cent. Would you accept given the following facts?

– Your normal selling price is $20.

– The gross margin at this price is 55 per cent.

– You want the order, but only if the $ gross profit on the deal is maintained.

4 An instruction has come from corporate HQ that every effort must be made to maintain $ margins, even at the expense of losing small volume increases. One of your customers tells you that he will place an order either for 500 units @ $10 per unit or 600 units @ $8.50 per unit. The gross margin on the $10 is 30 per cent. Which alternative will you choose?

Exercise 1 – Answers

1 100 units @ $10 = $1 000 sales.
Gross margin is 40 per cent i.e.: $4 per unit
: $400 for 100 units
If the price is reduced to $9 per unit, the gross margin is reduced to $3 per unit. Therefore in order to make $400 gross profit on the deal you need to sell $\frac{\$400}{\$3}$ = 134 units

2 100 units @ $50 = $5 000 Sales
Gross margin is 20 per cent i.e.: $10 per unit
: $1 000 for 100 units

If the price is reduced to $45 per unit, the gross margin is reduced to $5 per unit. Therefore, in order to continue to make $1 000 gross profit on the deal you need to sell $\frac{\$1\ 000}{\$5}$ = 200 units

3 If your normal selling price is $20 and the gross margin is 55 per cent, then the gross margin per unit is $11. If you reduce your price by 5 per cent (i.e. $1), your gross margin per unit is reduced

to $10. You therefore need an increase in volume of 10 per cent to maintain your original $ gross profit. As your customer has offered a 10 per cent increase in volume in return for a 5 per cent reduction in price, you would accept.

4 You will choose the first alternative (500 units @ $10 each) because it gives you $1 500 gross profit. If you accept the second alternative you will sell 600 units, but your gross margin per unit will drop to $1.50, producing a total gross profit of only $900.

Volume

Introduction

1 Together with price, costs, and mix, volume is a significant influence on profits:

Volume × Price = Sales

Volume × Unit = Cost of Goods Sold

2 Volume is extremely important to you because of the need to make productive use of all of the money invested in the manufacturing units.

Similarly, high-volume sales lead to lower unit costs which create either higher margins or permit competitive pricing.

Unsold volume creates high stocks leading to high financing charges — money is being used to make products which is not being recovered in sales.

3 Normally, therefore, you will want to achieve volume sales and you may be prepared to make concessions in other areas to get them.

4 However, before any negotiation that can involve volume:

- Check that volume is a priority.
- Know the gross margins of the products involved.
- Know the effects on profit of changes in price: volume relationships.

Points to remember

1 Volume increases are always emotionally attractive to sellers. Buyers know this fact and trade on it:

- They suggest volume increases are possible 'if only you can . . .'
- They offer volume increases in return for price reductions which may not be attractive to you.

2 Volume increases are attractive to you when:

- Stocks are too high.
- Manufacturing capacity is under-utilized.
- Delivery vehicles are under-utilized.
- You want market penetration.
- You want to hold market share.
- A new product is being launched.

3 Volume increases are less attractive to you when:

- The customer wants too big a price reduction in return.
- The customer is unwilling to give you other concessions to compensate for the large price reduction.
- The extra volume has to be manufactured at an uneconomic cost.
- The extra revenue does not cover possible uneconomic use of transport.
- The customer wants to delay taking delivery, thus making you liable for the cost of carrying excess stocks.
- The increase in one product will be offset by decreases in other products that carry higher margins.
- The product is being phased out to liberate manufacturing capacity for new products.

Conclusion You will be able to negotiate successfully on volume if:

- You know how important a priority it is.
- You know the margins of the products under discussion.
- Volume increases are not being bought at too high a cost to you.

Timing

Introduction 1 The phrase 'Time is money' is as true for negotiators as it is for everyone else:

- Money values decline over time.
- Positive cash flow is essential, particularly in times of high interest rates.

2 Important aspects of timing for your negotiators are:

- Timing of price increases and other agreements (effective date).
- Phased increases.
- Length of agreement (stability period).
- Credit period.

This section covers the first three. Credit periods are dealt with separately.

Effective date 1 Both parties to a negotiated agreement commit themselves financially from the effective date, i.e., the date that the agreement comes into force.

2 The timing of the effective date is important to you particularly when price increases are being negotiated.

The usual notice period for price increases is 28 days. Any delay in implementation will reduce sales values, adversely affect cash flow, increase interest charges, and reduce profits. (See Exercise 2.)

3 If the customer increases his purchases in the month before the price increase, you will benefit from reduced stocks. But the beneficial effect will be minimal if the customer delays payment.

Phased increases

1 You may occasionally be forced to phase the increase over several months. If you do, remember that every month without the full increase being applied costs you money, as shown in Exercise 2.

2 Beware, too, of assuming an even sales pattern. If, for example, the customer is in a seasonal business, you may be committing yourself to phased increases which mean that most of the sales are invoiced at the lower rate and that only a few later sales are being invoiced at the full rate.

The financial effect of this can be worked out by using the calculations in Exercise 2, month by month.

Length of agreement (stability period)

1 The duration of an agreement or stability period for a price level are legitimate areas for negotiation within the overall corporate requirements of each party.

2 When price increases are being negotiated a customer will attempt to extend the stability period as far as possible.

There are three dangers in this:

- In times of high inflation, high interest rates and depressed demand, profits can quickly disappear.

- The concessions he is prepared to give you in return may be worth very little.

- The longer the period of agreement the less confident you can be that the concessions can be guaranteed. (For example, promises of volume increases.)

3 Therefore, you should resist attempts to increase the period of the agreement beyond your normal level.

Conclusion

1 Timing is as important to you as volumes, prices, costs and mix of sales.

2 Do not enter into time commitments without calculating the financial implications.

3 Make sure you obtain adequate concessions to compensate.

Exercise 2 Timing

A customer is spending $10 000 per month with your company.

A 7 per cent price increase is agreed but its introduction is delayed by one month over and above the normal 28 days' notice.

What effect will this delay have

- on sales?
- on cash flow?*

* Assume that interest charges on bank overdraft are 12 per cent per annum.

Exercise 2 – Answer Timing The effect of the one month's delay in implementing the price increase will be 7 per cent of $10 000 = $700.

If the interest charge on bank overdraft is 12 per cent per annum, the interest charge on $700 for one month will be 1 per cent = $7.

Thus the total cost to you of the delay will be $707 which is equal to 7.07 per cent of the monthly sales.

Range

Introduction 1 Your company's investment in manufacturing capacity is used to produce a wide range of items.

Many of these items use the same raw materials and share the same manufacturing processes.

2 Whilst some customers only need one item, many need a range.

3 Manufacturing and sales productivity are improved when the widest possible range is bought by the widest number of customers. Plant and equipment is highly utilized and Selling and Advertising expenses are reduced.

4 It is therefore your responsibility to ensure that, wherever possible, customers take the full range of your products. The exceptions to this are items that you want to phase out. Because there is often a difference between your objectives and the customer's objectives, range becomes a negotiable area.

Negotiating on range 1 Many users are unwilling to get all their requirements from one supplier. They will 'dual-source' on individual items where quantities are large and they will rarely take the full range from one supplier.

2 In trying to negotiate additional types you will prefer to get acceptance of those items which have the highest profit potential for you.

These will be items that are characterized by;

– High volume potential.

– High margin.

– Low cost of support.

– Relationship with other items in the range.

– Replacement sales.

Conclusion 1 The most valuable sources of increased sales and profit are additional items sold to existing customers.

2 Increases in the range sold should always be a priority.

3 Know what range your customer is buying from all sources and try to sell additional types that offer you the greatest profit potential.

Mix

Introduction

1 Because different products have different margins, the mix of products you sell has a significant impact on profit.

For example, two companies can have the same sales but different profits because their mix of sales is different.

2 What this means to you is that you may want to negotiate a change in mix to achieve higher profits without forcing your customer to spend more in total.

The profit impact of changes in mix

1 If we examine a company's financial results we could find the following pattern:

	Product A	Product B	Product C	TOTAL
Sales	50 000	20 000	30 000	100 000
Cost of Goods	36 000	8 000	16 000	60 000
Gross Profit	14 000	12 000	14 000	40 000
Operating Expenses				35 000
Net Profit				5 000

2 A change in sales mix, without a change in total sales, could have the following impact:

	Product A	Product B	Product C	TOTAL
Sales	30 000	50 000	20 000	100 000
Cost of Goods	21 600	20 000	10 667	52 267
Gross Profit	8 400	30 000	9 333	47 733
Operating Expenses				35 000
Net Profit				12 733

This example assumes market opportunity, production availability, and no increase in Operating Expenses. In practice, you are unlikely to achieve such big differences, but even marginal improvements are worthwhile.

Negotiating on mix

1 Whether or not you should aim to change your sales mix with a particular customer will depend on a number of factors:

- The need for profit in preference to volume. (Normally, products with higher margins sell in lower quantities.)
- The customer's ability to change his buying mix.
- The effect on competition – opportunity or threat?
- Production availability/stock availability.

2 Recognize, however, that the gross margins on individual products that you sell can differ widely.

Therefore, if your objectives and your client's can be achieved by a change to a more profitable mix for you, be prepared to negotiate on it. (See Exercise 3.)

Conclusions

1 Change in mix is often overlooked as a means of improving profit.

2 If your customer has a budget limit and wants concessions from you, consider changing the mix that he buys from you as a means of meeting your mutual objectives.

Exercise 3 Mix An engineering customer regularly buys from you and a competitor. His purchases are:

10 000 Item A @ $22	220 000
4 000 Item B @ $26	104 000
2 000 Item C @ $35	70 000
	$394 000

The gross profit margins at these prices are:

Item A $5 per unit	50 000
Item B $13 per unit	52 000
Item C $7 per unit	14 000
	$116 000

Your sales director has asked you to increase the gross profit from $116 000 to $132 000, but you know that the customer will not increase his purchases above the current level of $394 000.

You also know that:

1 The demand for Item A is likely to fall to 9 000.

2 The application for Item B is likely to grow.

3 You cannot increase his purchases of Item C.

What mix would you attempt to negotiate?

Exercise 3 – Answer You have two basic alternatives, both of which will meet your and his objectives:

1 To change the mix but still supply all three products, for example:

	Sales	Gross Profit
9 000 Item A @ $22	$198 000	$ 45 000
6 154 Item B @ $26	$160 004	$ 80 002
1 000 Item C @ $35	$ 35 000	$ 7 000
	$393 004	$132 002

2 To drop Item C entirely, your least profitable product, and go for a much larger increase in Item B, your most profitable product, for example:

	Sales	Gross Profit
9 000 Item A @ $22	$198 000	$45 000
6 693 Item B @ $26	$174 018	$87 009
	$372 018	$132 009

If you have no particular preference, it is good negotiating tactics to offer both alternatives and let him choose the one that suits him best.

Stocks

Introduction

1 In order to provide a competitive level of customer service and take advantage of sales opportunities your company carries stocks.

2 In accounting terminology stocks are *assets*. In a negotiating context they can be a bargaining point, incurring costs for you and offering values to the customer.

3 The problems of stocks are:
   - They may never be sold.
   - They cost money to produce.
   - If reserved for a particular customer, they are unavailable for someone else.
   - Customers like to have immediate availability, but are often unwilling to pay for it.

4 Consequently, it often happens that:
   - Stocks are held for particular customers, either on your premises, or on the customer's premises, or in an independent warehouse.
   - They are not paid for until they are used.

5 The profit implications of stocks can therefore be significant, both for you and your customer.

Financial implications of stocks

1 For negotiation purposes you need to be aware of two factors:
   - Time
   - Cost

2 Time

   If a customer wants you to hold stocks you need to know what it means in time.

   For example, if a customer wants you to hold 500 units of an item in stock, and his annual usage is 1 500, he is effectively asking you to carry four months' stock. You can then calculate the cost involved.

3 Cost

   To continue the example, if you agree to carry four months' stock, remember what it is costing you in interest charges, e.g.

   500 units @ $20 unit production cost = $10 000 cost of goods.

   If the interest rate on short-term borrowing is 15 per cent per annum, it is costing you $500 to hold 500 units in stock for four months, i.e.

   $$(\$10\ 000\ @\ 15\%) \times \frac{4}{12} = \$500$$

Such an amount is a significant drain on the profit from the sale. (See Exercise 4.)

Negotiating on stocks 1 If customers want you to carry stocks for them, do not agree to it without considering the financial implications.

What that means is that you must know:

- The unit costs of the various items to be stocked.

- How long they will be held in stock.

- Current interest rates on short-term borrowings.

2 You can then calculate the cost to you of carrying the suggested level of stocks and the benefits to the customer of doing so.

3 If you decide to agree to his request you should attempt to obtain from the customer a concession that compensates you for the cost involved.

Conclusion 1 Concessions on stock are often given away in the euphoria of a potential sale.

2 Sometimes it is well worth doing:

- it helps the customer run his business;

- it keeps your competitors out;

- it clinches the sale.

3 But remember, that it costs you money to do it. Therefore, know the cost and take it into account when negotiating the final details of the deal.

Exercise 4 Stocks A washing-machine manufacturer is about to launch a new model. His production schedules are clear and you have no problems in that respect.

He has asked you, however, to supply an extra quantity of an item to provide him with a stock buffer in the event of a possible demand for spares.

He has suggested that this extra quantity is stored on his premises and paid for as demand is called off.

The total quantity is 840 and he expects to use them at the rate of 70 per month.

What would it cost you in interest charges to agree to his request?

Assume that the unit production cost is $14 and that the interest charge on short-term borrowings is 15 per cent.

Exercise 4 – Answer The total cost in interest charges would be $955.50 i.e.: The cost per month for 70 units is $12.25

$$(70 \text{ units} \times \$14 @ 15\%) \times \frac{1}{12}$$

The total cost, based on the customer's rate of use, is as follows:

	Usage	Time in Stock	$ Cost
Month 1	70	1 month @ $12.25	12.25
Month 2	70	2 months @ $12.25	24.50
Month 3	70	3 months @ $12.25	36.75
Month 4	70	4 months @ $12.25	49.00
Month 5	70	5 months @ $12.25	61.25
Month 6	70	6 months @ $12.25	73.50
Month 7	70	7 months @ $12.25	85.75
Month 8	70	8 months @ $12.25	98.00
Month 9	70	9 months @ $12.25	110.25
Month 10	70	10 months @ $12.25	122.50
Month 11	70	11 months @ $12.25	134.75
Month 12	70	12 months @ $12.25	147.00

Total Cost $955.50

If the selling price per unit is $19, the sales value of the order would be $15 960.

If the gross margin is 40 per cent the total gross margin would be $6 384.

Not only would agreement to the customer's request seriously reduce the gross profit, it would also eliminate the net profit.

Credit period

Introduction 1 'The sale is not made until the money is received' is an old saying with a contemporary significance.

Some companies are very profitable because they control credit tightly. Others have ceased trading because they paid little attention to it.

2 Credit periods are a vital part of any sales agreement because they fundamentally affect profitability, even more so when interest rates are high.

The cost of credit 1 You can see the effects of credit periods on corporate profitability by studying a company's annual accounts. By taking the sales figure from the profit and loss account and the debtors (receivables) figure from the balance sheet you can work out the average credit period:

e.g. Sales $12 000m

Debtors $ 2 750m

$$\text{Credit Period} = \frac{\text{Debtors}}{\text{Sales}} \times 365 = \text{Number of days' credit}$$

$$= \frac{2\ 750m}{12\ 000m} \times 365 = 84 \text{ days}$$

If the interest rate on your company's overdraft is 15 per cent per annum, you can work out the cost of the credit:

e.g. Debtors $2 750m $\times \frac{15}{100} = $412.5m$

Thus the 84-day credit period is costing the company $412.5m per year in bank charges.

If you could reduce the average credit period from 84 to 56 days, the interest charges would be:

$412.5m $\times \frac{56}{84} = $275m$

The saving is therefore $137.5m which can be added directly to the company's net profit.

If the company had made a net profit of $480m, the addition of $137.5m would have been very significant (i.e. a 29 per cent increase).

Negotiating credit periods

1 Like other companies your company includes a credit period in its standard terms and conditions. In your case it is normally 28 days after the end of the month of despatch.

In practice the actual credit taken by customers is much longer.

If the profitability of a deal is small under the normal credit terms, it can be eliminated entirely by delays in payment.

Therefore, you must make it clear to the customer that the other details of the deal are conditional on the agreed credit terms being met. (See Exercise 5.)

2 If the customer agrees to pay within a certain period and then fails to do so, you cannot ignore it. You should bring it to his attention immediately and warn him that continued delays will result in the withdrawal of other agreed concessions.

3 If previous experience tells you that he always takes extended credit, it may be preferable not to make an issue of it in the negotiations, but get the money back in other ways, e.g.,

 – give him lower discounts than other customers of similar size.

 – give delivery priority to customers who pay on time.

 – reduce the amount of support.

4 Remember that buyers will often agree to payment terms, knowing that it is not they, but their accounts department, who are functionally responsible. They will, however, issue instructions to their accounts colleagues about payment, if the achievement of their own goals is affected by it.

5 Similarly, if payment terms are an integral part of a negotiated agreement, instruct your accounts department to notify you of any delays.

Conclusion You will be able to negotiate successfully on credit periods if:

- You recognize that delays in payment are very costly to you.
- You know current interest rates on short-term borrowings.
- You can calculate the cost of extended credit in actual money.
- You ensure that your customers do fulfil their obligations and pay on time.

Exercise 5 Credit Period

Your company's cash flow is tight and profit margins are low due to strong competition and price pressure from customers.

Across the company as a whole the average credit period is currently 48 days.

After several weeks of intense negotiation you have concluded a deal with a customer for a range of items which will produce sales of $40 000 per month at average gross margins.

Your accounts department informs you that the company is paying 13 per cent interest per annum on its bank overdraft.

1 What would be the annual cost to you in extra interest charges in $ if this customer took 78 days' credit?

2 How much extra profit (i.e. savings in interest charges) would you make if the customer only took 30 days' credit instead of the average 48 days?

3 Last year the company's Return on Sales after payment of bank interest charges was 4 per cent. What would have happened to company profit last year if all customers had taken an average of 78 days' credit?

Exercise 5 – Answers
Credit Period

1 Total Sales for the year @ $40 000 per month = $480 000.
The interest charge on 78 days' credit would be:

$$(\$480\ 000 \times \frac{78}{365}) \times 13\% = \$13\ 335$$

The interest charge on 48 days' credit would be:

$$(\$480\ 000 \times \frac{48}{365}) \times 13\% = \$8\ 206$$

Therefore the extra interest charges for a full year would be $13 335 − $8 026 = $5 129

N.B. A quicker method to calculate the difference is:

(i) Take the difference in days

(ii) 78 days − 48 days = 30 days
Multiply the sales by $\frac{30}{365} \times 13\%$

i.e. $(\$480\ 000 \times \frac{30}{365}) \times 13\% = \$5\ 129$

2 The difference between the normal credit period (48 days) and the actual credit period (30 days) is 18 days.

Therefore the extra profit (saving in interest charges) would be:

$$(\$480\ 000 \times \frac{18}{365}) \times 13\% = \$3\ 077$$

3 Your customer's purchases are at average margins. Therefore a Return on Sales of 4 per cent on his purchases would be:

$480 000 @ 4 per cent = $19 200

If he takes 78 days to pay, instead of the average 48 days the extra cost would be $5 129, thus reducing the Return on Sales from $19 200 to $14 071.

This represents a reduction in net profit of 27 per cent.

If all customers last year had taken 78 days credit the company's Return on Sales would have dropped from 4 per cent to 2.9 per cent.

Delivery

Introduction

1 In recent years the cost of physical distribution has become a major topic of analysis in many companies.

2 Increases in oil prices in particular have made the delivery of products to customers a very expensive business.

Wherever possible, you have tried to minimize these costs by better vehicle utilization and delivery scheduling, but they still have a significant impact on profit.

3 In many companies, delivery charges are included in the selling price. Exceptions to this rule are small-quantity orders and unusually fast delivery requirements.

4 Since most eventualities are covered in these standard terms and conditions, delivery is rarely the subject of negotiation. It can, however, be a variable that incurs a cost to you and offers a value to the customer.

Negotiating on delivery

1 Delivery can be a negotiable area when:

– You want to use it as a means of resolving a problem.

– The customer wants something unusual in delivery.

– You want to ensure that exceptions to the rule are identified in advance and negotiated separately.

2 *Resolving a problem*

Sometimes negotiations reach an *impasse* and there seems no way out. In such cases you may be able to use delivery as a variable to break the deadlock.

For example, suppose you cannot reduce your price to the level demanded by the customer. A quick mental calculation may tell you that you can reduce it to that level if he will agree to take full delivery on an early date convenient to you. It will keep your delivery costs down and bring the money in faster.

Alternatively, you may ask him to accept part deliveries that fit in with your delivery commitments to other customers.

3 *The customer wants something unusual*

During the opening of a negotiation when you are listing all the points he wants to discuss, you may find that the customer's delivery requirements are outside your standard terms and conditions.

You can work out what this is likely to mean financially and use it as a bargaining point, in return for other concessions from him.

4 *Exceptions to the rule*

If your profit margins are very narrow, any unforeseen extra costs can easily convert the profit on a deal into a loss.

If you know that this is a possibility, it may be valuable to get firm commitment that the deal is subject to your normal delivery terms and that any exceptions will be chargeable.

Conclusion
1 Delivery can be a variable in negotiation, just like price, volume, credit, etc.

2 Remember how expensive delivery is and be prepared to negotiate on it when you know it will have a serious effect on the profitability and operational acceptability of the final agreement.

Support

Introduction
1 Much of any company's business success is built on the twin pillars of technical excellence and customer support.

2 Support, covers a wide range of activities. Most often it is seen as technical support of various kinds – applications engineering, trouble-shooting, after-sales service, testing, etc.

There is also the large area of sales support, particularly to distributors.

3 In all cases support is an investment intended to produce a commercial return. It is not an end in itself – you do not provide support purely to create job satisfaction for its applications engineers, important though that is.

For example, consider the cost of providing support by means of:

– Extra visits	– Product design work
– Management involvement	– Samples and drawings
– Higher levels of service	– Technical literature
– Special packaging	– Product trials
– Training	– Test equipment
– Demonstrations	– Internal meetings

Negotiating on support

1 Support is not something you withhold from a customer simply because it represents a high hidden cost. On the contrary, the selective use of support can and should be a powerful sales tool.

Equally, it is not something to give away.

2 When considering support as a negotiating variable always bear in mind your objectives and those of your customer. For example, how important is it to you that you should provide it? How important is it to your customer that he should receive it? To what extent does mutual satisfaction and profit depend on it?

3 What this means is that support may be crucial in an integrative negotiation.

4 The danger signals arise when your customer wants a lot of support without any guarantee that its cost will be recovered in future sales.

Perhaps, your company does not normally charge for it.

In future there may be occasions where you take a more flexible approach, e.g.

   – Make the provision of free support conditional on some kind of firm commitment from the customer.

   – Charge for it, but credit the cost when the customer places the order.

   – Agree to provide a base level of support but charge for anything extra.

Conclusion

1 Your company is proud of the support that it provides to all kinds of customer. It is a competitive advantage which cannot be matched by many other suppliers.

2 Recognize its cost and sell its value. Do not devalue it by letting your customer take it for granted.

3 Whenever you are asked to provide support over and above normal levels, ask yourself this question:

   – If I provide it, will it produce volume sales?

If the answer is 'No' or 'Uncertain', consider charging for it or requesting a concession from the customer in return for providing it.

Conclusion

1 The financial implications of negotiation are considerable:

   – Every concession from you has a cost to you and a value to the customer.

   – Every concession from the customer has a cost to him and a value to you.

   – The final deal will have a significant impact on total company profit.

This means that, to be a successful sales negotiator you must be aware of the financial implications of your discussions with customers.

2 Specifically, you should *KNOW*:

- The cost to you of any concession you may give.

- The value to the customer of any concession you may give.

- The value to you of any concession the customer may give.

- The cost to the customer of any concession he may give.

- The profit margins you are working with.

3 When planning and conducting a negotiation you should *BE ABLE TO*:

- Calculate the costs and values of concessions given and received.

- Calculate their impact on profit.

4 Remember that whilst the final agreement must meet the *financial* needs of both parties, it must also meet the *operational* needs of both parties.

Long-term, mutually satisfying agreements are important to you and your customers.

Consequently, make sure that the details of the agreement not only make money but also make good business sense.

Some examples The following examples of four different types of business illustrate the degree of preparation that can be done before entering into negotiations with buyers:

1 *Agriculture*: Acquisition/disposal of pastoral property (Table 6.1).

2 *Food/Livestock*: Purchase of grain/livestock (Table 6.2).

3 *Meat*: Lease of abbatoirs and/or boning room (Table 6.3).

4 *Meat products*: Sale of meat products (Table 6.4).

Table 6.1 **Acquisition/disposal of pastoral property**

Main negotiating points	Buyer's view	Seller's view	Concessions given		Concessions obtained	
			Type	Amount	Type	Amount
1 What is included in vendor's price (a) property bare (normally would include all buildings, fences, and plant being integral to building, i.e. shearing plant, lighting plant); (b) farm plant, in or out of sale;						

Table 6.1 **cont'd**

Main negotiating points	Buyer's view	Seller's view	Concessions given		Concessions obtained	
			Type	Amount	Type	Amount
(c) livestock, in or out of sale;						
(d) stores, in or out of sale;						
(e) fodder and fertilizer stocks, in or out of sale;						
(f) growing crops;						
or (g) walk-in-walk-out.						
2 Where consumable items included, the delivery quantities.						
3 Price for 1, above.						
4 Allocation of purchase price in contract.	Buyer wants market value or higher for depreciable assets, livestock and other items to obtain tax advantages.	Seller wants tax written down values or less to obtain tax advantages.				
5 Who has right to harvest growing crops, if any.	Buyer may want crop to offset some of purchase price.	Seller may want growing crop for cash-flow purposes.				
6 Vacant possession.	Buyer may wish to obtain possession before settlement to (a) avoid agistment; (b) have somewhere to live; (c) harvest growing crop for which he may offer a rental pending settlement.	Seller may not wish to give possession to avoid performance of contract without payment of purchase price or may find it convenient to give possession to avoid paying carrying on expenditure.				
7 Settlement, time, place, method, i.e. cash, bank cheque, terms on satisfactory security.	Buyer may want settlement, say after 31 December, to avoid land tax on land held at that date. Buyer may want short- or long-term finance of	Seller may want settlement prior to 31 December to avoid liability for land tax. Seller may want cash or accept terms to provide income from an investment or as				

Table 6.1 **concluded**

	Main negotiating points	Buyer's view	Seller's view	Concessions given		Concessions obtained	
				Type	Amount	Type	Amount
		balance of purchase money.	a means of selling rather than hold out for cash buyer.				
8	Adjustment clause for differences between actual and contracted deliveries of livestock, plant, stores and fodder in 1, above.	Buyer would want some protection and compensation for deliveries less than quantities contracted.	Vendor may not wish to receive less for stores, fodder and other consumables used in maintaining stock and crops from date of contract to date of settlement.				
9	Easements and encroachments and minor tenure matters.	Buyer may want some reduction of purchase price for give-and-take fence lines, neighbour's irrigation channels traversing property.	Vendor wants buyer to accept give-and-take arrangements for fencing, easements and encroachments.				
10	Employee's accommodation meeting requirements of Rural Workers' Accommodation Act.	Buyer may require an indemnity as to costs of complying with act.	Vendor may wish to sell on an 'as is' basis with the buyer to satisfy himself on compliance with the act.				
11	Liability to continuing employees for annual, sick, long-service, and other leave.	Buyer does not accept liability without indemnity or adjustment on settlement.	Vendor wishes to terminate employees' services rather than pay purchaser the liability.				
12	Other conditions and warranties.						

Table 6.2 **Purchase of grain/livestock**

Main negotiating points	Buyer's view	Seller's view	Concessions given		Concessions obtained	
			Type	Value	Type	Value
1 Description, quantity and other specification. Is sale based on sale by sample description or buyer's inspection?	Full description and specification to be in writing.	Sale as inspected. Caveat emptor applies.				
2 Price.						
3 Delivery:time, place, to whom.	Delivery at buyer's premises within two weeks of acceptance.	Delivery at seller's premises on acceptance.				
4 At whose risk pending delivery?	Vendor's risk until delivery.	Purchaser's risk on acceptance.				
5 Right of rejection: (a) inferior to sample; (b) blind, lame and diseased.	Has rights under Sale of Goods Act. Usual for buyer to reject lame, blind and diseased livestock.	Inspection 'as is' without right of rejection and caveat emptor applies.				
6 Payment:time, place, method (i.e. cash or terms).	Half purchase price on delivery, balance within one month.	Cash on acceptance.				
7 Other conditions and warranty.						

Table 6.3 **Lease of abattoirs and/or boning room**

Main negotiating points	Lessor's view	Lessee's view	Concessions given		Concessions obtained	
			Type	Amount	Type	Amount
1 Description, area and other details of buildings, plant and facilities to be the subject of a lease.	Lessor wants to provide all facilities for exclusive use by lessee.	Lessee wants to lease all facilities for his exclusive use.				
2 Engagement and cost of labour where labour facilities being hired: (a) slaughtermen, boners, etc.; (b) supervisors; (c) Management.	Lessor to provide all labour, supervisory staff and management.	Lessee wants to use own labour.				

Table 6.3 **cont'd**

Main negotiating points	Lessor's view	Lessee's view	Concessions given		Concessions obtained	
			Type	Amount	Type	Amount
3 Who is entitled to by-products?	Negotiate with 7, below.	Lessee entitled.				
4 Who is to control operations?	Lessor controls operations.	Lessee to control.				
5 What rental concessions are to be given for break-downs of machinery, and interruptions (perhaps industrial)? Is there any abatement of rental in event of close-down for any reason or certain reasons?	Lessor wants no abatement.	Lessee wants abatement of rental for all lost time through circumstances beyond his control.				
6 Consideration for the granting of the lease. Consider: high rental and low cost per head of through-put; low rental and high cost per head of through-put.	Lessor wants high minimum rental and not concerned with through-put to cover overhead.	Lessee wants low rental but fixed cost per head to facilitate costing procedures.				
7 Term of lease	Five years.	Two years.				
8 Options, if any, on termination of lease.	No options.	Option to purchase at fixed figure or renewal of lease for further two years.				
9 Capital expenditure. Who pays? Where incurred by reason of compliance with statutory requirements and licensing authorities. Consider:	At lessee's expense					
(a) percentage per annum of cost;		10 per cent per annum of cost provided maxi-mum rental, not in excess of additional $5 000 p.a.				
(b) if more than, say, $20 000, cost is to be paid by lessor; if less than, say $20 000, cost is to be paid by lessee.						

Table 6.4 **Sale of meat products**

Main negotiating points	Buyer's view	Seller's view	Concessions given		Concessions obtained	
			Type	Amount	Type	Amount
1 Typical costing of selling price bases on kill, bone and export CIF.						

Live animal cost 20c per lb
Freight to
  abattoirs   1c per lb
Raw material
  cost   21c per lb
Killing costs   4c per lb
Handling to
  distribution   2c per lb
Boning   5c per lb
Packing and
  wrapping   1c per lb
Freezing   2c per lb
       35
70% yield (saleable
  products) say 50c per lb
Overhead:
  Rent, supervisors,
  insurance, telephone,
  electricity: 8 cents
  Fixed   6c per lb
  Variable   2c per lb
Charges to wharf and load
  on ship
  Freight
  Wharf overtime 2c per lb
FOB cost   60c per lb
CIF: Insurance
  and freight   9c per lb
CIF cost   69c per lb
Profit margin   2c per lb
Selling price   71c per lb
Based on through-put
  4 000 animals per month
	Too dear – offers 70 cents CIF.	Wants to sell at 62.5c FOB. Consider: higher through-put should over-absorb fixed cost and benefits of economies of scale; lower through-put should under-absorb fixed overhead and perhaps strain recovery semi-variable costs.				

2 Delivery:timing.	Commence delivery within two months.	Commence delivery 90 days.				
3 Right of rejection.	Not equal to sample or specification.	At least equal to sample or specification.				

114

Table 6.4 **cont'd**

Main negotiating points	Buyer's view	Seller's view	Concessions given		Concessions obtained	
			Type	Amount	Type	Amount
4 Settlement.	Cash on delivery at destination port, in buyer's currency.	Cash on production of shipping documents in seller's currency.				
5 Quantity.	Minimum 500 tonnes per month.	Minimum 650 tonnes per month				
6 Duration of contract.	Four months.	Six months.				

Table 6.5 **Illustration of costing control**

Gross margin of target deal

20% of £1 000	200	
Less:		
1 *Cash conceded*		
Price discount of 2½%		25
Over-riding discount 1½%		15
Advertising support		20
		60
Remainder	140	
Less:		
2 *Costed non-price concessions*		
Split delivery		5
Non-standard pack		20
Two weeks extra credit		5
Additional merchandising support		20
		50
Net gross margin on deal	90	
=9% retained (11% given away)		

Table 6.6 **Negotiation principles: checklist**

Principle	Comments
1 Negotiation is the act or process of bargaining to reach a mutually acceptable agreement or objective.	Both sides must feel they have won, but not regret what the other side has achieved because it is not seen as gained at his expense. Each side achieves what it feels is most important.
2 Negotiation must take place between equals – in each other's eyes.	Although titles may be different, the ability of either side to make matching decisions is essential, as is the mutual respect between negotiators that both count as equals.
3 Negotiation is based on a common respect for the rules of the game.	Be yourself. Discuss rather than debate. Neither side must attempt 'one-up-manship'. At the same time neither side yields anything that is really important to him, although he may well indicate the opposite. Avoid domination.
4 Put your cards on the table.	Do not pretend negotiating powers you do not possess. Declare what you can do and what you cannot do.
5 Be patient.	In negotiation, rushed decisions are rarely good ones that satisfy either side. Be prepared to take time and do not hurry. Delay is better than a bad decision.
6 See the other side's case – unemotionally.	Often called empathy, being able to put yourself in the negotiating position of the person opposite you without being blinkered or emotionally involved, helps your assessment of his position.
7 Communicate to advance relationship and negotiation objectives.	Be open and disclose your motives and self-interest. Lay it on the line and let the buyer do so in turn. Do not be obscure.
8 Avoid confrontation.	Do not put yourself in a position from which you cannot retract. If you have a row things are said which can make negotiating impossible. Avoid showdowns. Stand firm but always state your position calmly.
9 If you disagree do so as from a devil's advocate position.	Be prepared to disagree by looking at your case from the buyer's point of view. This enables you to say things that neither confront the buyer nor give rise to a confrontation.

Table 6.6 **cont'd**

Principle	Comments
10 Give a bit at a time.	Never concede everything or nothing. Give slice by slice, but for every concession you give get one back: 'If you do this I will do that'.
11 Know when to leave well alone.	In negotiation there is rarely an ideal solution, so do not pursue one when it is beyond your reach, too costly or takes more time than you can afford.
12 Declare company strategies if you must, but not objectives behind them.	Company strategies and plans become public knowledge as soon as they are implemented, but the objectives, personal motivations and needs that give them birth, impetus and fuel them should be kept secret.
13 Don't compromise your ultimate objectives.	Set your highest and lowest negotiating objective, then do not settle below the lowest point. Lose rather than gain a worthless deal.
14 Never relax your guard.	Stamina is one of the hallmarks of a good negotiator. Your opponent may stall for hours just to find out when you will crack. If you cannot bide your time in such duels do not negotiate.
15 Always rehearse your case.	Tell yourself what you are going to say, how you are going to say it and when. Then rehearse how your opposite numbers will do the same.
16 Do not under-estimate other people.	Many negotiators pretend not to know or to be foolish. Some are fools, but others may appear so to mislead you.
17 Respect confidences given in negotiating.	Do not ever betray a confidence learnt during negotiation. The essence of negotiation is mutual trust.
18 End negotiations positively.	Satisfactory negotiations should end when both sides can part without regret. Try to end all negotiations on a positive basis of satisfying the needs of all parties.

7

Buyer behaviour

The traditionally trained salesman has some fairly clearly defined objectives: to identify the needs of customers within the limits of those his products or services can meet and satisfy. Then he has to persuade a sufficient number of people to buy to enable him to meet or exceed his sales target. His two weapons are the *products* he sells and his *persuasive skills*. The salesman, on balance, will tend to succeed more often than not if the *product inspires confidence* in the purchaser or user by living up to, or exceeding, the promises or claims made about it. That confidence once established, repeat sales can be expected just so long as the product performance remains good or exceeds expectations. Problems will undoubtedly arise if there are technical failures, administrative muddles over the customer's account, or when a competitor comes along with an identical product at a cheaper price or offers one that is better. Nevertheless, the two essential elements are confidence in the product and the persuasive skills of the salesman.

In negotiation, however, the starting-point is not confidence in the product because product and service performance are for the most part no longer in question. They are accepted. And so confidence shifts from product performance to the salesman.

The very essence of negotiation is that it is concerned with *profit* and all that influences profit. Therefore the *negotiating salesman must inspire confidence* in those with whom he negotiates that he understands the customer's profit needs, the mechanisms that influence profit, and that he can communicate and negotiate about such matters and establish confidence in the different levels of people he deals with in customer companies. The product salesman who directs his selling towards groups of buyers with common needs will be tempted to treat customers as though their behaviour patterns were the same.

The negotiator's relationship with buyers is not just a persuasive one. Indeed he must, if he is to succeed, change the buyer's perception of him from being a persuader to being a problem-solver, a profit-improver. He must be perceived as being positively related to making profits – for the buyer.

Different levels of negotiating relationships

This perception must be shared by more than one person in the customer organization. Rarely are negotiated decisions the result of dealing with one person. So the negotiator must be able to deal with and relate to:

1 Different levels of personnel, from directors to operatives.
2 Different groups of decision-makers; some will be generalists, others will be specialists concerned with technical part-decisions.
3 Different disciplines; marketing men, financial experts, engineers, production, personnel.
4 Different backgrounds and motivations.

The negotiating salesman not only moves between these different groups, but also has to understand the factors that influence their behaviour patterns and how these affect his relationships with them. Since these behaviour patterns alternate between official roles and personal roles, the salesman must be sensitive to and understand deeply but not censoriously. In particular, he must identify in each important customer organization:

1 Company personality and philosophy.
2 Company's management or leadership style.
3 Personality and needs of buyers involved in negotiation.

Company personality and philosophy

Commercial organizations are made up of groups of people who work together to achieve a variety of objectives, of which the need to survive, and/or to prosper, will depend upon those in whose hands power lies. Like salesmen, customer companies seek to satisfy their needs. For some this may be survival, or the avoidance of failure, whilst for others it is the constant search for success, the need to be top in everything, to achieve.

A.H. Maslow's *Theory of Human Motivation* gives us a valuable insight into what stimulates human behaviour towards certain goals, and provides clues to a company's as well as to an individual's behaviour. He suggests that man's needs are organized in the form of a pyramid or hierarchy (see Figure 7.1). At the most basic level our needs are those essential to sustain life – our physiological needs for such things as food, shelter, water, clothing. At the next level, once these basic needs are satisfied, come our safety needs. The average person needs and prefers to have a safe, orderly, predictable and organized life and to reduce to the minimum the unpredictable, dangerous things. If both the physiological and safety needs are being satisfied then man turns to the need to belong, to love and be loved and to have a recognized place in a group. At its most basic, as a member of a family, in the larger context in the social community within which the family lives and then in the work group. The satisfaction of this need to belong, established, gives rise to another need – the need for respect, for self-esteem, for the esteem of others, for the satisfaction of one's ego.

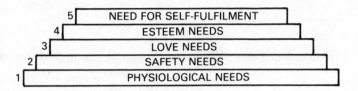

Figure 7.1 **The hierarchy of needs**

The satisfaction of these four sets of needs, on a continuous and fairly uninterrupted basis – the *physiological, safety, love,* and *esteem* needs – leads ultimately to discontent unless an individual is doing that which he really feels he is fitted for and wants to do, as opposed necessarily to what he is doing.

These needs vary from person to person. Likewise, in commercial terms they vary from company to company and the negotiating salesman should consider the needs of key account customers in terms of the following:

1 Is the company's profitability so low or non-existent that the dominant need is the basic one of survival, or is the chief executive hell bent on beating his only rival in the market, or obtaining public recognition?

2 Except in extreme circumstances, most customers' needs are a mixture to be satisfied, ranging from improving security of a division's survival to gaining the approval of the local community, so that a favourable climate of opinion will sway the local authorities to grant permission for a factory extension or new office block.

3 A satisfied need is not a motivator. Whilst for all practical purposes every company has needs to be satisfied, it is the degree and extent that the negotiator must be aware of.

4 The lower the level of customer need, the easier it is to satisfy. But most customers' needs tend to be at the higher levels which are more complex to understand and more difficult to satisfy.

The achievers and the failure avoiders

Companies can also be identified in their philosophy by whether they are actively and aggressively seeking to achieve larger profits, market dominance, be the first to invent a new product or process, or are merely trying to avoid failure. To some extent these two extremes mirror the age of the company and the drives of its directing executives.

Styles of leadership

The way in which a customer company reaches buying decisions usually reflects the style of management or leadership that exists. There are three main styles characterized by clearly recognizable differences:

1 Autocracy or dictatorship

Here the chief executive lays down the policy by telling everyone what he wants done. He is rarely receptive to people telling him what they think, and so when negotiating with companies where this style exists, it is a waste of time dealing with intermediaries; you must deal with the principal. But you will also notice that in sub-groups in such a company, the leader in each one tends to exhibit a dictatorship style and this will be common throughout the organization.

2 Democratic

At the opposite extreme to the autocratic dictatorship style is what is known as the democratic, committee or bottom-up style of management. In such a company, management puts all its decisions to groups at every level of decision-making. The groups arrive, by a process of majority choice, at decisions, usually the least risky of those open to them, and their choice becomes the management's decision. It is always pleasant dealing with such companies. The staff are friendly and not threatening, the management open and usually approachable. But from a negotiating angle, decisions tend to be long-drawn-out and conservative in character. Innovation and taking calculated risks are seldom the characteristics found in companies managed over-democratically.

3 Participative or benevolent autocracy

This style is where senior management is usually decisive but seeks the positive participation of its staff in the decisions that are reached. Management asks staff for its views and comments on vital decisions and, in the light of these comments, decides upon a course of action which may reflect some, all or none of the ideas that have been fed to it. But the act of consultation provides a positive environment wherein there tends to be creativity and the taking of calculated risks; ideas are explored and innovative approaches are encouraged.

The organization's profile

All these factors contribute to the profile of a customer organization in terms of the climate in which its people work, the way decisions are made, the urgency and tempo of work, how people communicate with one another; the way power is distributed and the amount of it that is delegated and to whom; the characteristics and personalities of the important personnel with whom you have to negotiate and the roles people play in the various groups in which you meet them.

Buying decision groups

Negotiating is a complex art and, because of the far-reaching implications of principal negotiations, many people are concerned in a customer company and contribute to the final decision. For these reasons, you must not only know what groups are involved in reaching negotiated decisions but equally who else, either individually or as groups, influence buying decisions. You need to identify:

1 What are the decision-making groups and the levels of decisions they reach?
2 What are the specialist/expert groups who influence the major decision-making groups?
3 Who are the leaders in each group?
4 Who are the members of each group?
5 What types of decision does each group make and take?
6 What are the behaviour patterns of each group? For example, does a product planning group always meet at a certain time before the buying committee meets with suppliers, etc.?

Where does power reside?

At a certain negotiation meeting the leader of one side of the negotiations became so incensed by the apparent inability of the other side to come to a decision that he spat out the question: 'Am I dealing with the engine driver or the oil rag?' *Negotiation can only succeed between equals with equal power to reach a mutually acceptable decision.*

If one side or the other does not possess such power then inevitably the negotiations break down. So it is essential to understand the distribution of power in its various forms in essential customer companies and to have an up-to-date intelligence of the coming generation of power-holders. You should know:

1 Power of position: Do the people with grand-sounding titles always have the power to match them? Titles are too often exchanged for power!

2 Power behind the throne:
(a) Who are the people whose opinion is always asked before major decisions are reached?
(b) Who influences the decision-makers?
(c) Whose opinions help to frame policy?

3 Power of expert:
(a) Some decisions are made by experts behind the scenes and the decision-makers just pass on what the experts say.
(b) Some decisions are never reached without clearance by the experts.

(c) Who are these experts and what is the source or basis of their power? Frequently, it resides with the financial adviser or director.

Power is not an easy thing to define or to perceive. If it is held by one person then there is precious little for anyone else to exercise. But because it tends to be distributed in different ways in different companies, look for clues that provide the answers to four questions:

Table 7.1 **Customer organization profiles: checklist**

	Yes	No	Notes
Management style			
Autocracy-Dictatorship			
Democratic			
Participative			
Irrational			
Decision-making process			
One-man			
Committee/bottom-up			
Consultative			
Specialist			
Company character			
Aggressive			
Conservative			
Creative			
Risk-taking			
Traditional			
Communication system			
Free and open			
Friendly			
Formal			
Guarded-defensive			
Bureaucratic			
Image-personality			
Achievers			
Failure avoiders			
Inventive/innovative			
Imitators			
Co-operative			
Success-seeking			
Other factors			

1 Who has the power to compel others to do things?

2 Who has the power to influence or decide what is done?

3 Who has the limited power in certain circumstances to influence?

4 Who has expert power?

A checklist has been constructed (Table 7.1), to help you to analyse customer organization profiles, behaviour patterns and motivations, and power.

Table 7.2 **Negotiation strategy checklist**

Strategy	Comments
1 Have a total negotiating plan.	Always know what you are going to do. If you have to break off to get further instructions because you get stuck through lack of planning you weaken your bargaining strength.
2 Sit where you can command meeting	Always place yourself if you can where you can see, watch and hear everyone else at the meeting.
3 Keep numbers to the minimum	The fewer the participants the sooner agreement can usually be reached.
4 Learn all the key facts.	Only when you possess *all* the facts do you know what you can give or concede and afford to.
5 Do not be afraid to make an opening concession.	One of the arts of negotiating is knowing how to open. Be ready to make an opening concession. Use a minor one to show flexibility or to achieve a significant compromise from the other side.
6 Be specific.	Every point agreed should be agreed in *specific terms*, so that there is no re-opening of discussion when the final agreement is turned into a written contract for signature.
7 Promise only what you can do.	Long-term business relationships can only be built on mutually fulfilled promises. Do not promise something you cannot do. Never over-sell.

Table 7.3 **Checklist for negotiation planning**

Questions	Answers	Planning implications
1 What are the customer's marketing policies?		
2 What are his major marketing strategies?		
3 What marketing tactics does he use?		
4 What sort of customers does he have?		
5 What are the trends in his market?		
6 What are the commercial needs of the buyer?		
7 The major negotiation ingredients are?		
8 What are the costs and value of concessions involved?		
9 How do you assess the buyer's stances?		
10 How do these relate to your own objectives?		
11 What should your stances be?		
12 How will you control the negotiation?		

8
___

Conducting negotiations

As we have seen, successful negotiation entails planning, and the plan must be based on a coherent strategy. In this chapter we look at the process of negotiation itself and see how various tactics can be used to achieve desired results.

At the end of the chapter are descriptions of two actual commercial situations, with the relevant negotiating points analysed, by way of example, from the point of view of both buyer and seller.

What are the principal strategic elements of negotiation?

Actual stances   Given the underlying common needs, the strategy of negotiation is concerned with the actual and stated magnitude of those needs on both sides.

S ——————— NB ——————— B

Actual supplier stance   ↑   Actual buyer stance

Point of need balance

At the start of a negotiation there will normally be a gap between the terms and conditions the buyer says he wants and what the supplier says he is prepared to offer. The major strategic task of the sales negotiator, whether the subject under negotiation is price or a non-price factor such as delivery, is to judge accurately the *actual* gap that exists between the parties, as opposed to the *stated* gap. The major initial strategic ploy in negotiations is for both sides to *exaggerate* the distance between them.

Initial stances   Sometimes (not always) a buyer will open up a negotiation by deliberately (or automatically) exaggerating his stance: 'Before we start, if you think I'm going to accept that price increase that came through the post the other day, forget it. It's high time somebody took a stand against this constant pushing up of prices.' Or he may attempt to suggest that he is not likely to come to an agreement because of other negative factors which he raises at the beginning of the interview.

If (as is often the case) this is a strategic ploy, he will, if you allow him to save face while doing so, move from his initial stance to an actual stance quite quickly and with little encouragement: 'Alright, let's talk about prices, but I warn you, you'll have to think very hard about that ten per cent increase.'

You must be clear about the reasons for initial stance. It is done purely to disconcert the salesman. This can be seen clearly in an example of a trade union/management pay negotiation, where the opening stance comes from the trade union.

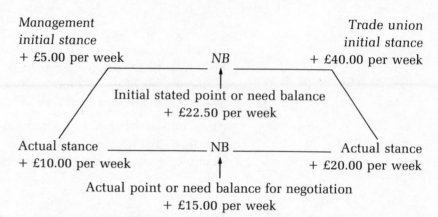

Management
initial stance
+ £5.00 per week   NB   *Trade union*
initial stance
+ £40.00 per week

Initial stated point or need balance
+ £22.50 per week

Actual stance ——————— NB ——————— Actual stance
+ £10.00 per week   + £20.00 per week

Actual point or need balance for negotiation
+ £15.00 per week

Thus, the first task is to establish by discussion the *actual* gap which exists between yourself and the buyer. This is invariably achieved by a mutual examination of the needs and covering benefits on both sides. But you must ensure that you limit the loss of position that this manoeuvring entails for both parties. Commonly, the parties will take up their actual stances with ritualistic face-saving comments, which are important if the fabric of the negotiation is to be preserved. The negotiation then moves into its tactical stage.

Tactics of negotiation

You are now concerned with reaching, from the actual points of difference between the parties, a mutually acceptable agreement. You can see at this stage that the essence of negotiation is *compromise*, actual or apparent. The discussion now proceeds in a highly structured way, each side reducing the gap by a series of mutual *concessions*. At this stage the skilful negotiator *trades a concession*, which in fact costs him little, but which has a real or implied high value to the other party, and brings a relatively more valuable concession from them.

Enhancing the cost and value of concessions

A great deal of skill is required on the part of the supplier in raising the apparent *cost to him and value to the buyer* of a concession he is trading. Remember that if there is no apparent cost to you then you are really conceding nothing.

Concessions *from* you *to* the buyer: with these concessions you must credibly *raise* the value to the buyer of the concession you are offering by applying the benefits of the concession to his needs. You can reinforce this value by stressing credibly the high cost of the concession to you. 'You will appreciate that increasing our promotional support to you for this product is not something I could easily agree to considering the cost and how my budget is already heavily committed.'

Concessions *from* the buyer *to* you: similarly the buyer will magnify the costs to him and the value to you of his concessions. You will attempt to qualify these statements by minimizing the value to you of his concessions.

Matching and trading concessions

Concessions must be traded carefully. That is to say you must not take your hands off your concession until the buyer has agreed on what he will do in return. (. . . 'I will do this if you will do that'.) If you habitually refer to your concessions alone, the buyer will accept them without reciprocation.

Maintaining the fabric of the negotiation

In many respects, negotiation is a vital game played for real consequence. Any unduly early attempt by either side to 'dig in their heels' by being genuinely inflexible will be met by reciprocal inflexibility from the other side, and the negotiation will break down. It is critical in these cases that at the conclusion of the negotiation both sides agree they cannot reasonably bridge the gap between them at this stage, or in this instance. Such a conclusion leaves open the possibility of further negotiation on the same subject, or new negotiations in another area.

A breakdown in negotiation caused by the unreasonable inflexibility of one party will not leave the possibility of new negotiations for the future so open. At all times, even when you have reached a point beyond which you are not prepared to go, you must appear to be reasonable. Remember that you are playing a ritual game which is firmly based in hard financial reality. For many buyers much of their sense of achievement comes from playing the game well.

The definition of a successful negotiation from the supplier's angle is one which ends on your side of the point of need balance, but where the buyer believes that the deal favours him. The steps and methods to be used in achieving a successful outcome are as follows:

1 Allow the buyer to do most of the talking in the early stages, but do not frustrate him by refusing to answer his questions.

2 Move the discussion from opening stances to a clear statement of actual stances, taking care to limit your losses on both sides. It is your responsibility to 'save face' for the buyer:

    (a) A buyer first presents his stance: you have then a variety of possible responses to it:

        (i) accept it and persuade him that the negatives are greater than the positives;

        (ii) accept it and go back to initial problem with alternatives;

       (iii) ignore it and take own stance;

       (iv) take opposite stance;

       (v) accept it and use 'suppose' technique.

  (b) You present your stance first: you can:

       (i) take exaggerated view;

       (ii) take actual stance (when your case is strong);

       (iii) 'give' buyer his stance (i.e. indicate your initial acceptance);

       (iv) 'give' both stances in the current environment: both initial; sales initial/buyer actual; both actual.

3 Avoid premature stance on any point which might result in reaching a point of no return too early in the negotiation. It is easier for the buyer to walk away than it is for you in most circumstances.

4 Try to close on a clear statement of the actual gaps between you.

5 Trade any concessions *one at a time*, ensuring that you raise the value of your concessions to him above their cost to you. Make a small move on your part seem large to him.

6 Tactics of devaluing cost to buyer and value to salesman of the buyer's concession, viz.:

  (a) treat it as given (assumption) that there is no real concession;

  (b) competitors always expect it (or more);

  (c) there is benefit to the buyer in agreeing;

  (d) 'we've got the benefits anyway';

  (e) 'you'd incur the cost anyway';

  (f) look for a major concession then suggest the 'minor' one as an alternative;

  (g) it is normal practice.

7 Increasing the value of concessions given to the buyer, and the cost of giving it for the salesman:

  (a) imply that you cannot really give it;

  (b) refer to main problem that will be solved by the concession;

  (c) refer to saving gained by the buyer;

  (d) calculate the financial results of the concession;

  (e) refer to loss if concession is not given;

  (f) refer to past gains from similar concessions;

  (g) imply loss that you will incur by giving concessions;

  (h) build up notional cost or oppportunity cost of giving the concession;

  (i) start by implying you are going to give a small concession, then give a large one or enlarge the small concession;

  (j) not normal practice ('competitors don't do it').

8 Handling situations where the buyer is asking for concession that you cannot give:

(a) build up cost of giving the concession;

(b) minimize the importance to the buyer of the concession;

(c) 'persuade' the buyer that the benefits of the deal without the concession still justify acceptance;

(d) offer an alternative concession;

(e) summarize the problem area and offer alternative concession or a choice of alternatives;

(f) show the concession would put the buyer at a disadvantage.

With each and every concession made, whether from you or the buyer, it is essential that you summarize the details agreed. This will prevent misinterpretations later. It is further advisable that having agreed the concession details you should make *written* notes.

9 Have facts and figures fluently to hand – but not 'pat' or 'glib' ones.

10 Avoid emotional reactions, but satisfy the buyer's emotional needs. The good buyer/negotiator will try to put you under emotional pressure.

11 Allow the buyer to save face in giving you a concession.

12 Ensure that the buyer is given the 'value satisfaction' he needs, and that you confirm it.

13 At the end of your negotiation interview summarize totally the agreements made, both by you and the buyer.

Conclusion

Negotiation relies on you accurately identifying, at the *preparation* stage:

1 The buyer's needs.

2 Your needs.

3 The point of balance.

4 The value of your concessions to the buyer.

5 The benefits to the buyer of your concessions that will increase their value.

6 The concessions he will give, and how their 'cost' to him can be minimized.

7 The buyer's likely initial stance.

8 How you can move the buyer from his initial stance to the point of balance.

You are then in a position to meet the buyer without fear of conceding points for no reasons. You will be able to meet a point of balance where the buyer is satisfied, and you have achieved your objectives. Always summarize agreements as soon as possible *in writing*. List the points of explanation, clarification and understanding. Include *all* conditioning and mutual concessions.

The following two examples (Tables 8.1 and 8.2) indicate the chain of negotiations between the supplier and a soft drinks manufacturer and the consequential negotiations between the soft drinks manufacturer and the typical food chain through whom he sells his products.

Table 8.1 **The contact between buyer and supplier in the plant. Soft drinks situation: supplies**

Main negotiating points	Buyer's view	Supplier's view
Quality of supplies being purchased	What variance in quality can be expected from the supplier in question? Are the variances that may be expected critical to our own process? Will quality problems at supplier's plant restrict supply and interfere with production of company goods? Is the quality of the supply favourable to that from competitive suppliers? Will the supplier provide goods in accordance with a quality acceptance plan? Does the supplier employ Quality Control procedures in his plant? Are the Quality Control procedures adequate?	How reliable is the production output from our plant? Will our plant be able to maintain a consistent supply of material within the accepted quality level? What is the quality level of our competitors product? What quality aspects can we use to persuade the buyer to take our product in preference to that of our competitors? Can we agree on a quality acceptance plan with our client? Can our plant adhere to the Quality Adherence Programme? What Quality Control procedures are practised in our plant? Are they adequate or will they need to be expanded?
Price of supplies being purchased	What price negotiations can be made with the supplier in question? Does he hold a monopoly? Does he hold the only patent or agency for the material? Are other sources of supply available? Are volume discounts available? Are package type discounts available?	What price negotiations can we make to the buyer? Are we the only supplier? What other competitors do we have for our range of products? Are we aware of the price/volume discounts of our competitors? What types of packaging are available?
Ability of supplier to maintain adequate supplies	What capacity has the supplier available within his plant? Are any constituents of the	What components do we use in the product? Are they easily obtainable?

Table 8.1 **cont'd**

Main negotiating points	Buyer's view	Supplier's view
	product imported? Are there any world shortages of this commodity or any of its constituents? Is there any suspect key point in the supplier's plant that will cause breakdowns, and cut off supplies? What arrangements are made by the supplier if there is a serious breakdown or an annual shutdown of his plant?	How many suppliers of raw materials are there? Is there an alternative supplier of raw materials? If this material becomes unavailable, is there a similar product we can offer that will perform the same function? What arrangements do we make regarding supplies at times of important breakdown and annual shutdown (if any)?
Technical specifications for supplies	What specifications are available for the material to be purchased? What processes of manufacture are used? Does the selected supplier use the best process? Are the specification ranges tight enough for our operation? Can the supplier produce product fairly easily within the specification range or will we need to spend labour on monitoring his supply?	What are the product specifications for raw materials used in manufacturing the product for the buyer? Will extreme variance in raw material quality vary specification of final product? Are we able to provide a product specification? Are we able to check that our product conforms with the specification required? Is the process we use the most up to date? If not, what plans are in hand to convert to a more up to date process?
Terms of payment for supplies	What terms are available for payment: 30-day, 60-day or even 90-day credit arrangements? Can we arrange to pay as we use, not for unused stocks? Is there a discount on payments within 30 days, 7 days, etc.? Are these annual/quarterly/ monthly rebates available on volume? Does supplier have a good credit rating? Is he a reputable organization?	What terms can we offer the buyer that will put us at an advantage? What discounts/rebates can we offer? What is the buyer's credit rating? What are other suppliers' knowledge of his performance? Has he been listed for any adverse reason in any credit publication? Is the buyer a profitable, liquid company and what are its immediate performance projections?
Stockholding of supplies	What stocks of material are held by the supplier in terms of week's	What warehouse space is available that can be allocated to the buyer's

Table 8.1 **concluded**

Main negotiating points	Buyer's view	Seller's view
	cover of our production? Do we have to hold any stock? What maximum and minimum levels does the supplier work to? What stocks of important ingredients does the supplier hold? Will outside warehouse space be required?	product? What does this mean in terms of the buyer's plant production days? What stocks of raw materials can we hold? What is the recovery time of our plant in regard to replenishment of stock levels? Will outside warehouse space be required? How will the above affect the price of the product and has it been allowed?
Packaging of supplies	What range of packaging is available? Is there a range of cheaper bulk packages? Is there a bulk delivery facility? What degree of handling does the packaging of the material withstand? Can material be handled easily within plant? Can it be removed easily from packaging without losses?	What range of packaging material can we use for this product? Is it the most convenient? Are there other mediums available? Will it stand up to handling? Can it be conveniently handled by the buyer? Can the buyer take bulk deliveries. Can we supply the product in bulk? What future plans are in hand to improve supply?
Delivery of supplies	How is material delivered (packs, pallets etc.)? Is there returnable packaging involved? Who does the delivery? Is freight an additional cost to quoted price? Can national FIS price be arranged? Is delivery service reliable? Can urgent deliveries be made? How is return of suspect product arranged?	Is our delivery fleet working to full capacity, or can problems be seen in not meeting prompt delivery times? Is any special type of truck required to deliver the goods (e.g. what can supplier handle)? Can contractors be used? What is our current reputation in the trade for meeting delivery targets? Do we have to rely on other instrumentalities to provide transport (rail, shipping)? Has adequate provision been made in our costing for product delivery?

Table 8.2 **The contact between buyer and seller in foodchain. Typical soft drink situation**

Main negotiating points	Buyer's view	Seller's view
Price of supply, terms and conditions	Seeking stability of price and additional discounts and deals. To ensure we get the best price in relation to our competitors. We are aiming for maximum turnover with high profit per unit sale. Best possible credit facilities and terms. We are advised as early as possible on price increases or other charges relating to price and terms.	To obtain maximum price from dealer consistent with fullest support and stocking capacity. To keep tabs on competitive terms and conditions. To ensure they are not gaining an advantage with buyer. To ensure documentation flows smoothly.
Delivery	Reliability of delivery. Goods properly identified on delivery notes. Delivery at times convenient to buyer. No hold up on supplies. We want prompt service.	Ensure we have sufficient floor stocks. That potential stock problems are known in advance so buyer may be notified. We have dependable delivery service with minimum union problems and other disruptions.
Stockholding levels	Minimum stocking levels required commensurate with sales off-take. To guard against over-stock but take advantage of vendor's deals when available.	To ensure maximum stocking levels in order to force and maintain high distribution and stocks at forward selling areas.
Defective and obsolete stocks	Ensure replacements carried out effectively. To ensure slow sellers are liquidated with supplier's participation. We want prompt service in this area and if product does not sell to be able to return to vendor.	Whilst offering a replacement service keep returns to a minimum and ensure that job lines are kept to absolute minimum by alerting buyers to situation in his stores. We do not want to take back stock unless absolutely necessary.
Store merchandising and distribution	To permit supplier's merchandisers into our stores to help with stock replacement and merchandising. This saves us labour providing it is properly controlled. Supplies must not overstep our company policy in respect of allotted shelf facings and display material, etc. Also merchandiser's presence must not disrupt our operation in	Excellent opportunity to do PR job with section leader and store manager. We aim to have maximum shelf exposure and displays. Also to cement relations down the line. Educate section leader to advantages of stocking our product – to obtain maximum shelf and off-location display. Also good opportunity for intelligence work on competition

Table 8.2 **cont'd**

Main negotiating points	Buyer's view	Seller's view
	any way.	(i.e. checking competitive price 'specialling' – new products, etc.).
Co-operative advertising	We wish to obtain maximum support from the supplier in monetary terms so our prices may be discounted and co-operative advertising and promotion may be arranged. To ensure the participants in our total co-operative advertising package are major lead lines where 'specialling' will bring the customers into our stores.	To maximize our share of total availability of soft drink promotional programme. To ensure our company focuses attention on to the right products/ brands (the largest and most profitable). To ensure that our co-operative advertising programmes are policed – they are carried out in accordance with our pre-agreed plan. Also to provide fullest on-the-spot help in the form of store merchandising.
Contact	Phone orders to plant are handled efficiently. Are personal calls necessary – we are busy. There must be a purpose to the call. We are interested in industry trends by flavour and package and what our competitors are doing.	We need to keep best possible rapport with buyer and HQ personnel so that our product is uppermost in their minds and we gain maximum support. We also need to form close liaison at store level to get best results possible. This contact is a useful source of competitive information.
Packaging and warehousing	Packaging must be convenient size and shape and easily disposed of. Ease of warehouse handling, fork on, fork off. We need to minimize breakages and spillages and packages must be easily identifiable for warehouse picking, and packaging must be robust and withstand humidity and heat.	We must make sure our packaging reaches forward selling areas. Identification of contents must be good otherwise they are overlooked by warehousemen. Packages must be robust so that stock reaches store racks in mint condition. Poor presentation puts customers off.
Variety of product to be carried	To confine selling range to minimum variety and size consistent with maximum turnover. At same time to take into consideration our involvement with major competitors in similar product category.	To maximize range so far as possible, to achieve maximum shelf facings to detriment of competitive brands.
The new product/ packaging introduction	Caution in purchase of new lines, reassurance needed regarding off-take. Why should we stock product? If	Most important to obtain maximum co-operation right at start. We need largest possible opening order to force maximum

Table 8.2 **concluded**

Main negotiating points	Buyer's view	Seller's view
	really new product, has it been test marketed? In the case of 'me too's' why should we stock this product in preference to established products because we are sure to delete something else to put a 'me too' in? The 'me too' has to be cheaper than established product or have a real and definite advantage. We want to know how the product will be advertised, where and when and how long the ads will last. We also require samples. We require information about how many products to a carton and how big the outer carton is – how many cartons to a layer – and layers to a pallet. We do not wish to see elaborate presentations in our office – or sit and watch TV ads. We do not have the time. What are the prices for quantity buys including any opening deals, and how long will the deals last?	shelf facings and distribution through all stores. We need co-operative advertising promotion to achieve maximum publicity coincidentally with start of advertising campaign. Our objective must be to get buyer to ensure that all outlets are thoroughly briefed on details of new product and importance of launch. To obtain best store grading (classification) with the new product we are offering.

Table 8.3 **Negotiation tactics: checklist**

Tactic	Comment
1 If you know your objectives don't be afraid to start suggesting major terms.	You know what your next move is.
2 Always start high and trade-down.	Use your highest figures first then trade-down if you have to. You can rarely trade-up from a lower figure.
3 Conceal your emotions.	Try to keep a poker face. Avoid expressing relief, disgust, elation. It will give clues to your opponent. If you do any of these things it becomes an act which it

Table 8.3 **cont'd**

Tactic	Comment
4 Use silence.	is difficult to sustain for long. When an unacceptable offer is presented, silence is the best reply.
5 Be prepared to break off negotiation when the alternative is having to retract later.	If the unexpected arises, it is better to confer with your colleagues, if there are others in your team, and agree the next step than to go on and then have to retract in front of your opponents.
6 Delay sensitive issues to avoid confrontation.	If you risk a direct confrontation by raising a delicate issue early either delay, of if necessary defer meeting.
7 If a negotiation is deferred decide basis for next meeting.	Always agree the next step or objective if more than one meeting is necessary to reach agreement.
8 Do not exaggerate facts.	Never exaggerate what can later be verified about your company. *Be frank.*
9 When agreement is reached leave.	To delay your departure can expose you to danger of someone wanting to revise the terms of an agreement.
10 Respect buyer's conventions.	Be watchful to ensure you do not offend: 'When in Rome do as the Romans do'.
11 Use simple language.	Negotiation above all else requires clear thinking and clear speech. Keep your language simple.
12 Do not be greedy.	Everyone has his breaking point. If you push too far or too hard you may succeed *once* but only once.

Table 8.4 **Negotiation details: checklist**

Detail	Comment
1 Record all points agreed as you go.	Avoid the need to meet again to renegotiate what was not noted down.

Table 8.4 **cont'd**

Detail	Comment
2 Keep negotiating team even.	Do not be over-powered or over-power.
3 Choose negotiating team carefully.	How technical will the discussions become? Take technicians for technical advice *only*.
4 Do not assume anything.	Clarify each point agreed including the limits and the precise latitudes.
5 Do not send subordinates to speak for you if you can help it. If you must delegate, make sure you confirm your subordinates' authority in writing, stating the scope and limits of their power.	As a rule, only equals should negotiate. Besides, what your subordinates say they said, and what they *actually* said, rarely are the same.
6 Negotiate on your own ground.	But if your objective is to get to know your opposite number visit him on his home ground.
7 Do not embarrass others who make mistakes.	Do not draw attention to their errors and do not knock other people. If you make mistakes do not over-react but do not make too many.
8 Avoid personal opinion about others.	Unless you know people very well your personal opinions can swing a fine-balanced decision against you. Be sure that you understand the 'chemistry of vibrations'.
9 Expect negative reactions in negotiating.	No one wants to give the impression of pleasure at decisions reached in case it alters balance of advantage.

Table 8.5 **Negotiation warnings: checklist**

Warning	Comment
1 If you decide to be provocative or unpleasant know what you are doing.	Such actions should be very controlled. If you make someone lose their temper they could cause you to lose yours and you may throw away all your negotiating advantages.

Table 8.5 **cont'd**

Warning	Comment
2 Watch for wandering eyes.	Some people are very good at reading upside down print. They may read your next negotiating point and answer it before you are ready.
3 Do not sign anything in haste.	Always read the small print. It can often contain unnegotiated surprises.
4 Avoid the hospitality trap.	Try and negotiate before lunch.
5 Never be superior.	In negotiating stick to *your objectives*. If you cannot reach the minimum, the timing is wrong or your overtures are unwelcome, better to lose with a good grace and live to parley on a better day.

Appendix: A planning format
for major customers

Negotiations between suppliers and their major customers often span several meetings before agreements are reached; in some industries and public authorities the discussions can even last several years.

However short or long negotiations are, systematic planning will yield a number of benefits.

1 It forces you to consider all the issues involved on paper and, as a result, highlights the costs and values of each and every concession and the contradictions. Without planning, some of these contradictions can arise in the middle of negotiations with customers, leading to confusion, loss of face and of bargaining position, and frequently to unprofitable business.

2 When, as is often the case, you are a member of a negotiating team, a planning document provides a disciplined agenda and co-ordinated plan for all concerned and avoids the danger of any one person going off at a tangent. It ensures that issues are covered and pinpoints possible areas of duplication.

3 It provides a disciplined approach for reviewing each stage of a complex, long-drawn-out negotiation and, where you changed direction from the plan, what are the implications for future meetings.

The following pages contain a major customer planning format together with explanatory notes to help you complete it. This system of planning has been tested in over 52 countries and is now used to plan the activities of sales personnel responsible for many hundreds of millions of pounds of sales each year.

The appendix concludes with an example of a completed format.

Situation analysis

This first section of the plan examines your trading performance with the customer to date, your position in relation to your competitors and the present and future business environment in which both the customer and you as supplier are operating.

The Situation Analysis is divided into four sections: Introduction and summary, Historical trading analysis, Environment summary and Competitive comparison. Each section concludes with a suggested format for recording the relevant information.

Introduction and summary

The purpose of this section is to provide a descriptive overview of the customer and important information related to your selling activities.

This will encompass:

– Key customer contacts.
– The type of business the customer is in.
– His business objectives.
– The principal buying considerations.
– The customer buying decision process.
– The customer attitude to your company.
– Terms and services currently provided by your company.
– Main competitors and their products.

Customer profile

1.

Name of customer:

2.

Key contacts:

	Name	Position
1.	_____	_____
2.	_____	_____
3.	_____	_____

3.

Type of business:
Products/Services:

4. Commercial description:

(a) Chief business objectives:
- Financial
- Marketing
- Production

(b) Key buying considerations:

(c) Buying decision process:

(d) Attitude to our company:

(e) Other significant factors:

5. *Terms & services currently provided by us*

Price:

Credit:

Delivery:

Technical service:

Promotion:

Financial support:

Other:

> **6.**
>
> *Main competitors & their products*
>
> *Direct:*
>
>
>
> *Indirect:*

Historical trading analysis

The purpose of this section is to provide a broad picture of the customer's trading history over the past three years. In particular, we are concerned to identify what proportion the company has been obtaining of the customer's purchases for the type of products you can supply.

The analysis is designed to answer the following questions:

- What total actual sales have we achieved each year in both value (revenue) and volume (e.g. tonnes)?
- What sales value and volume have we achieved by product or major product range?
- What is the customer's potential for the type of product we sell?
- What is the trend of the customer potential? (growth, decline, static)
- What is the trend of our sales? (growth, decline, static)

Environment summary

The purpose of this section is to show factors coming from outside of the customer or our own company which are having, or will have, a positive or negative impact upon future sales expectations.

These external factors should be looked at in the light of two questions:

- What is happening or will happen that will affect the customer's trading future with *its* customers?
- What is happening or will happen that will affect our own trading position with the customer?

You are therefore identifying a range of future business opportunities and threats.

The main opportunities and threats for the future are likely to be identified from:

Value: $ Volume:

Customer purchases from all suppliers of type of products you sell	1987	1988	1989	Trend
Value Volume				
Total sales achieved by you at this customer Value Volume				
Share of total purchases Value % Volume %				
Sales achieved by you at this customer by product or product range				
1. Value Volume				
2. Value Volume				
3. Value Volume				
4. Value Volume				
5. Value Volume				
6. Value Volume				
7. Value Volume				
8. Value Volume				
Others Value Volume				

Historical trading analysis

(a) Economic factors

e.g. – growing/declining population;
  – inflation;
  – exchange rates;
  – energy and labour costs;
  – raw material costs;
  – others

No one is expecting you to be an economist; what you should be thinking about is what do you know, or have you heard, that is going to affect your business area? What is the trade talking about? Are your customer's sales growing or declining?

(b) Political/Legal

e.g. – taxation;
  – legislation;
  – regulations;
  – government philosophy.

(c) Technological

Consider advances in product or production technology that affect your company or your customer's business. New products on their own are not to be considered here, unless they represent a significant technological advance e.g., a revolutionary new material, compound process or chemical entity which offers the potential for a significant change in your customer's market or production.

Environment summary
Future business opportunities
Future business threats

(d) Social

Possible developments in distribution/trade channels

e.g.   −   growth of retail multiples;
     −   growth in healthcare expectation;
     −   increasing interest in safer, cleaner working conditions.

(e) Others

Competitive comparison The purpose of this section is to establish how well your 'package' (products, services, people, support), meets the purchasing needs of your customer compared with your competitors.

It therefore seeks to identify the following:

− What are the key factors that influence
  − his choice of suppliers?
  − the volumes purchased from each supplier?
− What importance does the customer attach to these factors?
− How well do your products meet the customer's needs in each area?
− Are the other competitors just as good as we are? Better or worse?

For such an analysis to be useful it is essential that you complete the information as though you were the customer and as objectively as possible.

It is clear therefore that a good level of knowledge is required about your customer's buying considerations, needs and the competition (generally and in relation to this customer).

Eventually, the conclusions from this form will be used to identify areas of relative strength, which we can use in negotiation and selling, and areas of weaknesses which will need to be addressed in the future plan.

Summary So far we have reviewed the current situation and looked forward to identify any known areas of change.

The information and statistics prepared have formed our database on *'where are we now?'*

The more accurate we can make this phase of our plan, the greater is the likelihood of our action plan being realistic and achievable.

Each of the four analyses we have completed (Introduction and summary, Historical trading analysis, Enviroment summary and Competitive comparison) has been prepared independent of the others.

The next step will be to interpret each analysis and identify the issues which should be addressed in the future, as a matter of priority.

Competitors: 1 _____ X
                2 _____ Y
                3 _____ Z

	Importance Rating	Company	Competition			Implications
			1	2	3	
Prices						
Discounts						
Payment terms						
Product performance						
Deliveries						
Sales presentation						
Promotional support						
Technical support						
Others						

IMPORTANCE RATING

A = Very important – Essential
B = Important – Desirable
C = Low – Importance

CUSTOMER VIEW

1 = Consistently and fully meets need
2 = Meets needs inconsistently
3 = Fails to meet needs

Competitive comparison

Planning implications (strengths, weaknesses, opportunities and threats)

The purpose of this section is to produce a summary of the key issues arising from the Introduction and summary, Historical trading analysis, Environment summary and Competitive comparison against which our future customers plan will be prepared.

This analysis is more commonly known as a SWOT analysis as it identifies strengths, weaknesses, opportunities and threats.

The important issues are therefore summarized under each of these four headings.

(a) *Opportunities*

Opportunities for future business are created by factors or changes outside and are therefore not directly controllable by us. Typical examples would be growth in the customer's market(s), new processes planned by the customer, customer dissatisfaction with an existing competitor etc.

When completing this section you will need to refer back to the following:

– Introduction and summary

    e.g. – Chief business objectives.

       – Key buying considerations.

– Historical trading analysis

    e.g. – Is the customer's potential trend increasing over the last three years – is this likely to continue.

– Environment summary

    Of the opportunity factors listed, which are the most important to you?

When selecting the key opportunities always keep in focus:

– Are they compatible with your company/division/business area strategy?
– Are they realizable within the resources of your company?
– Do they conflict with the customer's business objectives or buying considerations?
– Are they commercially worthwhile?
– How long will they take to be realized?

Finally, since not all the opportunities represent the same scale of commercial value to you, you will need to categorize the list into:

– High commercial opportunities.
– Medium commercial opportunities
– Low commercial opportunities.

(b) *Threats*

As with opportunities, threats are created by factors outside your company.

You will again need to refer to the

– Introduction and summary.
– Historical trading analysis.
– Environment summary.

In each case now you are looking for the significant negative influences on your future business.

Again, the commercial impact of these key threats will probably vary. Assuming that all these key threats will materialize in the period covered by your plan, categorize the list into:

– High commercial threats.
– Medium commercial threats.
– Low commercial threats.

Base this judgement on the commercial effect each threat will have on your business.

(c) *Strengths*

Strengths are derived from your products, services, people and support activities and are therefore controllable by your company.

To complete this section you will need to refer to the Competitive comparison section.

When selecting main strengths, try to see your company as your customer does. If your delivery service is consistently good, but so is the service provided by all your competitors, then the customer does not see this as your exclusive strength.

List only those strengths therefore where you could claim to be better than most or all of your competitors. In other words where you have a differential advantage.

(d) *Weaknesses*

To complete this section follow the same guidelines as for strengths, except that you are looking for areas where you are worse than any of your competitors.

A suggested outline for completing the analysis is given on page 151.

Planning implications for year

Preparation of planning implications or a SWOT analysis is a vital stage in putting together 'where we are now' and 'where we could go'. It is the principal document for determining the future action you take with the major customer.

OPPORTUNITIES		THREATS	
HIGH		HIGH	
MEDIUM		MEDIUM	
LOW		LOW	
STRENGTHS		WEAKNESSES	

In setting your future sales objectives and actions for the customer you will need to make judgements regarding:

— which opportunities am I going to focus on?
— do these build on my key strengths as seen by the customer?
— which weaknesses will need to be addressed in relation to the opportunities?
— will action on our current weaknesses reduce threats?
— what other actions could be considered to reduce threats?

You must balance opportunities against threats. *Do not* be carried away by size of the opportunity (volume or cash) alone, thus ignoring the impact of threats or weaknesses.

Objectives   This is the cornerstone of the plan – deciding what your sales achievement needs to be with this customer in the future. This is the stage of specifying *'where do we want/need to go?'*

The sales objectives you set need to be: S M A R T

S Specific	–	product/product range
(at least by)	–	volume
	–	where possible value (revenue)
	–	share of customer potential
M Measurable	–	i.e. quantified and within your ability to gather information;

A Achievable – within your company/division/business area competence;

– compatible with the customer's business objectives and his buying considerations;

R Realistic – commercially worthwhile to your company/division/business area;

T Timed – within the time frame covered by the customer plan.

Sales objectives will flow from the:

(a) – Historical trading analysis.

– Projecting forward the customer potential trend for all the types of products you sell.

– Projecting forward the customer potential for each product/product range you can supply.

(b) – Planning implications (SWOT analysis).

– Adjusting current year's actual sales trend (Historical trading analysis) in light of the opportunities you have selected.

	Customer potential	Actual sales	% share	Customer potential	Target	% share	Customer potential	Forecast	% share
Maximum customer purchases available for the product you sell Value Volume									
Value Volume									
Value Volume									
Value Volume									
Value Volume									
Value Volume									
Value Volume									

Sales objectives

Sales strategies Simply stated, strategies describe how you intend to go about achieving the objectives you have set, in broad terms. They should not specify the detailed activity you will undertake.

For each product/product range that will be sold to the customer we will need to produce a strategic statement (say two or three sentences) summarizing the direction we intend to follow to achieve the product/product range sales objective.

Figure A.1 shows diagrammatically a range of strategic decision options you consider frequently.

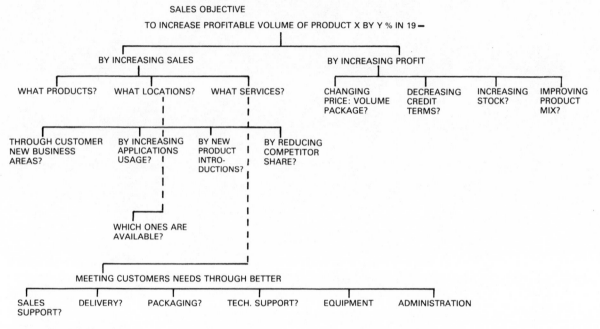

Figure A.1 **Strategic decision options**

To achieve our sales objective we have two broad options – to increase volume and/or improve profitability. Each route subdivides providing a comprehensive range of decision options.

You clearly could not address every option – you must make judgements based on your knowledge of:

– the customer's purchasing needs;

– his buying considerations;

– competitor reactions;

– your capability/flexibility;

– our present strengths and weaknesses as a supplier etc.

When you have written your strategy statement it is worth asking the question 'will this strategy give me a differential advantage over my competitors in the customer's eyes, thereby leading to the achievement of my sales objective?'

A suggested outline for preparing sales strategies is given on page 154.

Sales strategies *Customer strategy:*
Product strategies: Product:
Product:
Product:
Product:
Product:

Action programme The action programme is the outcome of the customer planning process. It extends from the objectives and strategies you have prepared, and describes the specific actions/activities you will need to undertake to implement the strategy, when they need to occur and who is responsible for implementing them.

In preparing your action programme ask yourself the following questions:

(a) What changes are we trying to achieve with the customer?

These answers form your *ACTION OBJECTIVES*

Remember that you must quantify these objectives for them to have any meaning i.e. 'To reduce late deliveries' means nothing, but 'To reduce late deliveries so that 90 per cent are delivered on time as against the current figure of 40 per cent, during the whole of 1992' – means something.

If you have quantified the objective you can measure it.

(b) What do we need to do to fulfil each action objective?

These answers form the *ACTIVITY REQUIRED*

(c) When do these actions need to be completed?

These answers give you the *TIMING*

To achieve your objectives you will probably have several actions to perform. Some of these might be consecutive, some might need time to have the full effect. This column allows us to place a deadline on the activities.

(d) Who should undertake the actions?

These answers specify the responsibility of each *person*

All of the planned actions need not necessarily be under your control i.e. technical support, discounting, distribution, promotion etc., but it is your responsibility to ensure that they are carried out by the appropriate people in so far as you possibly can.

You will need to identify who is responsible for the action and show up areas where you may need to co-operate.

(e) When should I monitor the progress of the plan and how will this be done?

These answers indicate the necessary *REVIEW ACTIONS*

Failure to achieve the desired results on one Action Objective can often affect other objectives you have set. Monitoring performance is therefore crucial to taking early corrective action.

A suggested outline for preparing an action programme is given on page 156.

CUSTOMER:_____

Action objective	Activity required	Timing	Person responsible	Method of Review

Action programme

	You	Customer
Long-term Check the annual report and other published inform-ation		
Short-term		
This negotiation		

Negotiation objectives

YOUR OBJECTIVES: _____

_____

_____

_____

NEGOTIATING ELEMENTS: *YOUR STANCE*
                                 (position/attitude?)

1. _____   _____
2. _____   _____
3. _____   _____
4. _____   _____
5. _____   _____

Elements	Concessions by you	Agreed	Cost to you	Benefits to customer
1	1 2 3 4 Fall back position			
2	1 2 3 4 Fall back position			
3	1 2 3 4 Fall back position			
4	1 2 3 4 Fall back position			
5	1 2 3 4 Fall back position			

Negotiation strategy

	Estimated	Stated
Customer objectives:	_____	
	_____	
	_____	
	_____	
Customer minimum:	_____	
	_____	

Customer stances:	Element	Stance
	_____	_____
	_____	_____
	_____	_____
	_____	_____
	_____	_____
	_____	_____
	_____	_____

Concessions from customer	Agreed	Cost to customer	Benefit to customer
Fall-back			
Fall-back			
Fall-back			
Fall-back			
Fall-back			

Negotiation strategy

January	February	March
April	May	June
July	August	September
October	November	December

Action plan for 1992

Major customer planning
Worked example

Introduction and summary

| 1. | Name of customer: | Terrytex Ltd
Anytown
Anywhere |

| 2. | Key contacts: | Mr Girvans – for general policy
Mr Willcox – day-to-day business |

| 3. | Type of business: | Distributor of products & associated equipment – partly to trade and partly direct to end users |

4. Commercial description:

(a) Chief business objectives:
- Wants to maintain average gross margin of 30 per cent.
- Wants to maintain rate of growth as per last five years
- Wants to maintain position as first in size, quality, prestige

(b) Key buying considerations:
- Past proven sales performance carries great weight
- Terms and conditions must meet Terrytex objectives
- Resistant to new products prefers trial market rather than major stockholding
- Not restricted to price alone will consider other ways of achieving profitability

(c) Buying decision process:
    Repeat orders – Mr Willcox new products/changes – Mr Girvans

(d) Attitude to us:
- Generally friendly and positive – likes products but becoming more aggressive on prices and threatening to switch
- Expects us to act as partner to help him reach objectives despite changing competitive circumstances

(e) Other significant factors:
- Increased competition to Terrytex over past two years – mainly lower prices – includes our products. Competition and Terrytex same as our price level but Terrytex not convinced

5.

> *Terms & services currently provided by company*
>
> * Price: Obtains our best Terms Across Range
>
> Delivery: Products 1 & 2 & 5 delivered against monthly orders
> Product 3 Called off on 48–hour notice
> Product 4 Against fortnightly stock control order
>
> Technical service: – Head Office 'Hot line' For urgent questions
>   – Quarterly onsite visit
>   – Special advice & instruction for new products
>   – annual training of sales staff by me
>
> Credit: Standard terms – but actually takes 60 days
>
> Promotion: – Onsite material plus point of sale material
>   – Special credit note discount for his key accounts to meet his competition prices
>   – onsite equipment for our products
>   – mailings to customer for special offers
>   – use of our facilities to prove special features coupled with written reports
>   – PR trips for both prinicipals
>
> Financial support: – Promotion budget for customer activity
>   – Our loan in early days helped with start-up
>
> Other:

6.

> *Main competitors & their products*
>
> * Direct   Company X Product a)
>   Brand 1
>   Company Y Product b)
>   Brand 2
>
> Indirect   Company Z Product c)
>   Brand 3
>   Company X Product d)
>   Brand 4
>
> – No knowledge of competitors' actual sales and prices
> – No hard knowledge of competitive service

Historical trading analysis

Value: $000   Volume: Tonnes

	1987	1988	1989	Trend
Customer purchases, from all suppliers, of the type of products you sell				
Value	2752	3033	3178	13.4
Volume	1690	1721	1747	3.4
Total sales achieved by you at this customer				
Value	1974	2014	2112	7.0
Volume	980	1012	1036	5.7
Co share of total purchases				
Value %	72	66	66	(8.0)
Volume %	58	59	59	1.7

		1987	1988	1989	Trend
Sales achieved by you at this customer by product or product range					
1. Product 1	Value Volume	1078 490	1107 527	1220 610	13.2 24.5
2. Product 2	Value Volume	303 200	351 185	242 110	(20.0) (45.0)
3. Product 3	Value Volume	224 115	205 105	175 90	(21.9) (21.7)
4. Product 4	Value Volume	218 100	144 95	155 76	(28.9) (24.0)
5. Product 5	Value Volume	151 75	207 100	320 150	111.9 100.0
6. Product 6	Value Volume				
7. Product 7	Value Volume				
8. Product 8	Value Volume				
Others	Value Volume				

Environment summary

Future Business Opportunities

- Increase in consumer spending and leisure time should result in growth in volume.
- Age-band boom will increase number of potential customers hence increase volume over next two years.
- Need to comply with environmental legislation could increase dependence upon our technical know how.
- TERRYTEX need to improve efficiency of operation and reduce costs in response to their competitor's pricing policy.

Future Business Threats

- No new technical advances are foreseen to challenge our company position or products.
- High interest rates and rising labour costs will increase customer pressure to reduce prices to maintain profitability.
- Increase in environment interest could increase customer's costs and therefore price pressure.
- Increase in direct competition via imports and third world 'cheap' manufacturing will increase competitive price pressure.
- Competitors are increasing their visibility through increased advertising, trade deals, and contact frequency.

Competitive comparison

Competitors: 1 Company X
2 Company Y
3 Company Z

	Importance Rating	Company	Competition			Implications
			1	2	3	
Prices	A	2	1	2	1	Need to avoid head to head comparison
Discounts	A	2	1	2	2	Need to tailor to customers' needs
Payment terms	A	1	1	1	1	Slack enforcement satisfies customer
Product performance	A	1	2	2	2	Best product on head to head
Deliveries	A	2	2	1	1	Generally OK but 48 hour sometimes late
Sales presentation	A	1	2	2	1	Better contact more frequent calls
Promotional support	B	1	2	1	2	Better quality helps to sell out

	Importance Rating	Company	Competition			Implications
			1	2	3	
Technical support	B	1	3	2	3	Improves efficiency and reduces costs
Others						

Importance rating	Customer view
A = Very important – essential	1 = Consistently and fully meets needs
B = Important – desirable	2 = Meets needs inconsistently
C = Low importance	3 = Fails to meet needs

Planning implications for year

	Opportunities		Threats
High	– Potential growth for products 1 & 5 – No technically superior products expected – Customer's image objective	High	– Rising costs could encourage move to low price competition – Increasing competitive activity on prices
Medium	– Probable legislation needing technical support	Medium	– Customer's total volume static – Customer's profit objectives
Low	– Need to reduce operating costs through better systems	Low	– Increasing competitor visibility

Strengths	Weaknesses
– Products meet needs better – Frequency and contact – Sales promotion support especially mailings and point of sale – Technical service/support – Product 5 has proved very successful – Product 1 is maintaining growth – Are dominant supplier – Record of assistance in past	– Higher prices than competition – Less flexible discounts – 48 hour delivery service must be consistent – Products 2, 3, 4 being replaced by competition – Lack of knowledge of real competitors' performance

		1990–91			1991–92			1992–93		
		Customer Potential	Actual Sales	% Share	Customer Potential	Target	% Share	Customer Potential	Forecast	% Share
Maximum Customer Purchases Available for the Product you sell	Value	3178	xxxx	xxxx	3432	xxxx	xxxx	3737	xxxx	xxxx
	Volume	1747	xxxx	xxxx	1750	xxxx	xxxx	1750	xxxx	xxxx
Product 1	Value	1220	1220	100	1529	1529	100	1919	1919	100
	Volume	610	610	100	695	695	100	793	793	100
Product 2	Value	592	242	41	495	218	44	295	196	66
	Volume	310	110	35.5	250	110	44	166	110	66
Product 3	Value	526	175	33	482	282	48	396	260	66
	Volume	381	90	23.6	350	150	43	305	200	66
Product 4	Value	520	155	30	435	155	36	371	155	42
	Volume	296	76	25.7	245	76	31	192	76	40
Product 5	Value	320	320	100	491	491	100	756	756	100
	Volume	150	100	100	210	210	100	294	294	100
Others	Value									
	Volume									

Sales objectives

SALES STRATEGIES

Customer Strategy:

To penetrate this customer further by emphasizing the strengths of the product range coupled with our technical support to reinforce the customer's image need and to offset the competitive threat through a flexible product pricing and promotion support.

Product Strategies:

Product: *Product 1*: To emphasize historic growth of this product coupled with promotion support to justify a continued price increase.

Product: *Product 2*: To hold the actual volume by emphasizing the company image and responding to competitive pricing pressure.

Product: *Product 3*: To penetrate the volume business through an aggressive discounting and promotion policy and by improving delivery service.

Product: *Product 4*: To maintain the volume value position by selling our company 'package'.

Product: *Product 5*: To emphasize the launch success and the reinforcing qualities of this product to the customer's image and to use the value of this product to aid the sales of the rest of the range.

Action objective	Activity required	Timing	Person responsible	Review action
1. To gain target volume & sales figures a) Prod 1 & 5 b) Prod 4	a) Develop & implement call & negotiation plans	2 months before current year end	Me & ASM	Monthly sales stats
	b) Obtain approval for price/discount levels on: Product 1 + 10% Product 2 − 10% Product 3 − 20% Product 5 + 10%	3 months before current year end	Me & ASM	Plan review with Manager
	c) Maintain calling rate	Monthly	Me	Call reports/diary
2. To identify areas for 'added value' technical support	a) Obtain evaluation of legislation changes	January	Tech dept	Monitor reply to memo
	b) Plan increased inter-face with customer	February	Me & ASM Tech dept	Monitor tech visits and customer attitude
3. To hold 3 promotion specials for product to achieve volume targets	a) Develop package linked to our plans but specific to product and customer	December of current year	Me & Mkt dept: ASM	Monitor before and after sales figures relate sales increase to promotion cost
4. To make 48-hour delivery consistent	a) To identify problem and remedy	ASAP	Me: Depot Manager	Monitor deliveries with customer
5. To increase knowledge of company sales and volume	a) Ask customer and Market dept	ASAP	Me: Mkt dept	Have full information by mid-year
6. To maintain our image at the perceived current level	a) Organize co PR trips	Spring Autumn	Me & ASM	Review customer attitude on each call

Action programme

Part III

The skills of negotiating

Introduction to Part III

The first problem with all human communications is that no one thinks that there is a problem. Whether we are talking to one person or to a group, we all too often think that they not only *hear* what we say but also, *understand, agree with* and will *act upon* what they have heard in exactly the way we think they should.

The second problem is that we are not very good at listening, *really listening*, when someone speaks to us and understanding correctly what we have heard. This is superbly summed up in the following words on a noticeboard in the Pentagon, Washington:

'I think you believe you understand what you think I said, but I am not sure you realise that what you heard is not what I meant.'

When we are involved in negotiations with either one person or a group of people; our success depends not only on how well we have planned them but on our understanding and mastery of *three* communication skills:

- EFFECTIVE LISTENING.
- INTERPRETATION OF BODY LANGUAGE – 'the art of seeing what other people are thinking'.
- EFFECTIVE PRESENTATION.

In the next two chapters we examine the barriers that create problems in listening and how we can overcome them and how to interpret the thoughts of others from their body behaviour. In the final chapter we deal with how to improve our skills when we communicate to others.

9

Effective listening

Of all the communication skills, *listening* is the one in which most of us receive no training, are the least efficient yet use the most!

Research shows that we spend 80 per cent of our lives communicating and about half of that listening. Studies of the four activities used in communication indicate that, and yet perversely our educational systems give priority in reverse order. Writing gets most, reading next and listening least attention.

	Listening	Speaking	Reading	Writing
Learned	1st	2nd	3rd	4th
Used	Most (45%)	Next Most (30%)	Next Least (16%)	Least (9%)
Taught	Least	Next Least	Next Most	Most

Why don't we listen?

There are many reasons why we don't listen when people speak to us. In many societies, particularly western ones, children are taught always to try to do better, to excel and to be assertive. So whilst speaking is a powerful means of asserting our will, our views and our authority, listening is too often thought to be a sign of passivity of compliance. When we speak we feel in control of events or situations. Yet when we are talking, whilst we may satisfy our own needs, we fail to consider the needs of others. Indeed the more we talk the less we learn!

From my observations all over the world and from other professional analyses, those who are good at listening tend to be good at selling, at negotiation and at marketing.

Barriers to effective listening

There are many common obstacles to good listening.

1 *The speed at which we speak in our own language.* We talk at between 120–150 words a minute. But the brain thinks at speeds of up to 500 words a minute. The consequences of this surplus capacity are that the brain uses it to:

– judge;

– evaluate;

– compile responses;

– become distracted and often bored whilst listening to the person speaking.

2 *Outside Distractions*

Fatigue, personal discomfort from seating, over-eating or drinking or lack of both, noise, telephone calls, or too much comfort all make it difficult to concentrate on the messages the person speaking to you is trying to convey. Unwanted messages caused by outside distractions keep intruding and superimposing themselves.

3 *Interpretation and Distortion*

The cultural and educational background of the speaker and, in the mind of the listener, the imprecise language he uses, can often mislead. A vivid example of this occurred within my hearing when the death of Anthony Eden (Lord Avon and prime minister of Great Britain in 1955–56) was announced on a television news bulletin in January 1977. On the same programme a tribute was paid to him by a close political colleague, Christopher Soames, who spoke of Eden as being always '. . . such a gay companion'. I knew exactly what Soames meant yet, in the hotel room listening to those same words, another hotel guest said 'Amazing. I never knew Eden was homosexual'.

Preconceived ideas from one's own past experience can distort or colour your reception of an idea, particularly if you associate it with one that failed or created problems for you.

Assumptions about what you hear, leading you to stop listening because you think you have heard it all before, can be very dangerous e.g., at the last round of negotiations, the purchasing director said in a loud voice, 'Pricing is *the* critical issue if you are to enjoy the same volume of our business'. 'This time round', he says in a lowered voice in the middle of other matters 'and in relation to the whole package, price is of course a factor to bear in mind'.

4 *Personal Barriers*

These barriers can block your ability to listen even before the speaker has said a word, e.g.

Prejudices: – against men or women;

– against white or black people;

– against people who are neatly dressed/scruffy;

– men wearing earrings;

– women with strong perfume or wearing nail varnish;

or as Emerson put it,

'What you are sounds so loudly in my ears that I can't hear what you say.'

After the speaker has begun to speak he or she may do or say things in such a manner that you 'switch off'.

This can happen because he/she:
— uses jargon;
— uses repetitious phrases;
— has a 'class' accent;
— has irritating mannerisms.

Inefficient listening resulting from any one of these barriers can be very costly to you and your company, e.g.

— letters to the team you are negotiating with or selling to containing errors, first because the shorthand or audio typist did not listen correctly to what you said and secondly, because you did not check the letters before signing them;

— appointments having to be cancelled or re-scheduled to your potential customer's inconvenience because you did not *listen* fully on the telephone when the secretary said that her boss *would not* be available on certain dates and *would be* available on other dates!

How you can develop your listening skills

There are a number of ways to improve listening skills. Firstly you should recognize that effective listening is hard work and needs your conscious and concentrated attention to succeed.

Avoid distractions   This is easier to control when negotiation meetings take place on your premises. First there are physical distractions that can impair effective listening, e.g.

* another conversation taking place in the same room with you half listening to it and at the same time to the person speaking to you;

* telephones ringing in the next office; traffic, trains passing, a police siren wailing in the distance.

Secondly, there are visual distractions which can interfere with your ability to listen, e.g.

* a glamorous picture on a Pirelli calendar behind the speaker;

* some arithmetical figure almost visible on a flip-chart;

* a chart amongst the papers in front of the speaker that may relate to what he is saying.

Physically attending to the Speaker   * *Face the speaker squarely* – sit where you can see and hear the speaker squarely. If you are negotiating seated at a round table and one of the team from the other side sits next to you, it is much more difficult to listen when he or she speaks to you.

* *Maintain good eye contact* – the good listener maintains eye contact that is neither fixedly staring at one extreme nor evasively avoiding eye contact at the other. You want to avoid being so different in your eye contact from what we are used to that your listener/speaker draws an unfavourable conclusion; 'She gives me the creeps with that piercing stare all the time', or 'He's a shifty customer. Never looked at me when I spoke to him'.

The psychologist, Michael Argyle, has provided, through his extensive studies, figures for the normal pattern of eye contact:

* we look at each other for an average of about 60 per cent of the time;
* about 75 per cent of the time while we are listening;
* about 40 per cent of the time while we are speaking;
* generally our mutual eye contact when we look into each other's eye is only about 30 per cent when we are speaking or listening to a particular person and then in short bursts which average no more than one to two seconds.

Eye contact should convey to the speaker the impression that you do not want to miss a word; that 'I am all ears' – and of course you must convey this by not:

* sitting back with your arms folded;
* half closing your eyes when you look at the speaker;
* fiddling with your clothes;
* looking at your watch or your nails;
* doodling on a piece of paper.

Look at the speaker so that you convey a picture of someone who is relaxed, still, and at peace with yourself, yet alert.

Psychologically attending to the speaker

Because of the differences to which I have already referred between the speed at which we speak words and can listen to them, you must learn how to use your surplus brain capacity effectively when listening.

What is being said? – Listen for the speaker's central theme not just the facts; the meaning behind the words even decoding what is not said or left unsaid.

– Keep an open mind and do not start drawing conclusions until you understand fully all that the speaker *wants* to say.

- Ignore the speaker's clothes, voice, accent, haircut, sex, poor presentation.

- Watch out for your emotional filters either producing a biased attitude either in favour of what is being said or against.

- Concentrate and listen to the message. When someone is speaking to you, he or she is usually engaged in one of *four* kinds of verbal communication. Firstly, introductory *'Getting to know you'* communication which has the simple objective of building relationships. Secondly, *CATHARTIC* communication when someone wants only a sympathetic ear to listen to pent up feelings which must be expressed. Thirdly, *INFORMATIVE* communications when ideas, statistics, information are conveyed to you. Fourthly, *PERSUASIVE* communications when the speaker seeks to reinforce or to change your attitudes, your perception, your behaviour.

- Do not judge the message you have heard until you have understood it.

- Use that part of your mind that is ahead of what the speaker is saying constructively by thinking ahead; make short notes of what is being said so that you can test your understanding and interpretation. Weigh up the evidence used by the speaker. Ask yourself is this complete or has something been left out? Is this a valid comment?

How is it being said?

- In the next chapter we will find out how to interpret accurately what people are thinking (but often not saying) from their non-verbal behaviour – from their body language. Listen to how the speaker conveys what he/she says and observe the physical movements that accompany the words, e.g.

  * tone of voice; loud, soft, agreeable, unfriendly, sarcastic;

  * facial expressions;

  * body posture;

  * use of hands.

What is NOT being said?

As you listen, ask what is the meaning behind the words used? Try and read the meaning between the words. These can be one or a combination which may include the following:

* justifying a decision or course of action;

* sowing seeds of doubt in your mind;
* trying to promote agreement;
* winning personal acceptance;
* concealing emotions;
* hinting at personal needs to be satisfied;
* promoting a viewpoint;
* imposing a viewpoint;
* trying to flatter you;
* gaining support;
* trying to deliberately provoke;
* gaining commitment;
* clarifying own thoughts;
* airing self-doubts;
* releasing frustrations;
* making light of serious position;
* rationalizing a position;
* instilling.

When you are concentrating on understanding what is *not* being said, beware of the dangers of listening in total silence.

The decision to adopt a non-intervening listening attitude is not very difficult to sustain, but it can provoke the following reactions by the speaker:

- you are not listening;
- you are not interested in what is being said.

Both reactions can result in the speaker distorting, by exaggeration, different words to obtain a reaction and feedback from you to break your silence.

Because of these undesirable consequences caused by total silence, it is better to listen *inter-actively*. This involves a form of listening which encourages the speaker to communicate with you, but neither diverts the flow of that communication nor causes the speaker to distort what he is saying. This is achieved by the following actions on your part:

- *eye contact* with the speaker;
- *body gestures* that indicate interest and concentration on what is being said;
- *encouraging speaker phrases*; e.g. 'That's interesting', 'Tell me more about that';
- *paraphrasing*: re-stating for confirmation or amendment the sense of what the speaker has said, e.g. 'so if I understand this

correctly is this what you are saying . . .', or 'in other words . . .';

- *note taking* occasionally, rather than continuously take a note, e.g. 'That is a very important limitation you have just mentioned. Let me make a note of that straight away'.

Conclusion

Because our listening habits develop more by chance than through any training, most of us are inefficient listeners. Successful negotiations hinge upon accurate mastery by you of *all* facts. When listening:

- attend physically;
- attend psychologically to what is being said; how it is being said and what is not being said.

Ask the right questions to ensure that you hear the *full* story before you start evaluating or drawing any conclusions.

Listening is an active occupation which, like friendship, is in constant need of repair. It deserves your concentration, your intuition, your open-mindedness and curiosity, focusing and listening with all your being.

Some common obstacles to listening

1 Making Assumptions, e.g. that the subject is uninteresting and unimportant, that you know what is coming.
2 Mentally criticizing the speaker's delivery.
3 Getting over-stimulated when questioning or opposing an idea.
4 Listening only for facts, wanting to skip details.
5 Outlining everything.
6 Pretending to be attentive.
7 Permitting the speaker to be inaudible or incomplete.
8 Avoiding technical messages.
9 Over-reacting to certain words or phrases.
10 Withdrawing attention, daydreaming.

Effective listening checklist

1	WANT TO LISTEN	Listening is hard work and needs to be done consciously and with the right attitude.
2	LOOK LIKE A GOOD LISTENER	Look alert, have eye contact with speaker, lean forward, look interested.
3	LISTEN TO UNDER-STAND	Keep an open mind, do not make judgements until you have understood what you have heard.
4	LISTEN ACTIVELY	Use eye contact, words, encouraging questions.
5	CONCENTRATE	Focus your attention on what is said, how it is said, words used, gestures and meanings behind them.
6	LOOK AT SPEAKER	Eye contact, look at his face, his eyes, his hands, how he is sitting.
7	DISCIPLINE YOUR EMOTIONS	Listen to what is being said, avoid being biased towards or against speaker because of sex, appearance, accent, presentation, words used.
8	AVOID PHYSICAL DISTRACTIONS	Choose, if possible, meeting place where ringing telephones, passing traffic, conversations that can be overheard, distract attention.
9	DO NOT ANTAGONIZE	Try to avoid actions which will cause speaker to conceal his ideas, emotions or attitudes such as arguing, threatening questions, note taking in an officious manner, criticizing, appearing not to listen.
10	USE SPEAKING /LISTENER DIFFERENCE	Because you can listen faster than speaker can talk, concentrate your attention, think back over what he has said, make notes, identify theme behind words.

10

Accurate interpretation of body language

We do not listen in a kind of mental vacuum. As we listen we look at the speaker, and the body movements that accompany the words spoken convey messages to us. Accurate interpretation of this non-verbal behaviour is an important skill to develop to help your negotiations. Indeed it has been established from observation of negotiation sequences that it is only by considering words spoken *and* the complementary body movements that the progress of the negotiation can be assessed. Furthermore, since most people are unaware of the tell-tale messages that their non-verbal behaviour communicates to the listener they are unlikely to control it.

Research has shown that we tend to give greater weight to the messages that are conveyed by non-verbal behaviour than to what is spoken. The following figures indicate the relative importance we give to the parts of a speaker's message:

* Words 10%
* Tone 35%
* Non-verbal behaviour 55%

Some researchers put the influence of body language on what is heard when we listen as high as 70 per cent.

Nevertheless, we need to beware of two dangers. First of jumping to hasty conclusions or of simplifying the array of human behaviour. Secondly of reading messages from *single* unrelated gestures. I remember an occasion when I was sitting in on a management workshop session conducted by someone who was rather pompously showing off his claimed expertise in reading body language. Turning to me he said, 'John I notice that you have your arms folded and your legs tightly crossed so you are critically weighing up what I have been saying. Am I right?' 'No', I replied, 'As a matter of fact my bladder is full to bursting and I am wondering how soon you are going to finish this session so that I can get out to the lavatory.'

Non-verbal aspects of behaviour form about nine-tenths of meaningful social behaviour but they are also extremely complex. So although we rely very heavily on non-verbal behaviour in our normal contact with others, to a large extent we are not aware of doing so. Rather like driving a car, it all seems to happen without our needing to think about it and only becomes the focus of our attention when something intervenes.

There are other factors which make the understanding of body language difficult such as behaviour which is confusing, contradictory or carries more than one message. Equally much non-verbal behaviour is ignored because it is thought to be meaningless or unintentional.

Finally, non-verbal behaviour may be disregarded because it is not socially acceptable to draw attention to it or to 'use' it in some way.

Because of its importance in helping us to understand those with whom we negotiate by own conscious attention to body language we can make available to ourselves a wealth of knowledge about people. In negotiations the words people use are accompanied by complementary body movements. You are looking for what are called 'clusters' of body gestures, for example the arms, the feet, the head, the inclination of the body.

Body language often belies the spoken words. Words usually follow our planned thoughts. Body language expresses our unconscious emotions and feelings. Because of this in negotiation, is what he is saying to you mirrored by what he is really thinking? What he is really thinking is conveyed by his non-verbal body language. Words can be chosen and expressed with the greatest care and deliberation. Facial expressions, the eyes and deportment are far more difficult to discipline.

To understand body language adopt the following six-step approach:

1 Keep an open mind.
2 Observe your own bodily postures and the gestures and the changes of mind, moods or feelings.
3 Ask yourself what are my body language behaviours?
   e.g. * Am I leaning back or forward?
         * Are the palms of my hands open or are my fists clenched?
         * Are my legs apart or crossed?
         * What am I feeling?

Speaker	Body Language Displayed	Feelings Behind Them	Right? Wrong?

4 Transfer this analysis to others' behaviour so that you develop a reliable dictionary of body language messages.

5 Put the messages you receive from body language together with the spoken words and draw conclusions.

6 In your negotiations learn to control your own body language so that you show to others only those signals you want to send.

To develop your knowledge and skill to recognize non-verbal communication, chart with colleagues what they say and how they behave bodily, then check with them how accurately you interpreted their body language.

Interpreting body language

Let us now examine the range of signals or body movements that most people display. These non-verbal signals, often called 'leaks', give the sharp observer information we may often wish to hide because we believe that to consciously expose our innermost feelings makes us vulnerable to exploitation or attack. The more unintentional a signal appears, the more it can be taken to reflect the 'real' person. People 'leak' their real feelings through their *legs*, *feet*, *hands* and *fingers* and particularly *eyes*.

Your interpretation will be more reliable if it is based on clusters of behaviour rather than isolated movements, e.g.

— eyes, face, head;

— body movements and posture;

— gestures (e.g. hand to face, chin, back of neck).

Concern for time

HUMAN FEELING	BODY LANGUAGE
Concern for time	1. Openly looks at watch – unconcerned about impact of action on others.

HUMAN FEELING	BODY LANGUAGE

Concern for time

2. Pretended yawn – attempt to disguise a look at watch.

Concern for time passing

3. Secretive glance at neighbour's watch – assumes that it will not be noticed – shy, sneaky attitude. Is this likely to characterize his approach to whole relationship?

HUMAN FEELING	BODY LANGUAGE
Concern for time passing	4. Fiddling with watch or moving hand over watch face – reveals preoccupation with time or another appointment but reluctance to offend by looking blatantly at watch.

Responding to the telephone
When you have meetings with business colleagues, the telephone can ring and interrupt your conversation. If your meeting concerns an important negotiation, then the telephone caller who has brought it to a momentary halt could influence how it continues afterwards. So it is worthwhile observing the behaviour by the person you are meeting, as he responds to the person who has telephoned.

Is the caller a superior, an equal or the individual's spouse or partner?

TYPE OF TELEPHONE CALL	BODY LANGUAGE
1. A call from a superior in the company	The telephone call is probably taken sitting down but as the conversation proceeds, the hand tightens, the individual stands up as if to attention and may well button up his coat. It is almost as if he is on parade before the eyes of a superior officer. Listen to the

TYPE OF TELEPHONE CALL	BODY LANGUAGE

1. A call from a superior in company

tone of voice and the upright stance of body and head. What is said may well affect what is said afterwards to you.

2. A call from a colleague of equal status

The body position, whether seated or standing, is relaxed. The legs are crossed, the coat is open or is unbuttoned, the face is relaxed or smiling.

TYPE OF TELEPHONE CALL   BODY LANGUAGE

3. A private intimate caller

A call from a spouse, partner or head-hunter often causes the body position to take a stance designed to achieve maximum privacy. If seated turns away from you, hands cover the mouthpiece of the telephone, the head is down and the voice is deliberately low to avoid being overheard. He is trying to shut you out. What is being communicated may well bring your meeting to an end. Or what has been said on the telephone will not have helped it to proceed positively.

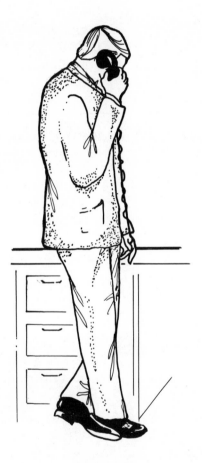

Eye contact

'The face is the mirror of the soul' and the eyes are the most compelling feature of it. Through them we can convey a variety of feelings: from boredom to greed, lust to listlessness, interest to displeasure. Just consider how much we depend on our eyes to add to our understanding of what someone is saying when speaking. Not only do we listen to what is said but we look at the eyes of the person talking to us. The extent to which the eyes are important to convey non-verbal messages can be experienced by closing your eyes for a conversation with another person. Try it out for as long as five minutes and then list the non-verbal signs and cues you have missed. The list will be surprisingly long and could include many of the following:

Anger	Fright	Pleasure
Annoyance	Frustration	Prejudice
Amusement	Gladness	Prudishness
Amazement	Hope	Pride
Antagonism	Hostility	Puzzlement
Approval	Humility	Regret
Boredom	Hurt	Resentment
Caution	Importance	Respect
Confidence	Indifference	Rudeness
Curiosity	Inferiority	Sarcasm
Despair	Joy	Shame
Disapproval	Loathing	Sorrow
Dislike	Modesty	Superiority
Friendliness	Nervousness	Worry

HUMAN FEELING	BODY LANGUAGE
When listening	People tend to look more at the person speaking whilst listening than when talking.
When pleased and when displeased	The pupils enlarge. The pupils contract.
Being evasive	An individual looks at the person he is speaking to for only a quarter to one-third of the time.
When more interested in the person than what is being said	The more interested, an individual will look more at the person speaking.*

* In normal conversations, people look at one another for about half to two-thirds of the time. Contrary to popular belief, it is abnormal to look at a person who is speaking the whole time.

HUMAN FEELING	BODY LANGUAGE
Acceptance of what is being read	Positively interested look in eyes or of pleasure; head is up, mouth may be slightly open and sometimes expressions such as 'yes' 'yes' are made.

HUMAN FEELING	BODY LANGUAGE
To: Reject what is being read	The mouth will be closed or teeth clamped together, the head down and the eyes less open – squinting or looking angry.

Hand movements

HUMAN FEELING	BODY LANGUAGE

Holding back a comment

One or both hands over the mouth accompanied by a frown or grimace.

Interest – Disinterest

Interest

Head up, voice up, palm of hands open as arms in upward direction.

Disinterest

Head down, voice down, arms and palms down.

HUMAN FEELING	BODY LANGUAGE

I want to:
Convey feelings of honesty
and sincerity

Moving close to the other person.

Touching the other person on the arm or back.

Hands held against chest or one held against heart but with fingers
or palm upward.

HUMAN FEELING	BODY LANGUAGE

I am:
Thinking about your
proposition

Stroking chin; when it stops a decision is likely to be made or action commences.

For those who smoke and are doing so, the cigarette is put out and he/she leans forward; the signs of a decision about to be made.

A deep sigh of relief or a deep breath are signs of someone who has decided on a course of action.

HUMAN FEELING	BODY LANGUAGE

I am:
Making a critical comparison of your proposition

Hand on chin with one or more fingers pointing up the side of the face; if accompanied by leaning back in the chair this signifies doubt or reservation.

Bored or dejected by you/or your proposition

Both hands clasping face or one hand.

Anxiety – uptight

Hands wringing – clenched fist.

HUMAN FEELING	BODY LANGUAGE
Attempts at self-control	Coat buttoned up; hands held together in front, in immobile stance; sometimes trying to avoid eye contact or staring in to space.

Sitting with hands clenched on knees; in a chair with arm supports tightly gripping both arm rests; with ankles crossed.

Defensive	Hands tightly folded across chest, leaning backwards in chair distancing space from speaker(s) with ankles crossed.

HUMAN FEELING	BODY LANGUAGE

Resentful

Leaning forward with arms tightly folded and facial expression to match.

Defensive

Head down on chest.

Awakening Interest

Head up and an open look on face, head inclining indicating to you 'I am interested'.

HUMAN FEELING	BODY LANGUAGE
I am: Evaluating your proposition	Head up, arms lightly folded, hands open or not clenched could indicate evaluation.

Seated body language behaviour

HUMAN FEELING	BODY LANGUAGE
I am: Enthusiastic open-minded about your proposals	Sitting forward, hands upturned, feet flat on ground, knees apart. When this is coupled with leaning forward – a favourable signal.

I am: Not convinced although attentive	Seated, feet out, ankles crossed or one leg crossed over other.

HUMAN FEELING	BODY LANGUAGE

Change in mental attitude

A pronounced change in physical body movement or the new arrangement of seating, arms and legs.

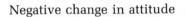

Negative change in attitude

Sudden leaning back in chair, touching the nose, folding arms – a negative shift in attitude.

Fingers to corner of eye; head downward.

Fingers to lobe of one ear.

HUMAN FEELING	BODY LANGUAGE

Negative evaluation of your proposals

Rubbing or touching nose with knuckles of index finger.

Disbelief – you exaggerate your claims

Running finger horizontally under nose.

Frustration – exasperation

Rubbing back of neck with palm of hand or running fingers through hair; hissed intake of breath through clenched teeth.

HUMAN FEELING	BODY LANGUAGE

Confident – superiority

Head well back; hands clasped behind head and body leaning back in chair; legs extended or on desk or resting on another chair; ankles crossed – general air of disinterest.

Bored – dejected

Hand supporting head; eyes half-closed; or doodling on pad with pencil.

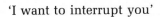

'I want to interrupt you'

Fleeting gestures of fingers raised to mouth indication of 'I want to say something'.

HUMAN FEELING	BODY LANGUAGE

Confidence

The listener/speaker forms a pyramid with the fingers of both hands.

Leaning back in chair with feet extended and ankles crossed.

Confident and interested frame of mind

Leaning back, feet apart, hands locked loosely together across the stomach.

Leaning forward in the chair, smiling and with hands clasped.

HUMAN FEELING	BODY LANGUAGE

Standing

Confident – Disinterested   Standing, hands behind back, shoulders set – 'seen it all before' attitude.

Ownership   Leaning against an object; wall, door.

Defensiveness   Buttons up coat, clenched hands, leg on ankle crossed, or an arm crossing chest; dark sunglasses.

Confident approach to you   Unbuttons coat, takes off glasses, puts down file unclenches hand, stance open and friendly, secure.

HUMAN FEELING	BODY LANGUAGE

ASSERTIVE ATTITUDE

Hand shaking – either first to extend hand to you or by refusing your offer of handshake putting you at a psychological disadvantage.

First through door when in a group crossing into a room; subordinates fall back for dominant member – often a clue to who holds power in a negotiating group.

HUMAN FEELING   BODY LANGUAGE

Using spectacles

Aggressive resistance to speaker or his proposals or both

Gaining time, usually to answer critically by sucking end of one frame and then folding them and placing in front of the speaker slowly and deliberately.

Slowly and ritually polishing the lens of the glasses – waiting for an opportunity or playing for time to challenge the speaker or stalling before coming to a decision.

Postures

Wanting reassurance

A man touching his tie, or signet ring or fiddling with cuff links; or a woman twiddling with a bracelet or necklace.

207

HUMAN FEELING	BODY LANGUAGE

Signs of dominance, of superiority or of indifference, sometimes of close friendship

Sitting astride a chair with hands resting on the chair back.

Sitting in a chair with one leg across the arm or sitting back with both feet on the desk/table in front, ignoring the usual courtesies afforded to a stranger.

Disapproving of what has been said, but reluctant to say so

Sitting looking down rather than at speaker, legs crossed picking real or imaginary fluff from suit or skirt.

HUMAN FEELING	BODY LANGUAGE

Reluctant to make a decision because cannot see how problem is to be solved

Head down and with hands and fingers across the eyes.

Eyes closed, head down with fingers pinching the bridge of nose – expect a request for further information.

Aggressive, defensive attitude

Head down on chest, arms tightly folded, sitting and leaning back with fists clenched and knees together, legs extended and ankles tightly crossed.

Still defensive – but interested

Same posture, but now head is up, legs are drawn up, knees apart, ankles crossed.

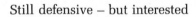

HUMAN FEELING	BODY LANGUAGE	
Interest developing	Head on one side, fist(s) un-clenched head on chin sitting more upright, legs apart and ankles crossed.	
Critical evaluation	Similar posture but with finger of the hand pointing upwards along cheekbone, head more inclined, legs apart, ankles crossed.	
Openness, enthusiasm, readi-ness to do business	Leaning forward in chair, or sit-ting on edge with knees apart and rubbing palms on thigh.	
	Or standing legs astride, hands on hips, coat unbuttoned and swept back, positive attitude saying 'let's get going'.	

HUMAN FEELING	BODY LANGUAGE	

Readiness to get going

Rubbing hands together, snapping fingers, hitting fist into palm of hand.

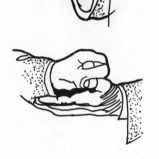

Sitting forward in chair, body inclined forward, head up, knees apart, feet flat on ground, forearm across one knee.

Superior, comparing, authoritative

Looking over rather than through a normal pair of glasses not half-moon ones.

Fingers upturned, leaning forward on palms of hands for support.

211

HUMAN FEELING	BODY LANGUAGE

Aggressive, dominant smug attitude

Hands in coat pocket(s) with thumbs outside and pointing down, coat buttoned up.

Thumbs in waistcoat pockets, or hands holding jacket lapels.

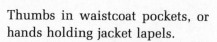

Signals of staged movement towards a decision after evaluation

Sitting upright with one hand on chin and hand across the chest.

To head inclining but still evaluating pros and cons of making a decision.

HUMAN FEELING	BODY LANGUAGE

Signs of staged movement towards a decision

Sitting forward, one hand still on chin the other comes down with flat of hand on desk. Mentally it is saying 'I know what has to be done'.

The following chart reproduced from *A Guide to Asking Questions* (BACIE 1980) provides a useful way of classifying the main types of non-verbal behaviour when you are negotiating.

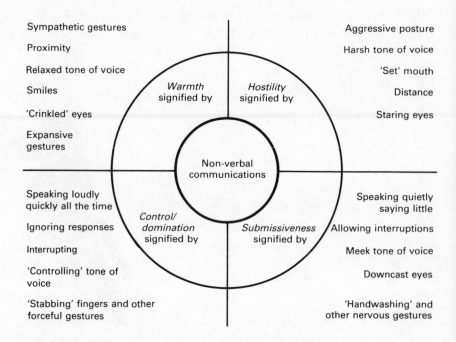

Conclusion

In this chapter we have put into place one of the last and most important pieces in the jigsaw puzzle that goes to make up the complex ways in which human beings express their thoughts, feelings and emotions. We use our bodies consciously and often unintentionally in communicating by modifying, elaborating and sometimes contradicting the words we use. Correct interpretation of body language is a crucial skill because it enables you to see what others are thinking and so smooth the pathway to successful negotiations.

11

Effective presentation

Historically, salesmen have been trained to deal with sales situations involving, in the majority of cases, selling to one buyer. In these one-to-one sales/negotiating meetings, there is usually a degree of informality and above all feedback from the buyer, in the form of questions and answers to questions. Now the salesman must be equipped to deal skilfully and successfully with group selling and negotiating meetings on an increasing scale. If you are not equipped and prepared for such challenges then you will consciously, or unconsciously, avoid group meetings even when opportunities arise. There are two main hurdles or fears you will have to overcome in preparing yourself to handle such multiple-sales challenges. First, the risk of being exposed to cross-questioning if you actively seek feedback from qualified technical people; and second, the lack of any evidence of success when making set presentations or speeches.

These two areas must be controlled or eliminated if you want to seize the opportunities these group-selling meetings offer you to sell effectively and successfully to a large number of people at one time. To help you to do this let us consider the main questions involved.

Who becomes involved in buying and selling decisions?

In both buying and selling situations, many people are involved in decisions:

Buying companies	*Selling companies*
Directors	Sales directors
Purchasing officers/buyers	Salesmen
Marketing staff	Sales managers
Technical staff	Marketing/product managers
Production staff	Technical advisers
Quality control staff	Installers/contractors
Operations/distribution staff	Distribution specialists
Computer staff	Financial analysts
Accountants	Computer staff
	Operations/distribution staff

Who should make or take part in group meetings/presentations?

Great care must be taken to choose the 'best' team to attend such group meetings or to make group presentations so that the subsequent buyer relationships run smoothly. The following factors should be borne in mind:

1 What type of meeting is it?

2 What will be the status and decision-making powers of those present from the buying group?

3 What type of decisions will the meeting reach?

4 What technical expertise will the meeting possess in the buying group? What therefore will it require from your side?

5 Can one man handle the meeting or should a group attend?

6 If a buying decision is likely to be made at meeting, who will run or service the resulting contract?

7 If a group is to present to the buying group, who should lead the group?

Remember: (a) that the on-going relationships with the customer will require the build-up and establishment of credibility of whoever will be chosen for this role; (b) the internal motivation of the salesman/ sales team must be considered.

What planning is necessary? The planning of such group meetings and presentations should cover two stages: first, the planning and preparation stage; second, the conduct and execution stage.

Planning and preparation There are two sets of factors to be reviewed at the planning and preparation stage: the objective/business elements and the subjective or human elements. The latter are the more difficult but if overlooked cannot only ruin one meeting but reduce the chances of a second one ever taking place.

1 Objective factors
   (a) What results do you want the meeting to achieve?
   (b) What will you present and discuss to reach this objective?
   (c) How will you present them?
   (d) In what order will you present them?
   (e) What key questions will you ask?
   (f) In what order/at what stage should they be asked?
   (g) What visual/display material should be prepared?
   (h) How will it be used?
2 Subjective factors
   (a) Who will take part in the meeting?
   (b) Who could be persuaded/influenced to take part?
   (c) Who could be persuaded/influenced to stay away?
   (d) What do these people think?
   (e) What do they *think* they know?
   (f) What do they *really* know?
   (g) What do they expect?
   (h) Who is likely to be an ally?

    (i)   Who is likely to be an opponent?

    (j)   Who is likely to be neutral or indifferent?

    (k)   How can these people be influenced or guided?

Dangers in presenting to groups Marketing specialists, particularly of industrial products and processes, always think they know their customers! They treat them as though they were completely rational beings and not susceptible to selling techniques beyond the bald presentation of product and technical features. Evidence to disprove this assumption can be found in Theodore Levitt's article entitled 'Industrial Purchasing Behaviour', *Harvard Business Review*, 1965. Salesmen and all others involved in group meetings and presentations must perceive the roles individuals play in such collective situations, seeking clues in their speech, behaviour to others and external status symbols.

Salesmen can be	*Buyers can be*
1 Information givers or just talkers.	1 Hostile, recalcitrant
2 Information getters, Listeners.	2 Self-important: 'Mr Big'.
3 Negative, nervous, afraid.	3 Joker, glad-hander, nervous, apologetic.
4 Meek, apologetic.	4 Silent.
5 Brash, 'Mr Big', too positive, over-powering.	5 Sceptical, suspicious.
6 Mature, poised, friendly.	6 Slow, methodical.
7 Joker, glad-hander, over-friendly.	7 Mature, poised, thoughtful.
8 Impulsive.	8 Impulsive.
9 Neutral, friendly.	9 Mr Average.
10 Goodwill order-taker.	10 Over-cautious.

These factors underline the importance of analysing the *attitudes*, the *knowledge, role expectations, status, position, personalities*, of all those whom the selling team will meet at a buying group meeting.

N.B. Bear in mind that even people you may know well on an individual basis are likely to adjust the way they behave as individuals to the role they play or are expected to play at a meeting. Beware, in particular, of the subordinate in a buying group who promises to pursue a certain policy or course of action at a meeting at which his manager or managing director suddenly decides to be present. The power to hire and fire can sometimes result in promises being forgotten and your erstwhile ally turning opponent.

What support is required? Most group meetings require support and the form this should take must be planned, for example:

1 Agenda.

2 Folders, with background about people, products, etc.

3 Samples.

4 Briefing of staff involved in providing support.

5 Implications of promises made at group meetings. Ensure that the staff upon whom such promises depend can and will be capable of fulfilling them.

Executing the group presentation

Whatever type of group presentation is to be made or meeting conducted with a buyer group, it requires structure throughout to reflect three factors:

1 Recognition by you that your audience as a whole and each individual member of it wants to feel important, be respected and for you to recognize this in your behaviour and conduct.

2 Ability through your words, your actions, your handling of questions and the solutions you propose to show understanding of the customer situation.

3 Creation of trust and confidence in you, in your company and in your solutions.

These factors pose challenging problems when presenting a proposition more formally to a group or to a larger audience. Frequently, at the conclusion of a successful round of negotiation meetings, the supplying company is asked to present the proposition agreed to the board of directors of the buying company or to the sales force. In such situations your presentation must be well planned, if it is to be effective; structured around the needs of your audience, if it is to be well received; and offer solutions in *their* terms, if the desired action is to be achieved.

Room	*Audience requirements*	*Meeting agenda*
Size	Notepaper/pencils	Finalise by
Layout	Product information	Circulated
Chairs	Refreshments	
Tables	Samples	*Meeting budget*
Lighting		£ amount
Electrical sockets	*Audience*	Approved
Window blinds	Notified – briefed	

Programme

1 Meeting's objective(s) ....

2 Information to be presented...

3 Methods ....

4 Visual aids...

5 Key discussion points...

6 Handouts – samples..

7 Possible objections ....

8 Close planned ....

9 Timing...

Figure 11.1 **Meeting planning and format**

The main problems in successful communication

The first problem is to recognize that, despite what many people believe, communicating successfully is not easy.

The second problem is to accept that the *onus* is on the *communicator* to achieve *successful communication*, and not on the receiver.

A number of specific difficulties arise that may prevent the achievement of each objective:

Objectives	*Difficulties*
HEAR (or see)	1 People cannot concentrate for long periods on the spoken or written word.
	2 People pay less attention to what appears to them unimportant.
UNDERSTAND	1 People make assumptions based upon their past experience.
	2 Often people do not understand the speaker's jargon.
	3 People misunderstand more easily when they hear but do not see.
	4 People often draw conclusions before we have finished talking.
AGREE	1 People are often suspicious of others with an interest in selling something.
	2 People do not like being proved wrong.
ACT	1 People do not easily change their habits.
	2 People fear the results of taking wrong action.
	3 Many people dislike taking decisions.
FEEDBACK	1 Some people deliberately hide their reactions and what they really think.
	2 Appearances can be deceptive – a nod may not always indicate agreement and understanding. It can mask ignorance or indecision.

These difficulties are common to both the communicator and the listener. Neither we who communicate nor our listeners:

– like to be proved wrong;

– pay attention to what seems unimportant;

- change our habits easily;
- understand other people's jargon.

If we examine the human communications process we can better understand how it works, how failures in communication arise and what we can do to be more effective and successful as communicators.

The way we communicate is illustrated in Figure 11.2. Messages are received through our senses of which we have five: *sound*, *sight*, *feel*, *smell* and *taste*. We then form impressions and assimilate or associate them with other information and ideas stored in the brain. Before we respond to what has been communicated, the brain reacts in a specific sequence to this new information.

It scans existing memories of past experiences and finds the frame of reference or memory which relates most closely to the new information received. The new information is sent to join the existing memory bank or frame of reference chosen.

If it is associated with what that memory perceived, the new information is analysed and subsequently fitted into the existing memory pattern. As a result of this filing system of the brain, the existing memory may:

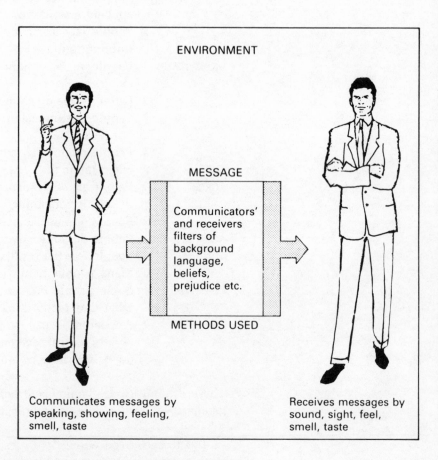

Figure 11.2 **How the human communication system operates**

1 remain the same but stronger;

2 change for the better;

3 change for the worse.

There are constant examples of the results of this memory bank at work. The politician, whose party is seeking office after five years in opposition, paints word pictures of carefully chosen unpleasant factors of life which his listeners will not only recognize but on which (he hopes) they will agree with him. The chief executive talking to his assembled management identifies with them as he describes some of the things he got up to as a young manager.

Apart from reinforcing what we believe, other factors influence the quality of our communications. There are five main elements that, as we have seen from Figure 11.2, can lead to failures in communication:

1 the value of standards of communicator and listener;

2 the message being transmitted;

3 the filters through which the message passes;

4 the methods of communication used;

5 the environment in which communication takes place.

The value standards of communicator and listener

Our backgrounds, education, beliefs, ethical standards and prejudices all affect the way we communicate with one another. Thus two people in an audience looking at the same object or picture or listening to the same story may perceive and react to it in quite different ways. Because of this, it is vital for a speaker to try to perceive the things he wants to say or to show through the eyes and mind of the people who will comprise his audience. The speaker's knowledge of the ideas and experiences of his audience will enable him to communicate successfully.

The message being transmitted

The same words mean different things to different people. When I was young the word 'gay' meant cheerful, full of mirth, exuberantly merry. Today, sadly, it is rarely used in that context but rather as a label for homosexuals.

Many speakers who have addressed American audiences have discovered that there are enormous differences in the meanings given to words by the Americans and the British. For example, to Americans there is no such word as *fortnight*; they say *two weeks*; we speak about *holidays*; Americans talk about a *vacation*.

Add to these complexities the jargon that frequently creeps into the language of business and the result is confusion. As a general rule in speaking, avoid the use of specialized words – or jargon – because there is a high probability that they will be misunderstood by your listeners.

The filters through which the message passes

Each person tends to think more often about himself than about the person or group he is communicating with or speaking to, and his words, how he expresses them and the meaning he imparts to them reflect this. Yet his own words, prejudices, beliefs and jargon can set up filters which confuse the message sent and received. One simple example of this is the word 'marketing', used by an ever-growing number of people to mean – what? To some people it is a word that defines what business is all about, e.g. *the identification and satisfaction of customers' needs at a profit*. Yet I know of at least one computer manufacturer with a worldwide reputation where the first-line managers responsible for the day-to-day management of teams of salesmen are called *marketing managers*. Very many businessmen invited to address groups of these marketing managers have prepared their presentations on the reasonable assumption that their audience would be familiar with such terms as marketing planning, strengths and weaknesses, opportunities and threats analyses, product mapping and so on, only to find that such areas of business are a closed book to them!

The methods of communication

No two individuals hear, see and feel with equal efficiency. You can tell some people something and they understand immediately. Others have to be told, shown and then asked to play back their understanding of what they have heard and seen before a message gets through. For this reason, when communicating ideas, a speaker making a presentation should always involve at least two of the senses through which listeners receive a message. A speaker can not only express ideas verbally; some at least of them – including the important ones he wants his audience to remember – become more firmly fixed in the minds of those in the audience if written down as a handout or shown as a chart, overhead transparency or slide.

The environment in which communication takes place

The environment can have a profound effect upon the outcome of a presentation. If you are addressing members of a company at which different levels of management are present, what you say is probably going to be digested at least *twice* by the junior managers. First, they will hear what you have said; then they will try to guess how it will be received by their senior management.

When a very large audience has congregated to hear you speak, it is likely to become almost one person. Indeed some speakers frame their presentation from the view of one person and the technique can be an effective one so long as your research into what your audience comprises and expects is thorough and accurate.

How can we communicate more effectively?

The communicator's role is that of a teacher educating his listener to his point of view. This process of helping people to learn can be made much easier by understanding and using the laws of learning: *effect, forward association, belonging* and *repetition*.

Effect A listener will more readily and willingly learn if your message shows how to satisfy an established need. The 'fireside chats' of President Roosevelt are an example of how to do this. When campaigning for election Roosevelt used to speak with tremendous effect on the radio to his unseen listeners. He never started by saying such things as 'I am standing on a programme of this, this and this, so vote for me'. No; he would begin by identifying the basic needs of average Americans and what they wanted. 'You good people of America, you need jobs to provide money to feed and keep your family clothed and to uphold your self-respect, you want . . . .' I have been told by older generation Americans who listened to these fireside chats that listeners not only started nodding as Roosevelt spelt out their needs, but then started saying 'Yes, yes, that's just what I want'.

Forward association People tend to remember things in the order in which they first learned them, especially if they are arranged in a logical sequence, for example:

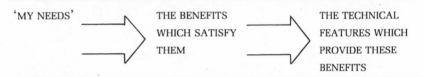

'MY NEEDS' → THE BENEFITS WHICH SATISFY THEM → THE TECHNICAL FEATURES WHICH PROVIDE THESE BENEFITS

The reason why so many speakers fail to tune into their listeners from the start is the fact that, unlike President Roosevelt, they talk about their needs, not the listeners', or they speak about technical features which are quite uninteresting from the listeners' point of view.

Belonging People learn more speedily and easily what relates to their own experiences, e.g. 'an air conditioner is like a refrigerator element with a fan to circulate the cooled air', or 'the plans I am about to describe are like those you make for your annual holidays'.

Repetition Contrary to what is often thought, constant repetition of a fact, a statement or a warning does not result in people learning, as pronouncements about dangerous driving, excessive drinking of alcohol, smoking etc. testify. Repetition is only useful as a means of getting people to learn if it is used in conjunction with one or more of the three laws already described. A speaker using repetition plus another law might say: 'So I repeat what I said at the beginning of this talk, if you are all really serious in your wish to cut down road accidents here, then this is what we have to do . . .'

Research shows how people forget what they learn:

— 38 per cent in 2 days

- 65 per cent in 8 days
- 75 per cent in 30 days.

But they tend to remember things which are important or of special interest to them. We can help them remember more by:

1 ensuring that our first and last impressions upon them are both favourable and positive;

2 starting a meeting, if possible, by summarizing progress made at earlier meetings;

3 giving them a general idea of a proposition before moving on to points of detail;

4 involving them from the start by:
   - talking about 'your problems' and 'your requirements' rather than 'what I want';
   - obtaining feedback, so that we know how well we are communicating, and thus can judge whether it is necessary to rephrase our remarks or repeat what has been said earlier;
   - using more than one sense (e.g. speech and visual aids);
   - planning to communicate.

Points to remember

1 Unless someone *hears* what you say, there is no communication.

2 You do not communicate just words. The whole person that you are comes with them.

3 Talk to people in terms of their own experience and they will listen to you.

4 When you have difficulties in getting through to people, it is a sign that your own thinking is confused, not theirs.

5 When you fail to communicate, it is not your sentences that need straightening out; it is the thoughts behind them.

6 Know what your listeners expect to hear and see before you start talking.

7 Your communication is always more powerful if it appeals to the *values* and the *aspirations* of your listeners.

8 If what you plan to say goes against the beliefs, the aspirations, the motivations of your audience, what you say is likely to be resisted or not received at all.

9 It is not what is written on the pages of your presentation that matters – it is what percentage comes off those pages and enters the listener's mind and stays there.

The listener's point of view

One of the results of the growth in communications, particularly those involving the visual senses, is that people have become accustomed to certain standards of performance from those who address them. They may not agree with what is being said, they may not even be interested, but they cannot fail to notice the style displayed by the speaker. They remember the image long after they have forgotten the content.

The effect is that it is impossible to say nowadays that any form of presentation will do. Right or wrong, an audience, whatever its composition, will judge a man's ability and that of his company by the kind of job he does on his feet. This is not to say that the substance of the speaker's proposals is unimportant, rather that the impact is disproportionately enhanced or diminished by the quality of his presentation. You are in a sense only as good as the ideas for which you gain acceptance. There are four categories of speakers:

1 Those who do not bother about what they are going to say or how they are going to say it.
2 Those who 'put on a show', but convey very little.
3 Those whose material is good, but badly presented.
4 Those who have something worthwhile to say and present it well.

The judge of a presentation is the audience. No two audiences are the same. The individuals within an audience differ in their attitude, but whatever their personalities and job responsibilities may be, they all react to presentations. There are certain mental demands which have to be met before they will give their willing acceptance. In addition, they are affected by what they see, what they hear and how they feel. All these can be summarized as the listener's viewpoint, whose basic elements form a sequence from which a speaker can prepare a structure for his presentation.

Thinking sequence The thinking sequence that the listener's mind follows consists of seven points. A presentation must take note of them all.

1 *I am important and want to be respected.* Each member of the audience wants the respect of the speaker. Without it the speaker is lost.
2 *Consider my needs.* Any proposal is judged by the listener in terms of his own priorities and sense of values. These are determined by what he wants to achieve:

   (a) in his work;

   (b) as a person.

The content of a presentation will have little impact if the listener cannot see that its theme is about improving his lot. In a business context his needs will be concerned with such things as improved profitability, higher sales, lower costs, better industrial relations, etc. He wants to know early in a presentation that the theme is of this type. If so, he will give the speaker his willing attention and interest. Likewise, his final decision will rest on his answer to one question: 'Will my needs be met by these people and their proposals?'

3 *Will your ideas help me?* If his attention and interest have been gained he is keen to know how the speaker's proposals will help him achieve the end results he and his company are looking for.

4 *What are the facts?* This step in his thinking process arises from the previous one. He wants to know how the speaker proposes to ensure that the promised results are forthcoming. Depending on the situation, he may also want evidence that the promised results have been achieved in other cases of a similar nature. He also wants to know his involvement – action to be taken, time commitment, etc.

5 *What are the snags?* It is an integral part of the listener's decision-making process that he should consider possible disadvantages arising from the speaker's proposals. If any come to mind, which he cannot see being overcome, he will frequently voice them in the form of objections. In a group situation there is a bigger chance that objections to the speaker's proposals remain unvoiced.

6 *What shall I do?* Provided all previous points have been covered he is now faced with a decision: 'Do I accept or reject these proposals?' In making the choice he will concentrate on his needs, job or personal, and decide accordingly. If he has several sets of proposals to consider, he will prefer the ones which, in his eyes, best meet his needs.

7 *I approve.* If Points 1 to 6 have been satisfactorily handled from his point of view, he will make a decision in the speaker's favour.

The importance of the listener's point of view

The seven points mentioned above represent the path that the human mind takes before it will give willing approval to proposals. The problem facing speakers, however, is that by nature they have difficulty in presenting their proposals in that kind of sequence and with that kind of emphasis. In many situations where proposals are being presented the speaker is concentrating on his company and his ideas while the audience is more interested in what they want to achieve. Consequently, the audience loses interest, their attention wanders, and they reject both the proposals and the speaker.

By structuring the presentation around the listener's point of view the speaker can go a long way to gaining the audience's attention and interest, persuading them of the value to them of his proposals, meeting their objections, and drawing them to a conclusion in his favour.

Other considerations

When presented with proposals the human mind not only thinks along certain lines, it is affected by what it sees and hears. To a lesser extent it is affected by sensations of touch, taste and smell. In formal presentations *sight* and *hearing* are of the most concern to a listener.

Sight. Listeners react to their first visual impact of you as a speaker. They expect your dress, facial expressions, and gestures to match their mood and the content of your presentation. They look for signs of confidence. Consider the position from the listener's viewpoint. He sees: (a) *How you are dressed.* Are you dressed up in bizarre clothes which will distract your audience from what you say to them? Try and dress neatly and like the group you will be with; (b) *Your mannerisms.* Always be yourself, but avoid distracting mannerisms. Some speakers wave their arms up and down whilst talking, like an Armenian shopkeeper. Gestures should be controlled, few and powerful, and used to emphasize specific points.

Eye contact. Listeners find it much easier to concentrate on and take greater interest in the things they can see. But what they look at must be *understandable, simple* and *professionally* handled. They have greater confidence in a speaker who looks at them. Keep in touch with your audience by looking at them.

Hearing. There are two major differences between a public presentation and a normal conversation. During a conversation you can ask your listener if he understands what you have just said, or alternatively he can ask you to repeat something if he did not hear you or understand. But in a public presentation this is not always possible or there may not be any interruptions. So you have to make sure that you get your message across and understood *the first time.* For these reasons, remember the following points:

1 Speak louder than you would in normal conversation. Adapt the scale of your presentation to the size of the room or hall and to the size of your audience so that everyone *hears* you.

2 Always make sure you pronounce words distinctly and emphasize the last words in each sentence. Inexperienced presenters have a habit of fading at the end of each sentence. If it contains the most important part of your message and no one hears you your presentation has failed.

3 Audiences expect you to speak in language they can understand. Avoid jargon which might confuse people.

4 Do not speak too fast.

5 Vary the pace and vary the pitch of your voice to maintain people's attention and interest.

6 Use *pauses.* Nothing is more effective in a presentation than the pause. It gives the audience time to digest what you have just said or shown, and you time to pick up the substance of your next point. It holds an audience expectant at what you will say next.

7 People dislike having to concentrate on a presentation that is read.

Conclusion Success in all formal presentation is founded upon understanding the listener, looking at what is *said* and *shown* from his point of view and endeavouring to meet it. Good ideas, however sound they may be, will not stand alone. They have to be presented *attractively, clearly* and *persuasively.* This means combining a listener-based structure with presentational skills so that your whole presentation achieves its objective.

Presentation planning

Why prepare? Presentations are selling situations. They are also unnatural social relationships because:

1 The speaker has usually sought out his listeners.

2 He wants them to act in his favour.

3 He may have to replace their ideas with his own.

4 Additionally, the speaker feels out on his own.

These problems create tension, which makes the speaker act out of character by talking too rapidly, avoiding eye contact with his audience, concentrating on his ideas rather than on the audience's needs. Planning helps to reduce tension and ensures an audience-orientated presentation based on 'your requirements' rather than 'our proposals'.

What should you prepare? Since planning is simply the thinking process that precedes purposeful action the first thing is to choose *your objective.* This can be a long-term objective covering a series of presentations or a single objective for one session. Having got your objective, you can then move to a structure for the presentation proper. For simplicity, this structure should be based on the listener's point of view and divided into three main parts, the *beginning,* the *middle,* and the *end.*

Listener's point of view		*Preparation points*
1 I am important and want to be respected. 2 Consider my needs.	Beginning	1 Getting attention. 2 Building rapport. 3 Statement of theme: audience needs.
3 Will your ideas help me? 4 What are the facts? 5 What are the snags?	Middle	1 Points to be made. 2 How they will benefit the audience? 3 Support material: examples; third party references; visual aids. 4 Possible audience objections: answers.

Listener's point of view		Preparation points

6 What shall I do?
 7 I approve.
	End	1 Résumé of theme.
		   Audience needs.
		 2 Summary of points.
		 3 Closing words:
		   commitment.

How does a structure help? Apart from reducing tension and ensuring an audience-orientated presentation, a structure has other important advantages for a speaker:

1 It enables the audience to follow easily, because it is based on an initial outline of the theme, followed by development of that theme. There is a summary of the theme, and the points made, with a request for action.

2 To ensure every mental demand by the audience is covered.

3 It provides a framework to fall back on if the audience leads the speaker astray.

4 It provides a disciplined and logical basis on which the speaker can plan his presentation.

The needs of your audience Sit down at your desk with pencil and notepad and imagine you are already in front of your audience. Ask yourself several questions:

1 Who are they?

2 What are their needs as businessmen; as individuals?

3 How much do they already *know* about the subject?

4 What do they *need to know* that I can tell them?

5 What are their backgrounds, culture, level of intelligence?

Preparing your notes One of the most important skills to develop is setting down what you want to say in notes, to which you can refer easily; and not become the prisoner of a sheaf of closely written material, and with the eyes glued to this not holding the attention of your audience. For a complicated talk write out what you plan to say in detail. Then select the key sentences or words that summarize each section and put these either on to cards or into checklist form on paper. Then take your notes and not your lengthy first draft with you; the notes will be easy to refer to without making you their prisoner.

Conducting the presentation: the beginning

Objectives At the start of your presentation you have to achieve three objectives:

1 Gain the undivided *attention* of your audience.

2 Build *rapport* between you and your audience.

3 State the *theme* in terms of the needs of your audience.

How do you achieve each of these objectives?

Methods 1 *Objective: To gain the undivided attention of your audience.* Before you start speaking the first impact you make on your audience will be through your appearance and manner. Audiences tend to make quick judgements on first appearances. It is important to:

(a) *Stand up straight* in a comfortable stance with your feet slightly apart.

(b) *Look at your audience* in a confident manner. It helps if you have learned your opening sentences by heart so that you do not at the very outset, when you want to hold your audience's attention, bury your head in your notes.

(c) *Talk louder than is necessary for normal conversation.* You have to make instant impact when you speak, so your voice must come out more boldly than you would pitch it in normal conversation.

When appropriate, drama, curiosity, a story, a checklist, or questions can be used to attract audience attention, for example:

Dramatic openings. Dame Agnes Weston, who will always be remembered by seamen for her work in collecting money for the Missions to Seamen, often found herself making appeals for money in church halls. If, when she was about to speak, she felt the audience needed galvanizing, she would deliberately knock over the lectern which was conveniently placed near her foot. The crash as it hit the floor brought everyone to the edge of their chairs and also woke those asleep!

Another excellent use of drama was used to show the value of training: 'Yesterday a plane, in which my wife was one of the 120 passengers, crash-landed at Heathrow Airport. My wife and her travelling companions owe their lives to the thousands of pounds spent on training the pilot of that aircraft who knew in that moment of crisis, when the undercarriage failed to operate, how to bring the aircraft in to land with the greatest chance of saving the lives of those on board. In that moment his training "paid a massive dividend".'

Curious openings. Audiences are always fascinated by the curious. Here are some examples: A salesman selling rock drills used to carry a huge leather bag into the room where he was invited to make his presentation. From this he would take a massive piece of rock, in silence placing it on a piece of cloth on the table, visible to his audience and then begin: 'Gentlemen, you see before you a piece of the hardest rock in the world. It is found in Jersey. Our rock drills are the only ones made that will break it.'

A pension insurance broker, presenting his scheme to a board of directors, took off the wrist-watch he was wearing and with great ceremony placed it in a glass full of water saying: 'On the back it says "this watch is waterproof". Let us see if the maker's guarantee stands up to the test of its promise. It is about the guarantees behind the pension scheme you are considering today that I want to talk.'

A story opening. A short, interesting story, well told and containing the message you want to convey, or which is linked to the theme of your presentation, can focus attention. Asked to explain 'why marketing is necessary' a sales director began: 'My company once sent me to America and I travelled to New York on the liner Queen Mary. It was at the height of the season, yet the ship was barely half full of passengers. As I puzzled over this on a walk round the deck on the first day out from Southampton, I glanced up into the sky and saw two aircraft winging their way in the same direction as this great ship. And then the penny dropped: overhead flew Queen Mary's erstwhile passengers and presumably her profits. That convinced me that marketing is necessary – that we need to look at tomorrow and ask ourselves how will we stay in business?'

A checklist. Another effective opening is to use a checklist which then becomes the framework of your subsequent presentation, for example: 'Gentlemen, you state that first you need to increase profitability – this scheme will help you do so. Second, you need the security of on-going business – this will give you it. Third, you want to be linked with a successful product – you can be.

2 *Objective: To build rapport between you and your audience.* A part of the secret of any successful presentation lies in the feeling of oneness between you and your audience. Your audience must warm to you. Never let it be said of you: 'He had everything except one thing. Nobody believed he believed.' Depending on the circumstances, one or more of the following will help build rapport:

(a) *Compliments*. If your audience belong to a company that has achieved something notable you can express your admiration or compliment on it. But compliments paid must be *genuine* and *specific*. Anyone can offer empty praises.

(b) *Mention a common interest*. If you and your audience have things in common these can be mentioned. They can be either *social* or *business*, e.g. 'Gentlemen, as an engineer it is a great pleasure today for me to be amongst professional colleagues'.

(c) Demonstrate your competence, without boasting.

(d) Radiate enthusiasm – it will make your audience enthusiastic. In your tone of voice, the occasional smile, you can bring a warmth to your presentation which is catching.

3 *Objective: To state the theme in terms of the needs of your audience:*

(a) This is very important because it sets the tone of the whole presentation. For maximum impact the theme should be stated, where possible, in terms of audience needs, for example, addressing a company's top management: 'With competition in your industry becoming stronger and the pressure on profit margins increasing every day, the effectiveness of the people in your marketing team is crucial to your success. It is about their performance, and how it can be improved, that I wish to talk to you today.' *Not:* 'I'd like to talk about our ideas on marketing training.' In short, if they do not understand what the subject means to them they will lose interest.

(b) If the presentation is going to cover several points it is helpful to mention them at the beginning so that the audience knows what they can expect.

(c) If it is a 'cold' presentation, where the speaker has little knowledge of the needs of his audience, he will have to probe for them by questions until he has agreement on what they are looking for. He can then structure his talk accordingly.

The opening of a presentation sets the scene for everything that follows. The speaker wants his audience to have confidence in him, he wants their undivided attention. he wants to establish common objectives. Above all he wants them to believe that he has something that they will want to know. To achieve these things he has to appear confident, enthusiastic and keen to help them. Above all else, remember this golden rule when preparing your opening words: if you don't strike oil in the first three minutes stop boring.

Conducting the presentation: the middle

Objectives
1 To present the proposals in detail.
2 To have each point accepted.
3 To keep attention.
4 To prevent or handle objections.

Methods
1 *Objective: To present the proposals in detail.* By this time the audience will know the theme of your presentation, and, if it has been stated in terms of their needs, they expect to be informed of the ways in which you propose to meet them.

For the sake of clarity and to aid acceptance it is best to take one point at a time and deal with it before moving on to the next. This can be done in two ways, depending on the subject matter. Either: (a) take one of the audience needs at a time and present the ideas you have for meeting that need; or (b) take each of your ideas at a time and show how it meets their needs. When the subject matter permits, it is better to structure the presentation around audience needs because these are the things uppermost in their minds.

2 *Objective: To have each point accepted.* Acceptance of your points depends on their being understood, seen to be of value in that they will produce a desirable result, known to be valid, and agreed.

(a) *Understanding* can be achieved by:

    (i) Using language familiar to the audience, avoiding jargon.

    (ii) Explaining ideas by using similes, or going into detail.

    (iii) Using actions or gestures.

Always make sure that an action or gesture does help to communicate the point you are making. To extend both arms to indicate massive size will be effective if you have not used this gesture before. If you have been waving them about all the time then it will not. Leaning forward on the desk from which you are speaking and then stating a serious point can be most effective if your audience has so far not seen you do this.

    (iv) Giving demonstrations.

Nothing directs the attention of an audience from one point to another so surely as a physical demonstration, or showing a piece of equipment. But always: be prepared; practise in advance what you propose to do or show; take your time; tell your audience what you are going to do before you start, and give your reasons for doing it.

For example, an accountant was asked to speak to a group of sales staff about money and what gives it value. He strode into the room carrying a large sack on his shoulder. Then he asked two or three members of the audience to check all the doors in the room and lock them. Assured that all the doors were locked he began: 'In this sack is £10,000 in used £1 notes. I am going to empty them all on to the carpet like this (he then did just that). Now any one of you could help yourselves to fistfuls of these notes. But as long as the doors leading from this room to the outside world where you could spend that money remain locked, those notes are just bits of paper without value.'

    (v) Using visual aids.

Like demonstrations, visual aids, skilfully introduced, can convey information and convince audiences. Keep in mind some basic rules about visual aids: uniformity of size is preferable; readability from the back of the room is necessary. Always go to the farthest point in the room and check that what you are showing can be *seen* and *understood* by everyone. If your visuals are not uniform in size then you must carry out this check for each one you propose showing.

Avoid too much detail on one visual aid. Whether it is a chart or a slide, keep information to about *four* lines and make letters three inches high. Sketches, pictures or diagrams linked to words convey your visual message more effectively. Keep numerical information on charts to the minimum since people cannot remember it. Use as few words as possible so that each one makes impact.

Do not apologize for your visuals; just make sure they are good. Keep them hidden until needed. If you are showing a series of charts, then have the top one covered by at least two thicknesses of plain paper; and interleave between the others you propose showing. This avoids the danger of the outline of your visual aids being seen through the flimsy chart paper that is sometimes supplied.

Here is another tip for when you want to write in free-hand three or four key points on a flipchart; and you are not too good at keeping them in your head; or you would like to illustrate a point by means of a diagram and are not sure that you can reproduce it without an outline. Take an HB pencil and very faintly draw on to the flipchart paper the drawing you want to reproduce; or if it is three/four key points you want to write boldly in magic marker pen, then faintly write in pencil the words in the top right-hand corner of the flipchart. From a distance your audience will not see or be aware of your self-prepared prompters. From your point of view they provide you with the guides you need without having to rush back to your notes all the time. Number each visual you propose showing and place the relevant visual-aid number beside the points in your notes where you want to show each one (see Figure 11.3).

Allow your audience to note your visuals without distraction. So many speakers ruin the impact of their excellent visuals by competing with them. A picture is worth a thousand words. Show each one and *shut up* whilst your audience takes in what you want to communicate.

Remove your visual aids when they have served their purpose. This rule is broken by so many speakers. Overhead projectors are left on: flipcharts with pictures on them, a model remains visible to the audience when the speaker has moved on in his presentation to deal with points totally unrelated to what these visual aids are saying. The result is that the attention of some members of the audience is distracted, and if the speaker is becoming boring, often the important things he wants to say are missed. Afterwards he blames the audience if they do not react as he had hoped. *As always the onus of getting your message across is on you as the communicator.*

Beware of handing out visual material during a presentation. If you want your audience to take away with them a visual reminder of what you have said, it is better to keep such material to the end rather than hand it out in the middle of your talk. Interesting brochures, photographs, diagrams, can often prove more absorbing than a speaker!

(b) *Acceptance* of the value of your proposals is vital. To achieve it: (i) tell your audience what your ideas will do for them: in their jobs; as individuals; or (ii) what your ideas will do for other people in whom your audience are interested, their staff, distributors, superiors, colleagues, customers, shareholders.

The audience wants to know what your ideas will do *in terms of what they want done*. For example, if they want to be certain that your equipment can easily be operated by semi-skilled labour, it is wasting time to emphasize that it fits into a small space thereby increasing production per sq ft. Therefore, if you want your proposals to be desirable to your audience: (i) select the results they will get that fit in with their need; (ii) arrange the sequence so that one result logically leads to another, so that eventually their need is met.

(c) *Validity* of your points may be questioned, albeit mentally, by your audience, especially if your proposals are new to them. Points can be proved by quoting examples of other cases where they have worked. When quoting these examples, or when referring to third parties who have adopted your ideas: (i) do not start with such references; instead, use them to support arguments you have already made; (ii) ensure that the company or people to whom you refer are respected by the audience; (iii) ensure that the circumstances in both cases are sufficiently similar to make your point acceptable; (iv) tell your audience the desirable results the third party obtained.

(d) *Agreement* on the part of your audience is not always visible. Blank silence can imply agreement, disagreement, bewilderment, or boredom. You need agreement on each point before moving on to the next one. It is useful to check it by: (i) constant observation of their facial expressions; (ii) asking questions, if their facial expressions create doubt, e.g. 'are you satisfied that you will have a quality image by using this design?'

3 *Objective: To keep attention.* It is usually in the middle of a presentation that attention declines. To keep it at a high level:

(a) Keep telling them what your ideas mean to them;

(b) keep their eyes occupied by using visual aids, demonstrations, etc.;

(c) where possible give them something to do;

(d) quote examples, stories, etc.;

(e) maintain your enthusiasm;

(f) involve them where possible.

4 *Objective: To prevent or handle objections.* In formal presentations the audience is just as likely to think of objections as an individual would in a face-to-face situation. The main difference is that objections are less frequently voiced in formal presentations. It is therefore important that possible objections are considered in

advance by the speaker and answers to them woven into his presentation. For example: 'Of course, the initial cost is high, but all the evidence shows that the return far exceeds that of other methods. For example, . . .'

If objections are voiced, the objector wants his views acknowledged by the speaker and answered sympathetically. It pays a speaker to handle objections by:

(a) pausing – this gives him time to think and prevents the temptation to crush the objector with a snappy rebuttal;

(b) acknowledging that the objector has a point, e.g. 'yes, that is an important consideration';

(c) answering by concentrating on what the objector wants.

If the objection is unclear, clarify it by getting the objector to explain what he means.

In many presentations, the middle is the part least remembered, the part where attention is lost, where credibility falls, where objections arise, and where rejection sets in. If the beginning has been good, the middle should be even better. Remember to:

(a) take one thing at a time;

(b) keep emphasizing what that point means to them;

(c) keep their attention with visual aids, examples, stories, involvement, etc.;

(d) conclude each point before moving on to the next.

Conducting the presentation: the end

Introduction

1 No matter how long a presentation has lasted, no matter what the subject is, the audience expects it to end on a high note. If it has been good at the beginning, better in the middle, it deserves to be best at the end. If it has been a battle, this is your last chance to make a good impression.

2 The end is where all the threads need to be joined together and all your presentational skills combined to produce a climax that leaves the audience impressed, convinced, and eager to act in your favour.

The psychological barrier

Many speakers feel uncomfortable at having to conclude a presentation. They fight shy of asking for a commitment. Yet a commitment is what they want. They fight shy because they are afraid of getting a rejection and they prefer to leave things open. Such an attitude is understandable, but weak. The audience expects the speaker to draw conclusions from his presentation. He should do so, and confidently ask for a commitment because a commitment is in their interest as well as his.

How to conclude a presentation

1 There are several techniques for ending, but in every presentation the speaker should be concentrating on the needs of his audience when he winds up, so that their minds are being focused on their objectives rather than his.

2 From a structural point of view it helps to:

(a) Refer back to the theme – audience needs.

(b) Summarize the points you have made.

(c) If presenting a plan of action, state it in an orderly fashion. Do not leave the audience with a bundle of generalities.

3 Asking for a commitment can be done by using one or more of the following methods:

(a) Direct request, e.g.: 'Can we take it then that you will want to go ahead?'

(b) Command, e.g.: 'Take my advice, adopt this campaign, and let the sales pour in.'

(c) Alternatives, e.g.: 'As you have seen, your problem can be solved by a comprehensive plan which will be ready in three months or by a gradual process starting now and phased over six months. Do you prefer to start now or wait for the comprehensive plan to be ready?'

(d) Immediate gain from immediate decision, e.g.: 'As you know, your competitors have been ominously quiet during the past year and it is believed that they are about to launch a new product at any time. To protect your share of the market, I suggest you start the campaign now and make things as difficult for them as possible.'

(e) Summary, e.g.: 'You want equipment which will reduce your production costs by a minimum of 10 per cent. It must be compatible with the equipment you wish to retain and must be fully operational within six weeks from your order being placed. Taking all these points into consideration your best approach will be to purchase our equipment because it will give you what you want.'

Conclusion

1 The end of a presentation should appear to be a logical development from what has previously been said.

2 Asking for a commitment from the audience does not mean that a favourable one will be forthcoming. Action will only result if the rest of the presentation has been audience-orientated all the way through. A rough check of its audience-orientation is to note the number of times 'you' and 'your' are used compared with 'I', 'we' and 'our'.

3 To ensure that your message gets across, remember the phrase: 'Tell 'em what you're going to tell 'em. Tell 'em. Then tell 'em what you've told 'em.'

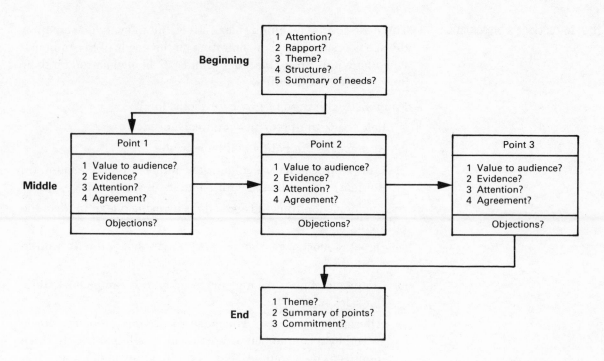

Figure 11.3 **Presentation planning chart**

		Visual aid
1	The title of my talk is	numbers

2 The objective(s) of my talk is/are ....

....

3 Who am I talking to? ....

4 What are their *needs*? ....

5 *Opening words*? (how am I going to gain their
  attention?) ....

....

6 *Middle*? (how am I going to maintain their interest?) do I need

.... charts or

.... props?

7 *Prevent objections*? (what objections will there be;
  how will I identify, acknowledge, handle/answer?)

....

....

8 *Close*? (how will I end my talk?) ....

  (a) by summarizing? ....

  (b) by a story? ....

  (c) by three-step formula? ....

  (d) by asking for action? ....

  (e) by assigning a task? ....

  (f) by alternatives? ....

....

....

....

Remember to:

(a) smile;

(b) keep eye contact with your audience;

(c) start good, get better as you end;

(d) end on a high note;

(e) write your talk as a checklist;

(f) keep your visuals simple;

(g) stand still.

Figure 11.4 **Effective speaking plan**

DO . . .

1 Get your suit pressed.
2 Dress as the group does
3 Look like an expert.
4 Get your back to wall or curtain.
5 Be yourself.
6 Write your talk as a checklist.
7 Smile from time to time.
8 Talk louder than normal.
9 Keep eye contact.
10 Face your audience.
11 Stand still.
12 Stand erect.
13 Stand slightly on your toes.
14 Lean forward a bit.
15 Leave your spectacles on or off.
16 Use variety of gestures.
17 Tell 'em what you are going to tell 'em.
18 Then tell 'em.
19 End by telling 'em what you told 'em.
20 Get a good ending.
21 Keep visuals covered till you need to show them.
22 Remove visuals when they have served their purpose.
23 Finish before you are expected to.

DON'T . . .

1 Write your talk as an essay.
2 Read your talk.
3 Talk to your notes.
4 Have distractions behind you.
5 Talk to your visuals.
6 Talk to the blackboard.
7 Walk up and down.
8 Lean on the lectern.
9 Fidget with yourself.
10 Play with your clothes.
11 Smoke.
12 Use the same gesture continually.
13 Compete with distractions.
14 Compete with your own material: if you pass an item out to be looked at stop talking till it has been examined by all.
15 Stand in front of a window.
16 Wear clothes that distract attention from what you are saying.
17 Fidget with your notes.
18 Over-run your allotted time.

Figure 11.5 **Effective speaker's dos and don'ts.**

Developing negotiating skills

This manual has been written with the aim of setting down guidelines and proven techniques which all of you who negotiate business for your companies will find helpful in developing your knowledge and sharpening your skills. This will enable you to be more successful in your negotiations, achieve more profitable business to the benefit of your company and of yourself and last, but not least, enjoy refining the art of negotiating.

For some of you this manual may simply confirm what you have almost instinctively been doing when faced with what you intuitively recognized and have responded to at negotiating meetings, although until now you may not have used such terminology. For you, please use this manual as a means of recording alongside the techniques described, your own approaches, stances, techniques, and those ideas you have adopted and which have succeeded, so that you can repeat them when the need arises again.

Some of you, having read this manual, will find it comparatively easy at once to develop and apply successfully the techniques recommended. But others, and you will probably be the majority, will ask how one can be trained to develop knowledge and skills so as to become an effective and successful sales negotiator?

You may, on the other hand, be the sales director of a small company responsible for negotiating some of the most important and profitable parts of your company's business. Or you could be the national accounts manager or one of a team of important account executives in a bank or a large company, or even a public utility.

External courses

For the one man or woman in a business who is responsible for key account negotiation, and where it would be expensive or impractical to have an individually tailored programme, there are external courses specifically designed to develop *sales negotiating skills and related financial knowledge*. Your choice must be made with care because otherwise you may find yourself sitting down with a group of delegates bent upon how to negotiate with trade unions! So here are some guidelines to help you make the right selection (see Figure 12.1).

Questions	Answers			
	Knowledge needs	Skills needed	Attitudes needed	Level of expertise
1 What do I need to know and understand about sales negotiation?				
2 What must I be able to do?				
3 What are the circumstances in which I must be able to do it?				
4 What standards of knowledge and skills must I reach to be able to conduct negotiations successfully?				

Figure 12.1 **Negotiating skills: personal training needs analysis**

1 *Define training objective:*

(a) What do I need to know and understand about sales negotiation?

(b) What must I be able to do? For example, read a balance sheet, work out break-even charts, prepare and conduct negotiation meetings.

(c) What are the circumstances in which I must be able to do it? For example, negotiate with buyers, intermediaries, directors, government bodies, etc.

(d) What standards of knowledge and skills must I reach to be able to conduct negotiations successfully?

This personal training needs analysis will help you to assess the objectives and content of any course you review much more effectively. Above all it will help you to pinpoint and answer *what you must be able to do at the end of the course.*

2 *Send for information about courses to develop negotiating for profit skills.*

Check with the course organizers:

(a) Who actually runs the programme? What are their qualifications as key account negotiators, in finance and above all as trainers? Have they been trained to train?

(b) Which companies have used the course regularly?

(c) Ask the course organizers for the names, positions and telephone numbers of at least three people who have attended the course in the last six months and to whom you can speak about the programme and its effectiveness in *developing skills.*

3 *Choose a suitable programme and attend it.*

4 *Decide what follow-up action is necessary after attending a course.*

How are you going to ensure that the time and money invested in attending a training course on sales negotiation yields a worthwhile return? Obviously by applying the techniques learnt on the job. But try and measure improvement if you can by self-appraisal. Write down at least ten and, if you can, 20 major prospects with whom you have been in negotiation up to the time you plan to go on the course and with whom you have so far failed to do business. Then when you have carried out detailed negotiations with them all, and in your judgement should have achieved some measurable objectives, add up your successes and failures. Be honest with yourself. Were the successes due to improved technique or were they fortuitous? Were your failures due to you or circumstances beyond your control?

How to structure a company programme/ workshop

A great number of fast-moving consumer goods companies, banks and insurance organizations and service companies employ a sufficient number of sales executives involved in major account negotiations to justify designing an in-company programme organized through their own training manager or commissioning a specialist consultant. Here are some guidelines on how a 'negotiating profitable sales' workshop might be constructed. The term workshop is used quite deliberately because it would be just that: it would be conducted in a workshop environment during which a small group of people would absorb new knowledge, examine systems and techniques and then practise and develop using them to the point of skilled application.

Workshop objectives By the end of the workshop, sales negotiators will have:

1 Developed a knowledge and understanding of the company's financial, business and marketing objectives and their role in helping to achieve them.
2 Developed the knowledge and skills necessary to assess the marketing and financial implications of negotiations and agreements made with customers and suppliers.
3 Developed their skills in their preparation of negotiations, particularly in trading and buying situations.
4 Developed and refined their skills in conducting effective negotiations to the point of practical application on the job, so that both volume and profit goals are achieved.

Content of workshop Based upon these objectives, the workshop content and material covered would include:

1 *The background to today's market conditions.* The development of the marketing concept; historical growth of marketing methods and organization structures; product and brand marketing; development of sales organization structures and methods; changes in the nature and scale of customer purchasing activities.

2 *Controlling the impact of selling activities on company profitability.* The problems of traditional budgetary systems; lack of genuine accountability for discretionary costs; the salesman as the final arbiter of the marketing mix offered to the customer; the dangers of standard discount systems; the relevance of incentive schemes to the salesman's real performance; the impact of costing systems on negotiation.

3 *Negotiation or Selling? Which technique for which situation?* What are the essential differences between negotiation and selling?; selling defined from a supplier's and a buyer's viewpoint; what relationship between supplier and buyer indicates a selling approach?; what relationship indicates the need for negotiation?; how do the two techniques and skills fit together?

4 *Negotiation – the techniques and skills involved.* A framework for viewing and understanding the process; the strategic elements of negotiation; the tactics of negotiation; the psychology of negotiation; negotiations in practice – an audio-visual example.

5 *The implications for the supplier.* Marketing and sales organization structures; a more accurate approach; budgetary systems for genuine accountability and more precise control; the selection, development control and motivation of negotiators.

Method The workshop will be designed to allow the maximum time for discussions and questions arising as each subject and session is presented and developed by the workshop tutor. It should be borne in mind that whilst the temptation to use the company accountant to handle the sessions on finance will be strong, it should be resisted unless your accountant is a natural teacher. Very few accountants can teach non-financial people finance in a simple way that all will understand.

The bulk of the workshop will be devoted to developing negotiating skills, using as a means of feedback closed-circuit television, so that negotiators can see as well as hear how they conduct a negotiating meeting and with their colleagues' and tutors' comments and analyses develop their skills.

Role-playing The most effective way to develop negotiating skills is for each sales negotiator attending the workshop to have the maximum amount of time and opportunity to practise the techniques he has been taught. To achieve this, in as realistic a way as possible, each person attending the workshop should be asked in advance to bring with him the details of two real-life negotiating situations in which he is currently involved where indicative costings have been calculated and submitted to the potential customers. In addition to these real-life commercial situations, the tutor conducting the workshop should prepare a realistic negotiation situation which can be used in the first stage of skill development. This case should be costed and in addition the concessions to be sought and conceded by either side should be itemized, their cost and value. Using this material, the workshop is divided into a buying and a selling group and each side is given the same information and asked to prepare themselves for a negotiation meeting. This meeting is conducted, recorded on closed-circuit television, played back and assessed.

Following the preliminary role-playing to familiarize everyone with the way negotiation meetings are prepared and conducted, the workshop is divided off into pairs, each pair taking one by one the real-life negotiation situations they have brought with them and preparing negotiation meetings based on them. Each pair works on *one* situation at a time. The person whose situation is chosen first will give his colleague all the necessary details he requires to understand the current customer position. Then each member at this point prepares how he will conduct the negotiation meeting, the buyer being played by the salesman whose customer situation is being used, his colleague playing the part of the salesman. Both are given time to prepare their respective positions to negotiate. Then each pair role-play their negotiation. The value of using real-life customer details is that they provide dress rehearsals for the actual negotiating meetings each salesman will conduct after the workshop.

Assessing the role-playing During the role-playing sessions, each member of the workshop carries out at least one assessment of a negotiation meeting. Through structured observation of negotiating techniques, his ability to analyse the cause and effect of relationships that are revealed and developed and how they influence the final outcome is increased. The manner in which the role-playing is conducted is as follows:

Phase 1. The seller leaves the room to enable the buyer to brief the observer(s) and others on the workshop as to how he proposes to conduct his part of the introduction and deal with the point-of-need balance and his ultimate objective. The buyer then leaves the room whilst the seller tells the group how he plans to conduct his part of the introduction and deal with the point-of-need balance and his selling objective(s). Phase 1 then begins and the nominated observer(s) uses a negotiation observation and evaluation sheet to record his comments on the check-points as shown in Figure 12.2. The tutor will judge and decide with the role-players the effective conclusion of phase 1. Phase 1 is recorded on closed-circuit television.

Phase 2. The phase 2 briefings will follow the same pattern as for the first phase, this time buyer and seller describing their tactics and the concessions they will seek, trade, and their value. The second phase is then conducted and recorded on closed-circuit television and the observer(s) use(s) the second section of his/their negotiation observation(s) and evaluation sheet to record comments on the tactics and concessions of buyer and seller (see Figure 12.3).

At the completion of each negotiation meeting, the participants are given evaluation sheets; then the recorded meeting is played back and participants' and observers' comments made. Finally the tutor summarizes the strengths and weaknesses revealed and where improvements in technique are needed.

Length and numbers on workshop

To cover the comprehensive material presented and develop negotiating skills so that they can be effectively applied on the job after the workshop means that numbers attending must be limited. An even number of delegates should attend and the numbers should not exceed eight as the absolute maximum.

Conclusion

The professional salesman or saleswoman of tomorrow will need much more than basic selling techniques to survive and compete successfully in the years ahead for worthwhile profitable business

Although you may have been trained in using the best and most effective selling aids available so far and these will still be needed, alone they will not be enough to help you to meet the changed markets and marketing conditions in which you will be operating from now on. Buyers of your products and services, like you, cannot

Check-points	Observer comments	
	The buyer	The seller
Clear objective		
Well prepared plan		
Well prepared facts		
Well prepared background		
Presentation of opening stances		
Recognition of need strengths		
Encouragement to others to talk		
Recognition of opposing tactics		
Treatment of exaggeration		
Move from opening to actual stance		
Avoidance of being 'concerned'		
Recognition of point-of-need balance		

Figure 12.2 **Negotiation observation and evaluation sheet: phase 1**

afford to be amateurs. They are becoming bigger in their responsibilities but fewer in number. They are becoming professionals in financial knowledge and increasingly skilled in negotiating the purchases of supplies and services. So must you.

Phase 1. Introduction and point-of-need balance recognition

What relevant background information is uncovered?

How well does each party 'position' himself in the estimation of the other?

Phase 2. Trading concessions

What use is made of negotiation tactics?

How are 'concessions' presented? Are they given or traded?

Check-points	Observer comments	
	The buyer	The seller

Tactics:
Over-statement
Under-statement
Face-saving
Emotional reaction
Use of trial close
Facial reaction
Bluff
Confidence
Credibility in use of facts/
   figures/third party

Concessions:
What type?
How traded?
What value?

Movement to conclusion
What snag objection?
How overcome?

Conclusion
Which side of need balance?

Figure 12.3 **Negotiation observation and evaluation sheet: phase 2**

Part IV

Case studies

Introduction to Part IV

The three case studies that follow are designed to illustrate the ideas and techniques presented in this manual.

In 1979 Video Arts asked me if they could make a two-part training film based on material from the first edition of this book. The result was two highly acclaimed films entitled: *The Preparation* and *The Negotiation*.

These two films, for which I was the technical adviser, were launched in September 1979. In January 1980 they had their American première at the Waldorf Hotel in New York.

Case Studies I and II comprise the original scripts. The first is an example of a traditionally trained salesman selling to a highly skilled buyer. The second shows a salesman trained in negotiation techniques negotiating with a trained buyer.

The final case study is an edited version of *Own Label*, a script written by Ric Vanes and made into a video programme for the Open College series *Reaching Agreement* by Yorkshire Television and produced by David Wilson. I was retained by Yorkshire Television as adviser for the series and edited the script to ensure that the appropriate teaching points were brought out.

Case Study I: A traditionally trained salesman selling to a highly skilled buyer

The buyer. Mr Johnson is the professional buyer of a large, well-known firm of plant and plant-hire contractors. His company operates machines ranging from small mechanically driven road-rollers to the largest industrial earth-moving equipment. He has asked a major plant manufacturer with whom his company has done business in the past to quote for the supply of an initial order of ten motorway construction machines. The list purchase price of each machine is £11 500 and, not unnaturally for an order of this size, the buyer has invited other manufacturers to tender. Mr Johnson has been trained in finance and purchasing.

The salesman. Mr Edmunds is an experienced salesman who has a background of factory experience. He was given a basic sales training course before taking over a sales territory. He is considered by his company to be a competent and reasonably successful member of the 12-man sales force. He has done a small amount of business in the past with Mr Johnson and has recently had a number of discussions with both operating and technical staff to obtain the necessary information needed to prepare the quotation to supply the ten machines.

Buyer's objectives

To obtain the best possible machines for his company on time to meet his company's financial and marketing plans. This company's machines are of the best quality and he will try and negotiate their purchase on the following terms:

1 To obtain the machines with the guarantee that 'C' part spares stock unused are taken back by the manufacturer at the end of 12 months free of charge.

2 To have the machines painted in the company's new livery free of charge.

3 To have the machines delivered to a number of different depots rather than all to one and so avoid carrying the cost of onward delivery.

Salesman's objectives

To sell ten new machines at the quotation price.

1 To arrange for the machines to be delivered to Birmingham within the price allowed for in the quotation.

2 To supply the recommended parts stock to the level specified in the quotation.

3 To ensure that arrangements are made to train the new machine operators to correspond with the dates of delivery.

Buyer's objectives **Salesman's objectives**

4 To have the operators and fitters responsible for the new machines trained on a special course laid on by the manufacturer free of charge.

5 To obtain the manufacturer's agreement in writing to a guaranteed buy-back figure.

6 To obtain a discount of 2½ per cent off the quoted price of each machine.

The costs involved in the transaction

1 Quoted price of machines: £11 500 each: 10 × £11 500 = £115 000.

2 Initial cost of recommended parts stock: £4 100 ('C' part spares value £2 800).

3 Cost of paint-spraying each machine: £35 per machine.

4 Cost of delivering ten machines to one point (Birmingham): £700.

5 Cost of delivering to separate points: minimum £100 per machine to a distance of 100 miles from plant (any distance over that 50p per mile extra).

6 Cost of operator training at company's training school: £35 per delegate.

The discussion **Notes**

Buyer Good morning Mr Edmunds, please sit down.

Salesman Thank you Mr Johnson. You have our quote I see.

Buyer Yes, thank you very much.

Salesman I hope you have found it interesting.

Salesman tests buyer's attitude to the quotation.

Buyer Oh yes, indeed. Not quite so good as some of the others I have received but nevertheless interesting.

Buyer emphasizes that other quotations are better, thus putting the salesman under pressure.

Salesman Oh! Which specific points were not as satisfactory as you might have liked.

Salesman rightly attempts to clarify the buyer's remark.

Buyer Well technically I think it's quite good in the sense that from our discussions last time you obviously understood our technical requirements very well and I have no quibbles in that direction. However, we are of course purchasing a total system and not just a machine. We are purchasing all the bits and pieces that go with it, commissioning and everything else and I

Buyer begins to soften up the salesman.

The discussion		**Notes**
	think it is in that area that you need to have a closer look.	
Salesman	Where were there any particular problems that you saw?	Salesman seeks further clarification.
Buyer	Well I think there are several areas, perhaps we should take them one at a time. Let's deal first of all with this question of parts stock. Now in your quotation you put a recommended parts–stock level, which is normal practice. But of course in this particular case we are talking about ten machines and also talking about a brand-new model and inevitably I think you put in a recommended parts stock which both in terms of quantity and value is relatively high compared with standard situations. That of course is going to involve us in a considerable financial commitment and one which quite frankly I am reluctant to accept at this point in time. So what I would like you to do is to have another look at the recommended-parts level, and in those cases where we don't use them during the first 12 months to come to some arrangement whereby you will take these back free of charge.	Buyer prefers to deal with one thing at a time and in the sequence of his choice. Starts with first point: *Parts stock.* Buyer emphasizes the cost of carrying the recommended parts stock. Buyer asks for a concession on parts stock.
Salesman	Yes, I see we're talking about the 'C' class spares are we?	Salesman clarifies.
Buyer	That's right and there were some of them which are not common to other machines, and it is those that I am concerned about.	
Salesman	Yes.	
Buyer	I don't think these will present you with any difficulty will they?	Buyer minimizes the effect of the concession on the supplier.
Salesman	Well the warranty will cover a fair amount of that and at the end of 12 months it may be that you are buying new machines and will need to balance the parts stock up, or otherwise I am sure we can produce a buy-back situation with no problem.	Salesman partly concedes
Buyer	Good, fine. Now that covers the area of the recommended parts stock. Another point which we need to talk about is the question of livery. I think I mentioned to you last time, when we were	Buyer confirms the concession. He now turns to his second point: *Livery.*

	The discussion	**Notes**

Salesman talking about the technical specification, that we have in fact been doing an analysis of our corporate image.

Salesman Yes.

Buyer That analysis has now been completed and as a result what we are going to have to do is change various parts of our corporate image. You know at the bottom end it involves very simple things like changing our letterheads and so on. It also means developing the speaking abilities of our people who take hirings over the telephone. But one major area where we are going to have to make a change is livery. We are currently re-painting all our existing fleet and with the addition of these new machines into the fleet what I am going to need is for them to be delivered to us in the new colours.

Buyer asks for concession.

Salesman That wasn't in fact in the original specification.

Salesman resists.

Buyer No, I am sorry about that but at that time of course we hadn't completed our analysis. So what I would like you to do is arrange for these ten machines to be painted in our new colours prior to delivery to us.

Buyer apologizes, but repeats his request.

Salesman Is the basic paint job apart from stencils still yellow?

Buyer Yellow will still be in the colours but the predominant colour now will be green, Lincoln green.

Salesman I see. I think we can arrange that without too much problem. You can let us have the exact code of the paint and the necessary artwork and so on, some stills of existing machines?

Salesman agrees to the change.

Buyer Yes indeed. And, as normally happens, you will of course do this free of charge?

Buyer requests it FOC.

Salesman Yes, we can I think accommodate that. There's no particular problem there and you want these then delivered through to Birmingham?

Salesman agrees.

Buyer's third point: Delivery.

Buyer Yes, certainly three of them will be required in Birmingham, but we want the others delivered to our other regional depots.

Buyer has changed his original delivery requirements.

The discussion

Notes

Salesman Mmm, I thought all ten were going through to Birmingham?

Buyer This indeed was our original thinking. However, we have looked at the situation again and we have had discussions with our various regional managers and they have expressed the view that there is a demand for these machines in their own areas. In addition, we feel that we would like to get some idea of how the machines perform under different geographic conditions, and also because if these machines are successful we will probably want to increase the fleet at regular intervals, we need to sound out the demand in particular areas to see where machines should go. Now this means that of the ten, three will be required in Birmingham, (you know where our Birmingham depot is, very close to you at Wolverhampton). Three will be required in London and I'll give you the details.

Buyer suggests possible future business as a lever to obtain a delivery concession.

Buyer minimizes inconvenience and cost of change in delivery specification.

Salesman I know the London depot well.

Buyer Well as you know it's at the bottom of the motorway so that's no problem. Two will be required in Manchester and our Manchester depot is about four miles off the Altrincham turn-off on the M6. One is required in Glasgow and one is required in Plymouth, and I imagine, of course, that you do make deliveries from time to time in these areas so this won't present any particular problem.

Buyer continues to minimize the cost and inconvenience of the geographic delivery scheduling of these machines.

Salesman They are quite widely spread.

Buyer Indeed, I think I should add that in the competitive quotes that we have had, delivery to these depots has been offered by the companies concerned.

Buyer makes salesman feel uncompetitive.

Salesman Free delivery?

Buyer Oh indeed, yes.

Salesman Then I think that we will have to make sure that that's done for you.

Salesman agrees to concession.

Buyer Thank you.

Salesman Fine (and makes a note as does the buyer).

The discussion		**Notes**
Buyer	Now one point I wanted to raise with you was the date of the training courses when you're going to send our people into Wolverhampton.	
Salesman	Yes. You'll be sending ten people into Wolverhampton for the operator training course?	
Buyer	Not quite. We have, as far as operators are concerned, between two and three people at each of the regional centres who will require training, so we're talking about 12 or 15 people. We also feel that it is important that the people who have to maintain these machines are also made familiar with their operation.	
Salesman	Yes.	
Buyer	That being the case, what we want to do is to train both the operators and the fitters. So this means we are talking in total of 20–25 people.	
Salesman	Well normally we offer a training for one person per machine.	
Buyer	Yes.	
Salesman	And we don't really want to over-load the training school. The school obviously has a limited number of places, limited amount of courses and numbers of lecturers, and we find that the training centre has been set up in fact to match the demands that are made on it against the sales forecast that we make on machines.	Salesman explains situation on training.
Buyer	Yes, I appreciate that because we have of course sent people on previous occasions where we have bought one-off items from you in the past. Now I have looked at this and I think there is one way that we can get round this which will cause you the minimum of inconvenience. What I would like to do is to pull them all together as a group. Now this, of course, will present problems to you on your normal programmes. So what I am going to suggest is that we pull them all together at one of our depots and obviously the most convenient one is Birmingham, because that's closest to you and your own training centre.	Buyer minimizes the cost to the supplier of his proposition.

258

The discussion		Notes
Salesman	Yes.	
Buyer	We will provide the accommodation facilities, we will provide the training environment, we will make everything just as you want it. All you would need to do is to lay on the trainer and because, by the time we do the training the machines that we need won't have been delivered to the regional centres, I would like you to lay on a demonstration training machine as well. So all you would need to do is to provide the trainer and to provide the machine and we'll provide the environment and everything else and the accommodation.	Buyer makes his request seem very reasonable.
Salesman	So what you are really saying is that instead of sending ten people in, you want the increased number of operators and fitters in your own location with the machine?	
Buyer	Yes. Let me elaborate on that. This is a large purchase by any standards. As you well know, on training programmes which are attended by people from various companies you have, inevitably people talk, and in fact I believe that this is a training method in which you do in fact encourage people to exchange experience. With the standards of maintenance that we have, and our methods of maintenance, I am very reluctant indeed to expose those to fitters and operators from competitive companies. In other words, I don't want this to get about well before the machines are available because some of our competitors may well take action to prevent us getting the level of business that we shall need for these machines. So that is another reason why I would like to pull all these people together under one roof and have this programme specifically for us.	Buyer emphasizes the size of the order to soften up the salesman. Buyer 'sells' his proposal.
Salesman	Well I will have to check it with my training centre to make sure that they do have a machine available because the machines are in great demand. But I would think if they will give it the O.K. we can promise you that and we	Salesman conditionally agrees.

	The discussion	Notes
	can put that together. That will be in early December?	
Buyer	I would think so. Of course we're not putting any strain on your training centre or its programme.	
Salesman	No, quite. So really we must look at the parts stock and get a guarantee buy-back there; the paint job; delivery to those centres and we will organize that special training for you. Can we then go ahead on that basis?	Salesman tries to close.
Buyer	Almost. Almost. I think we're almost there Mr Edmunds. There's just one area that I would like to tidy up before we make a decision, and even if we do tidy it up I think I should emphasize that I've still got to look at the other ones as well. As you know it has always been our policy in the past to hold our machines for a length of time and then to sell them off.	Buyer, having already obtained a number of valuable concessions, tries for another: *Buy-back agreement.*
Salesman	Yes.	
Buyer	Now this policy runs counter to the policies of many companies who hold the machines for a period and then under a buy-back arrangement that they have with the manufacturer the machines are taken back by the manufacturer at an agreed price, Now what I would like to do in this particular situation, because these are new models, is to have that arrangement with you, so that we will forego our normal procedure of selling them off and come to some arrangement now whereby we have a buy-back agreement.	
Salesman	Of course you are quite right we do have buy-back arrangements, though normally that is with contractor's own plant. The problem with plant hire, quite simply, is that the conditions are very variable, and the effect on a machine that works, for example, purely on overburden instead of high silica sand, can be quite different, which has a major effect on its value. In addition to which I think that when you sometimes simply hire the machine you don't always hire it out with an operator, and that of course, also as you	Salesman answers.

The discussion	Notes
know very well, with some of the cowboys they have about, has an effect. I think the company would be very reluctant to guarantee a buy-back, especially since this is a new machine and we're not quite sure of the demand levels in the present economic situation.	
Buyer Yes, I think you'll find however, there are more cowboys amongst the general contractors than there are amongst plant-hire people.	Buyer counters the salesman's argument.
Salesman Indeed yes. Yes, the point I was making was that if you do hire out machines without an operator then that is where the misuse so often takes place.	Salesman rephrases his explanation.
Buyer I'm sorry, you misunderstand me. With the contractor, practically all the time the machines are being operated by the cowboys, whereas with us, where we hire out for most of the time with an operator, the machine is under very close control. I think there are other considerations as well, which I think would influence your view here. One is that on many occasions we are hiring out for lengthy periods to people whom we know and in conditions with which we are familiar, and we know perfectly well that the machine is going to be well maintained and the conditions are not going to be arduous. That's one consideration. The other is that in plant hire we have the ultimate sanction as to whether we take a hire or not.	Buyer counters again.
Salesman Yes.	
Buyer And, of course, one of the major considerations in taking a hire or not is the conditions under which that machine is going to be operated. Now for those reasons I think that what you are likely to find, particularly bearing in mind our regular maintenance which we have to carry out in order to maintain the level of service that our customers need, also bearing in mind the corporate image I am talking about, that under most circumstances these machines are operated and maintained to a fairly high standard and therefore buy-back	

The discussion

Salesman under these circumstances should be relatively easy for you.

Salesman Yes, I can see that that is so. The real problem of course is that it would be very difficult for you at the stage we agreed the buy-back level to tell us what those conditions were going to be. Therefore we have a difficult situation of projecting exactly what that would be. At this stage my company would not be able to produce a settled buy-back figure. That really would be very difficult for us.

> Salesman resists buyer's pressure to agree a buy-back price for the machines.

Buyer You're saying that doing it in advance creates great problems because you don't know what the circumstances are going to be?

Salesman Really yes.

Buyer Well perhaps we can approach it from another angle. I take it that your company is interested in this business?

> Buyer has to accept salesman's answer, so he switches to a price objection.

Salesman Oh indeed, yes certainly.

Buyer Now that being the case, as an alternative if you can't do buy-back, and I must say I am very disappointed that you don't feel you can do anything along these lines, but as an alternative what we could consider is some form of discount off the purchase price that you have quoted.

> Buyer makes salesman feel he is being reasonable.

Salesman Well, as you know, the price that we put in originally was very keen. You are quite right we are very interested in getting this business indeed and I don't know that we have a great deal of leeway at the price we quoted.

Buyer Yes your price is keen, but I think that you should know that it has been bettered.

> Buyer puts salesman's quotation on spot by reminding him that competitors have quoted keener prices.

Salesman Well what particular levels of discount are we talking about?

Buyer Well I would imagine that while they've been tested, their performance still needs to be proved long term. With this type of machine in this kind of situation I would say that something in the order of 4½ per cent would be acceptable to me.

Salesman 4½ per cent is a great deal of money.

> Salesman resists.

	The discussion	**Notes**
	It's coming considerably outside my court. At this stage I am quite sure that we will find it very difficult to stretch to 4½. That really is a considerable discount.	
Buyer	How far could you go?	Buyer squeezes him.
Salesman	Myself? I think with the price that we have already I could not go beyond 2½ per cent at this stage. That would be my absolute limit.	
Buyer	And how far could your company go at the next stage?	Buyer presses to test if salesman's limit and his company's has *really* been reached.
Salesman	When I say at this stage, I mean that with this particular deal 2½ per cent would be as far as we could go as a company.	
Buyer	That's the limit?	
Salesman	That would be the limit, yes.	
Buyer	So you're saying that the company's limit and your limit are the same?	Buyer expresses doubt.
Salesman	Yes, it would be, with the concessions that we have already made on delivery and parts stock and so on, and the price that we had initially. I think that would be as much of a package as we would be able to put together, and indeed we only reached that level being pretty sure that this machine would prove very attractive to you and then would give you the purchase price.	
Buyer	I wouldn't want you to misunderstand me, Mr Edmunds. The package that you are now quoting to me is no better than the package that I have received from several of your competitors.	Buyer raises the spectre of lower competitive quotations again.
Salesman	But if we were to go to the extra 2½ per cent? Would that make it into a deal which would be acceptable to you?	Salesman tries to close.
Buyer	It might be. I must confess I am a little bit surprised that on the sort of contracts you negotiate your company doesn't give you more authority in this area.	Buyer tries to undermine the salesman's status.
Salesman	Well the authority does stretch a good deal further than 2½ per cent, but we already have discounted considerably on the quotation that you have. Indeed I am not sure that the 2½ per cent itself isn't a major concession. I am quite	

The discussion		Notes
	sure that we couldn't go further than that at this stage. The 2½ per cent would be as far as we would be able to go.	
Buyer	Don't forget of course that although we are talking about the initial purchase of ten machines I think you know only too well the rate of expansion that this company has enjoyed over the past few years, and I think it's also only fair to say to you that during that period you have had a larger slice of our initial plant purchases than you used to enjoy.	Buyer uses the 'I help you, why don't you help me?' technique.
Salesman	Yes, indeed.	
Buyer	Now that is the relationship that I personally would like to continue but of course I have responsibilities to the board. The other consideration is that the purchase of further machines of whatever type, as you well know, depends very much on which machines we buy initially, because if we are familiar with them, our customers are familiar with them, and so on. Now, that being the case, and I think we have come to a reasonable arrangement on the other areas, is there anything you can do about that 2½ per cent?	Buyer paints the picture of a possible rosy future. Tries again for a larger price reduction.
Salesman	Quite honestly, Mr Johnson, if I were able to take it further than that I would. I am willing to take it back to my company, but I think it exceptionally unlikely that they would make any change. Indeed, I am going to get my fingers caned quite hard for going so far as I have, but 2½ per cent would be as far as I would be willing to go.	Salesman refuses.
Buyer	Well I'll tell you what I will do. 2½ per cent is within your authority?	
Salesman	Yes, it is.	
Buyer	Let's make sure we have got these points right. You will take back from us after 12 months, if we have not used them, the Class 'C' spares at no cost to ourselves.	Buyer summarizes revised terms: *Parts stock.*
Salesman	Yes, we will.	
Buyer	You will paint these ten machines and any subsequent machines that we may	*Livery.*

The discussion		**Notes**
	buy from you in our new livery prior to delivery?	
Salesman	Yes, of course.	
Buyer	As far as delivery is concerned, we are talking about ten machines, three to London, three to Birmingham, two to Manchester and one to Glasgow, one to Plymouth, free of charge.	*Delivery.*
Salesman	Yes, yes indeed.	
Buyer	You're going to train between 20 and 25 people on our premises and all you need to do is to lay on the trainer and the machine to carry out the training programme.	
Salesman	Yes.	
Buyer	And as far as the initial purchase is concerned you will reduce that quoted price by 2½ per cent.	*Price.*
Salesman	Yes.	
Buyer	Well, I think on that basis, Mr Edmunds, if you can sign up this morning I am prepared to place this initial order with you.	*Buyer closes.*
Salesman	Well, that's fine. I am very grateful. I am sure that that will go very well indeed.	
Buyer	Good. Now you will confirm this to me in writing.	
Salesman	Yes I will. I'll do that today, as soon as I get back to the office.	
Buyer	I'll get your letter tomorrow?	
Salesman	Yes, yes you will.	
Buyer	On receipt of your letter confirming these points I will then send you the purchase order. Would you like it addressed to you personally at your head office?	
Salesman	Please, if you would. Yes.	
Buyer	Well, thank you very much.	
Salesman	I hope you'll be very pleased with it.	
Buyer	I hope so. You will hear from me if we are not.	
Salesman	Thank you very much, Mr Johnson.	
Buyer	Thank you. Goodbye.	

Case study II: A salesman trained in negotiating techniques negotiating with a trained buyer

The commercial ituation

This is identical to the one described on pp. 253–255. But there are two vital differences in the salesman, Mr Edmunds. Firstly, he has now been trained to negotiate deals of the type he is handling here; secondly (and arising from this), his negotiating objectives for this crucial meeting are now related to the profitability of the order rather than whether he gets an order at any price.

Buyer's objectives

To obtain the best possible machines for his company on time to meet his company's financial and marketing plans. This company's machines are of the best quality and he will try and negotiate their purchase on the following terms:

1 To obtain the machines with the guarantee that 'C' part spares stock unused are taken back by the manufacturer at the end of 12 months free of charge.

2 To have the machines painted before delivery in the company's new livery free of charge.

3 To have the machines delivered to a number of different depots rather than all to one depot and so avoid carrying the cost of onward delivery.

4 To have the operators and fitters responsible for the new machines trained on a special course laid on by the manufacturer free of charge.

5 To obtain the manufacturer's agreement in writing to a guaranteed buy-back figure.

6 To obtain a discount of 2½ per cent off the quoted price of each machine.

Salesman's objectives

To sell the ten new machines at the quotation price.

1 To arrange for the machines to be delivered to Birmingham within the price allowed for in the quotation.

2 To supply the recommended parts stock to the level specified in the quotation.

3 To obtain some form of public relations value from the supply of the new machines by trading help with the training of operators or painting them in the company's livery.

4 To ensure that arrangements are made to train the new machinery operators to correspond with the dates of delivery.

The costs involved in the transaction

1 Quoted price of machines: £11 500 each: 10 × £11 500 = £115 000.

2 Initial cost of recommended parts stock: £4 100 ('C' part spare value £2 800).

3 Cost of paint-spraying each new machine: £35 per machine.

4 Cost of delivering ten machines to one point (Birmingham): £700.

5 Cost of delivery to separate points: minimum £100 per machine to a distance of 100 miles from plant (and distance over that 50p per mile extra).

6 Cost of operator training at company's training school: £35 per delegate.

	The discussion	Notes
Buyer	Good morning Mr Edmunds, please sit down.	
Salesman	Good morning Mr Johnson. Thank you. You have our quote and so I hope we can reach a decision today because the demand on these new machines could put back your chances of delivery quite seriously otherwise.	Salesman tries to close on original quotation.
Buyer	Well I also hope we can reach a decision today, but in order to get to that stage there are some items in your quotation I would like to deal with.	Buyer indicates desire to reach an agreement provided terms are acceptable.
Salesman	Fine. What are they?	Salesman asks for details.
Buyer	Well let me deal first of all with the areas where I think we are all right. As far as the technical specification is concerned, and the machine capability, I am quite satisfied and so are our technical people. There are no problems there whatsoever. The areas where I think we need to have some discussions are in the total package as opposed simply to the machine itself. I am talking about bringing the machines in and then developing the staff and these types of things. Those are the areas where we need to talk because at the moment although I am quite happy with the technical side of the operation, competitively you are a bit weak on the other aspects.	Buyer tries not to be too explicit, except to emphasize the uncompetitiveness of the quotation and thus disconcert the salesman.
Salesman	Well let's have a look at them, shall we? Can we take them all and then we can look at them in the round?	Salesman asks for *all* the points, so that he has a full idea of what is involved.
Buyer	Well I think there are some that are of major importance and others that I would call of peripheral importance. Perhaps we could deal with the major	Buyer identifies one point only: *Parts stock.*

The discussion		Notes
	things first of all. One of them is the recommended parts stock.	
Salesman	Yes, what concerns you there?	Salesman asks for details.
Buyer	Well, as you know, these are new machines but they are also new models, and I think quite understandably in that situation your recommended parts stock is much higher both in value and in volume than one would normally have for a standard machine. That places on us a considerable financial commitment which I am not prepared to accept *in toto* at this point in time and I think we need to talk about how we can get that financial commitment down in some way or other.	
Salesman	Fine, that's point one, and what's next?	Salesman asks for other points before dealing with the parts stock.
Buyer	I mean what would you suggest as far as parts volume is concerned?	Buyer tries to get the parts stock cleared up before revealing the rest of his hand.
Salesman	Well, what I am suggesting, just at this stage, is let's take all the points because after all, as you say, we are looking at a total package. Let's take all of them. I think some of them will relate one to another.	Salesman refuses to be sidetracked. He needs the total picture so that he can identify the size of the gap between them and thus the mid-point where agreement should be reached.
Buyer	Right.	
Salesman	Therefore shall we talk about all of them in one go?	
Buyer	Well I certainly think as far as you're concerned this parts-stock area and the value of it is something we need to look at in some detail.	
Salesman	Oh I'm sure we do.	
Buyer	A second area is this question of delivery. Now when I spoke to you last time, I think you were under the impression that we would have delivery to our Birmingham depot. Since then we have had discussions with the regional managers in the other centres and it is clear that they have a demand in those centres, and also we feel that it is important that they should have the opportunity to try them out so that we can determine just what is the demand in those areas, so that if and when we decide to purchase more machines we will know where to place them and how many we need.	Buyer reveals second point: *Delivery.*

	The discussion	Notes
Salesman	Well how would you dispose of the ten?	Salesman asks for details.
Buyer	Well of the ten I have the split here. Three would go to Birmingham, as we originally agreed.	
Salesman	Yes . . .	
Buyer	We shall need three in London, two in Manchester, one in Glasgow and one in Plymouth. Now I imagine from your point of view that delivery to these centres doesn't present any major problems.	Buyer minimizes the problems created by his request.
Salesman	It doesn't present a major problem, it does present a certain amount of cost and availability of transport but that's fine, let's come to that as well.	Salesman indicates willingness to talk, without committing himself.
Buyer	You think you can meet that one?	Buyer seeks agreement.
Salesman	I'm quite sure we can deliver to those areas or that we can make sure that the machines arrive in those areas. That won't be a problem.	Salesman agrees that the delivery arrangements can be changed but does not commit his company to paying for it.
Buyer	Good. The other vital area is the question of the way in which we dispose of these machines when they come to the end of their normal life. As you know, our policy is that after two years we normally sell them off. Now in this particular case, bearing in mind that they are new models, what I would like to do is to adopt the policy of many of your customers which is to have some form of buy-back arrangement with you.	Buyer raises third point: *Buy-back*.
Salesman	Yes.	
Buyer	And so we need to come to some agreement on the level at which you would be prepared to take these back from us after two years.	
Salesman	Now those are the main points are they?	Salesman checks that there are no other major points for discussion.
Buyer	Yes.	
Salesman	Now what about the minor ones. Were there any significant ones?	He now moves to the minor ones.
Buyer	No I don't think so. One concerns livery – we will need to have them painted in our new colours which is a result of the corporate image study we have done.	Buyer raises fourth point: *Livery*.
Salesman	Is the basic colour still yellow?	

	The discussion	**Notes**
Buyer	No it isn't. There will be a certain degree of yellow in it but the predominant colour will be green, Lincoln green.	
Salesman	Which would mean us clearing out a paint shop and doing a total new job.	Salesman stresses the cost of the change.
Buyer	That's right. But I would imagine that you've done that in the past.	Buyer plays it down.
Salesman	We have done it indeed. Yes, yes.	
Buyer	We shall need to have that done – free of charge of course. And the other peripheral area is the question of operator training. I know that it is normal policy to train operators to operate the machines. In our particular case we're talking about two or three people per regional centre which means 12 to 15 people in all. But in addition we want to be sure that the people who are going to maintain these machines are trained at the same time so that both operators and fitters are familiar with them. So we're talking altogether about something like 20–25 people that need to be trained.	Buyer raises fifth point. *Training.*
Salesman	I see.	
Buyer	I think I may be able to save you a headache here. Normally you would pull people in one at a time?	
Salesman	That's right, yes.	
Buyer	And in pulling people in one at a time you have this problem that you are mixing them with other people's staff. I wouldn't want this to happen because I don't want our competitors to know quickly that we are anticipating this purchase. And I certainly don't want them to know what we've got in the way of maintenance facilities and maintenance procedures. So what I would like to do is to have a programme purely for our own people and I think the best way to do this is for us to lay it on at our own depot in Birmingham, which is close to you. We'll provide all the facilities, accommodation and everything else and all you need to do is to lay on a trainer, to provide the necessary training aids and also a	Buyer explains why he wants special treatment. Buyer implies that, as he is making the arrangements for the training, the supplier's role is considerably reduced.

The discussion	**Notes**

machine for demonstration and training purposes.

Salesman So we have these five points:

1 the parts stock;
2 the delivery;
3 the buy-back;
4 the paint job;
5 the operator training.

Salesman checks the complete picture. He now knows the nature and financial implications of the buyer's requests and can decide how to handle them, how big is the gap between them, and where the mid-point lies where agreement should be reached.

Buyer That's right. And of those the parts stock, delivery and buy-back I think are the most important.

Salesman Good. Well let's examine those because certainly there is quite a lot we can do for you in these areas. Can we take this parts stock one first because it is in many ways separate from the others? When we talk about parts stock we are talking presumably about the slow moving, the 'C' class spares?

Salesman chooses to deal with parts stock first.

He asks for clarification.

Buyer That's right. As you well know the 'A' and 'B' class spares are common to other machines. I'm mainly concerned about the 'C' class spares which are peculiar to this machine, and I don't want to have a situation where at the end of 12 months we have got a lot of 'C' parts on hand which we won't need to use, and therefore I would like to agree that at the end of 12 months any that we haven't used of the 'C' parts you will take back free of charge.

Buyer explains.

Salesman Well, I think there's no reason we cannot help you here. The quote includes 'A' and 'B' spares doesn't it?

Salesman is willing to be reasonable.

Buyer Yes quite clearly there will be 'A' and 'B' type spares that we already have.

Salesman Yes, there will. You know the thing that troubles me slightly. Obviously things like basic split pins I'm not so concerned about. Indeed, I think that in our original parts stock for these machines we haven't excluded these spare parts altogether. But if you are willing to take from us the total parts stock recommended both on the 'A' and 'B' and the 'C' class spares, I see no reason why we should not guarantee a buy-back on the 'C' class spares at the end of 12 months; unless, of course, you

Salesman offers a concession, provided that the buyer will take the total recommended stock.

	The discussion	**Notes**
	want to maintain that stock at that stage for further machines that you are likely to buy.	
Buyer	Yes, I think that's fair. If you can guarantee that you will take back any unused 'C' parts at the end of 12 months free of charge then we will be prepared to take the recommended total spares that you have laid out in your quotation.	Buyer agrees.
Salesman	That's fine. Now I am sure that's a wise decision because the machine is new, and needs even in the smaller areas the precise part that is necessary. That will help your people considerably with the fitting manuals because the parts numbers will correspond.	Salesman reinforces the buyer's decision.
Salesman	The delivery points do trouble me somewhat. You have run low loaders perhaps even more than we do and you know the kinds of costs. The original costs that we put in were based on delivery to Birmingham. This is what we were building in. I don't think that it is necessarily too great a problem and we could handle it one of two ways. First, we could agree that you collected, and you could collect very simply with your Plymouth loader taking two and dropping one in London, and your Glasgow loader taking two and dropping one in Birmingham. If you were to collect, then we could remove altogether the, well it's about 0.7 per cent but let's say 1 per cent, from our quote. Alternatively, we discuss an economic rate for adjusting the delivery costs as you now require them.	Salesman takes the initiative, and introduces the point of: *Delivery.* He offers two alternatives to meet the buyer's requirements but asks for reciprocal movement from the buyer.
Buyer	Well, I think I need at this stage to put you in the picture as far as the competitors are concerned. As you well know, there are several machines on the market which we could take as very suitable for this application. I think the significant difference is that they are prepared to deliver these quantities to the regional centres free of charge.	Buyer decides to use the competitive 'stick' to beat a better deal out of the salesman.

The discussion

Salesman That doesn't surprise me at all. Indeed with the demand that we have got for the 787 I can quite see that they are probably getting a bit desperate anyway. My problem is not just with the cost, though that's part of it. My problem is one of capacity. You know very well what it costs to keep a low loader on the road, and we quoted on the basis that the total delivery would be to Birmingham, which from Wolverhampton is a very easy and simple trip to manage. I doubt that I could really pull together the low-loader capacity to cope with so many locations at once. What we could do is take the situation as it runs and on these longer trips prolong delivery somewhat to the end of January, or early February, and in that way still deliver at a much reduced delivery charge.

Buyer How much? You said 0.7 per cent.

Salesman Yes 0.7 per cent to 1 per cent. I think I could arrange for us to simply deliver within what we have already built into the quote and make no extra charge if you were willing to delay delivery by about six weeks. On the other hand, if you've now got low loaders running light, as I imagine that in several of your depots you will have at this time of the year, I would be quite happy for them to come and collect and take that out of our quotation. The choice is really with you, but I would recommend that you took the earlier delivery. The sooner you get these machines on the ground, the sooner you get the element of surprise which is available to you with a new machine.

Buyer I think on balance, Mr Edmunds, I would prefer your previous suggestion. If you can deliver to these centres at this reduced rate then I am prepared to accept delivery for some of them towards the end of January.

Salesman Yes, I can do that.

Buyer Good.

Salesman Now, I will have to go back and re-

Notes

Salesman stresses the difficulties in delivering to several points. He suggests an alternative method: a reduced price in exchange for delivery when it suits his own company.

He offers a further alternative: No charge for delivery if the customer collects.

Customer accepts the first alternative.

The discussion

Notes

check our production scheduling be-cause they won't be exactly the same machines which I had scheduled for building mid-December.

Buyer Do they meet the specifications.

Salesman Oh yes they will still be 787s. Now, the next point you had was buy-back. It is not our normal practice with a plant-hire company to produce a buy-back price. The reasons I think are obvious. Some of the old machines naturally get a great deal more wear than others, and this is why you not only maintain such an up-to-date fleet, but also change your machines frequently. However, as arrangements stand, we would be willing at the end of two years to re-purchase these machines on an inde-pendent appraisal of their full market value. To produce a figure now might be unfair to you, or rather dangerous for my company, which naturally I would be unwilling to do. More worry-ing is that in two years' time you might be able to make much better arrange-ments elsewhere, because of the low usage or the very well-handled usage. We would therefore be prepared to buy back on an independent valuation at that time.

Salesman now decides to tackle:
Buy-back.

He argues for an independent valuation in two years' time rather than fixing a figure now.

Buyer I appreciate what you're saying, but I think we need to understand that plant-hire contractors do have buy-back arrangements with manufacturers. In our particular case, although we have had this arrangement with other people, we have never invoked it. In terms of an arrangement it is nothing new. I was hoping that what you would be able to do would be to give us a guaranteed buy-back price now based on a percentage of the purchase price that you've quoted.

Buyer asks for a price now.

Salesman That, of course, we could do, and that I would be quite willing to do. I think, however, that the price which we would be liable to present to you would not be altogether acceptable. That is why I suggested the indepen-

Salesman stresses the disadvantages to the buyer of fixing a price now.

The discussion

Notes

dent assessment in two years' time. Because of all the improbables involved, such as type of conditions, type of operator, the economic situation, new machine introduction, government grant, etc., I don't think we could do you a fair job at this moment in time. I agree with you there are companies who do produce buy-back figures, but whether they are fair or whether they are trade allowances in another form is, as you know very well, another matter altogether.

Buyer What sort of figure are you thinking of?

Salesman Figure of what?

Buyer A buy-back figure. You say an independent valuation. Would you be prepared to accept that it would be either a certain figure or the valuation, whichever was the greater?

Buyer tries to get the best of both worlds.

Salesman Well, that doesn't really solve the problem. That safeguards your side but it doesn't safeguard my side. I think the independent valuation would be at market rate at the time. You have taken a forward view of the market as we have. At present there is a demand in the market, but whether in two years' time that's going to still be the same, or whether we'll be in recession, or whether we'll be in a buoyant situation is very difficult to say. What I'm trying to do is to produce the fairest situation for both of us. Our used-machinery division are selling at best prices and would be quite happy to buy at an independent market rate, and whether we really broke even on it, or in fact lost money, that's up to them. That really doesn't bother me. What does bother me is agreeing a price now.

Salesman senses that the buyer's position is not very strong and therefore presses his point home.

Buyer But you will be prepared to accept a completely independent valuation?

Salesman Yes, indeed.

Buyer And if we could get a better deal ourselves selling it off elsewhere that would be all right?

Salesman We would be very happy for you.

The discussion

Notes

Buyer   Then on that basis I think we can agree.

Buyer accepts salesman's proposal.

Salesman   Good. Now there are two other points I think that you mentioned at the beginning. We called them peripheral points but I think they are in fact quite important and quite difficult too. The first was this paint job. Of course we can do a livery job and indeed we do often do it, though naturally we normally charge for it. After all it means stopping the paint shop, cleaning the guns, and getting the whole thing set up.

One thing does occur to me. I was talking to my advertising manager the other day about this job and he was saying how interesting it would be, and I think for your PR people as well, if in trying to promote your corporate image and in trying to gain the public relations value that we want for this new machine, we were able to come to some arrangement whereby we could use the machines in your livery, in the local and national press, certainly in something like Contracts Journal, and generate PR value from it. If you could work that out with your advertising people I reckon I might be able to persuade our people to accept the paint job free of charge.

Salesman turns to:
Livery.

First, he makes it clear that a change is not as simple as it sounds.

Then he suggests a *quid pro quo*: the possibility of free painting in the new colours in exchange for joint PR.

Buyer   I think from your point of view that may seem relatively simple, Mr Edmunds. In fact it is asking quite a lot because, as a plant-hire organization, we have to be extremely careful in our relationship with the manufacturers that we are not seen to tie ourselves too closely to any one of them. I don't want us to get into a situation where we are badgered right, left and centre to take machines in exchange for free advertising. However, this point about corporate image could be — I'm not saying that it will be — but it could be of interest. What I would need to do is to talk to our own advertising manager to see how far he would be prepared to

Buyer stresses the problem it would create for his company, but recognizes the possible value of such an arrangement.

The discussion		Notes
Salesman	go along with it. But I certainly think it's an area that we could talk about. Good. Clearly, we would have to liaise on things like copy and both of us would want to make sure that we were getting from it what we wanted. I doubt whether that is such a serious problem. If you can arrange it, I will undertake to get the paint job through for you.	
Buyer	Well, let's put it this way. If we were to agree, it would be a major departure from policy. Consequently, I would need a commitment from you that subsequent machines would be painted in our livery free of charge.	Buyer seeks a long-term concession in return for joint PR.
Salesman	That, I think would have to follow. Now, the training is a very difficult one. I quite understand your desire to get it. Indeed, this is why I was wanting you to take the machines earlier. Let's see how this strikes you. You want your men on a special course for this machine, with no outsiders. You want it done certainly in early December, and you want it done with the necessary machines, all the equipment and everything else there, and with properly qualified trainers. Now, if you can get your people together, over a weekend, either Friday/Saturday or Saturday/Sunday (it's a two-day course), in Wolverhampton instead of Birmingham, then I will make sure that you have the whole of the centre to yourselves. We will provide the machines, lay on everything else that you need, give them a good time, and generally look after them. That way, I think that we could probably manage the training without too much trouble. That way, we wouldn't have to release that machine out, and getting hold of a machine of course is almost impossible. But do you think you could get them to come?	Salesman accepts. Salesman now turns to: *Training.* He offers to run a tailored course, but over a weekend. This will avoid having to make a lot of special arrangements and moving the equipment etc. out of the training centre.
Buyer	Oh there's no problem in getting them in. The problem is that if we get men in over the weekend, they are going to	Buyer asks for a reduced cost per head to compensate for overtime payments.

The discussion

Notes

want the rate for the job: time and a half Saturdays, double time Sundays. Now, in order to pay them that kind of money, I imagine you'd be quite prepared, particularly in view of the fact that you're using your centre over the weekends – which normally you don't do, so you're getting added mileage out of it – to come to some arrangement on the cost of carrying out this training? In other words, some form of reduction in the course fee per head would go some way to subsidising the cost of taking these men out of their normally free weekends?

Salesman Well, if we took Friday/Saturday that would mean your cost would not be quite so high, and your staffing is not quite so heavy at the beginning of December. If you could do that, then I think we could discount the costs of the training by 20 per cent. We would carry our own staff costs and we wouldn't make any extra charge for having the staff over the weekend. Yes, I think we could that for you.

Salesman offers a reduced fee if the buyer can agree to a course on a Friday and Saturday.

Buyer Well on that basis I would be very happy.

Buyer agrees.

Salesman So, if we take the parts stock: we will supply the 'C' class spares and take them back at the end of 12 months if you buy to the full recommended parts stock level on the 'A' and 'B' spares. On delivery, we will work on that slightly extended period so that we can fit it in with our availability of loading and we'll make sure the last machine is with you by end of first week in February.

Salesman now summarizes all the points that have been covered.

Buyer And all machines will be delivered free?

Salesman All machines delivered as they are already standing in the plant. No extra charge. On buy-back, we will take an independent valuation at the end of two years, if you still want it then.

Buyer We will both take an independent valuation!

Salesman Fine, in fact if you have an independent

The discussion

Notes

valuer, we will take his valuation. On paint: if you can get your advertising people to agree the PR usage, we will manage the paint job free. On training: if the two of us can agree a Saturday early in December, then we will provide the training with 20 per cent off our nominal charge. On that basis perhaps we ought to think about going ahead. As I said to you at the beginning, I'm very worried that with the production schedule going forward there could be problems if we don't sign up today. So do you think we can go ahead?

Buyer   I think so. There's one thing I would like to discuss with you before we make any full commitment and that is this. These are brand-new machines, brand-new models; this is the first time we shall have had them, the first time in fact anybody in the market has had them. You've also suggested this idea of joint advertising. I'm not a marketing man and you know this far better than I do, but I would imagine that if you're going to do that kind of mixed or joint advertising the last thing you can afford, having blown your trumpet, is to find that you've missed a few notes. That being the case I think it's important to both of us that, in addition to the things we've already agreed, we as a company should be upgraded to the level whereby if anything should go wrong in the field that our people can't cope with, you will give us the level of service that your grade 1 customers get. By that I mean that your people will come out at a moment's notice, day or night, seven days a week and put things right for us. Now if you can do that, I might well be in the position to get this pushed through quickly. Obviously this level of capital expenditure needs board approval, but if we could just add that to the package that we have agreed today, I think I could get it through by the weekend.

Salesman closes.

Seeing the salesman's desire to get the order, buyer throws in an unexpected demand: Service upgrading.

Buyer suggests that the order is there if only the salesman will accept this final request.

The discussion		**Notes**
	Mind you my managing director will take a pretty tough view of the agreement we've reached because he will probably feel that we might have been able to do better elsewhere.	
Salesman	So what you are asking us for is a special technical back-up support programme?	
Buyer	No, not a special one. Just the normal level of service enjoyed by your grade 1 customers.	Buyer emphasizes that other customers get it.
Salesman	Well, I will stick my neck out and agree to this order being classified as qualifying for grade 1 customer technical support service provided you can confirm in writing over the weekend, together with the arrangements about the parts spares, the joint publicity on the painting, and the training course. You will appreciate that in making this offer I am taking a considerable decision on behalf of our technical service director.	Salesman builds up the value and difficulty of the unexpected demand, though actual cost is small. Reluctantly agrees.
Buyer	Fine, Mr Edmunds, Subject to the board approval, which I do not feel will present any problems, I will send you confirmation of this order and the points we have agreed by Monday.	The deal is concluded.

Case study III: A negotiation between two skilled negotiators in the fashion industry

The commercial situation

The customer Paul Stoker owns a successful, rapidly expanding chain of boutiques in London. As a part of this development he plans a spectacular fashion show. For this event, and the business that he hopes will flow from it, he is negotiating a deal with 'OWN LABEL', a small competitive clothing manufacturer. Mr Stoker has done some business with Own Label in the past that has been highly profitable to him. He wants to obtain a range of well-designed garments but at very keen prices to keep profits as high as possible to offset the fashion show costs. He is glib and very sharp.

The seller Own Label's managing director is Des Dixon. Own Label's success is due to good design and careful budgeting. He combines flair with a fairly sound business approach. He prepares well, though he is flexible enough to alter plans on the evidence of changes in the market. He has supplied Paul Stoker in the past but they have been one-off deals. It would be an important breakthrough if he could become a preferred supplier of designer garments and ride on the success of the boutique's expanding reputation into a higher quality market. He has a small workforce that is enthusiastic, well paid and highly motivated to make Own Label successful.

Subsidiary negotiations Like any business, Own Label has its quota of human relations tensions that arise at any time. The case study includes a number of sub-negotiations which mirror real life situations with which the reader will be only too familiar: an inefficient travel agent making an error with one of Own Label's executive flights; the consequences for Own Label and their fabric supplier of a mistake in quality and colour of cloth delivered and the initial failure of the managing director to understand that his designer's concerns are not always solved with salary or bonus offers.

Customer's objectives	Seller's objectives
To obtain an initial supply of uniquely designed garments for the fashion show to be mounted by his London boutique and to ensure a guaranteed supply of the same merchandise thereafter for the whole season on the following terms:	To supply all the designer garments for Paul Stoker's newly expanded boutique and thereafter become his regular source of supply.

Customer's objectives

1 To obtain supply of full range of garments of minimum 9 000 to meet date of fashion show and opening of three new outlets.

2 To ensure continuity and reliable supply of garments after show but at reduced prices.

3 To obtain free delivery of garments on first order and all future business.

4 To obtain keen prices for initial supply of garments to offset cost of fashion show.

5 To ensure that Own Label keeps their head of design so that a flow of quality garments is assured.

6 To obtain big discount on all follow-up orders.

Seller's objectives

1 To obtain the highest prices to act as a cushion in case there are unforeseen problems in garment making causing production delays.

2 To obtain largest volume of initial order garments from the boutique's expansion into new outlets.

3 To emphasize the quality of Own Label's designs to distance it from Venti's the only other known competitor.

4 To obtain this business as a basis for taking Own Label into a higher quality, less price-sensitive market.

Characters in order of appearance

Des Dixon	– Managing Director of Own Label Garments
Brenda Whitehead	– Garment Supervisor of Own Label Garments
Frank Charnock	– Buyer for Own Label Garments
Russell Ormsby	– Designer for Own Label Garments
Sharon	– Managing Director's secretary of Own Label Garments
Dudley	– Management Trainee of Own Label Garments
Mary Forbes	– Head of Design of Own Label Garments
Caroline Chard	– Customer's Assistant
Paul Stoker	– Customer
On the telephone:	
Mr Lane	– Jumpjet Travel Clerk
Jeremy Saunders	– Jumpjet Travel Manager

The discussion

Managing Director

These six garment designs are excellent. They should fit the bill for our customer Paul Stoker's new little empire. What do you think, Brenda? Do they give you any problems? After all you've got to make them, or at least your girls have.

Supervising Garment Maker (Brenda)

None as far as I can see. The stuff our head of design produces never gives me any trouble. Certainly not if the

Notes

MD prepares ground work for negotiation by probing areas where difficulties could arise or there could be cost implications.

	The discussion	**Notes**
	fabric samples our buyer showed me are anything to go by. Oh good, he's just getting out of his car and it looks as though he's got the samples with him.	
M.D. to Buyer	We were just talking about your fabrics, Frank. Have you brought them?	
Buyer	Yes, here they are. You can show the samples to Paul Stoker. As you can see and feel for yourself, it's good stuff.	Quality factor to build into negotiation.
M.D.	I can see that.	
Buyer	So it should be, with what I had to pay for it.	Price implication sign in this comment.
M.D.	You always do like value for money don't you. I always think that's a wonderful trait in a buyer. However, it's quite a light fabric, Brenda. You sure it doesn't give any extra problems?	Buyer's comment signals that fabric is expensive so double checks on garment make-up problems.
Supervising Garment Maker	Well it will take a bit longer to machine and press than a heavier fabric, but I've allowed for that in the costs breakdown I gave you.	Negotiation points here to stress to customer; need to check that cost breakdowns are accurate.
M.D.	Fine. So there are no problems on the make-up and design side. All we've got to do now is to convince our customer, Paul Stoker. Thanks everybody.	
Designer 1 (Russell Ormsby)	Mr Dixon – could I come back to your office. I would like a word with you, if I may?	
M.D.	Yes, Russell?	
Designer 1	Well, you know that Mary Forbes, our head of design is thinking of leaving. She has not been happy here for quite a while, I've done my best to jolly her along, but . . .	Opening statement to start negotiating a job promotion.
M.D.	Is she? I certainly didn't know that. Well?	
Designer 1	Well, if she did go . . . Where would that leave me?	
M.D.	How do you mean?	
Designer 1	Well, would I be considered for the job? After all I have been here *four years*, you know. It's quite a long time in the fashion business.	Question designed to find out what his chances of promotion are.
M.D.	Four years is it? That is a long time. Almost too . . . Look I have got to get ready for the Paul Stoker meeting. He will be here soon. We'll talk about your future with us some other time.	Clever response to avoid making promises and to weaken designer's case.

	The discussion	Notes
M.D.'s Secretary	Dudley you may be the management trainee, but I must get on. The MD will be here any minute. Although the meeting today should be all right. After all, he and our largest customer are old friends, aren't they?	Dangerous assumption that friendship makes negotiation easier.
Management Trainee	That may have been once, before Stoker moved up in the world. What was it that *Fashion* described him as? 'From rag-trade cowboy to top chain-store buyer. The remarkable success story of Paul H. Stoker'. He and our MD may be old buddies – but Stoker's top dog now and he knows it and is going to use that power. You see if I'm not right.	
M.D.'s Secretary	Please put those press reports down. I have just put them into chronological order so that the MD can brief himself about Stylarama, the new outlets Stoker has taken over. Oh here comes Mr Dixon now so please make yourself scarce.	Indication of MD's preparation.
Head of Design (Mary Forbes)	Mr Dixon, if you're not too busy, could I see you for a minute?	
M.D.	Yes of course. I am doing a bit of homework about Stylarama. Our friend Stoker is going to need something a bit special to live up to all this publicity he's been getting.	MD makes mistake of talking about his needs first instead of asking questions to find out what is on mind of head of design.
Head of Design	Well he's going to get something more than a bit special from us isn't he? At least, I think so.	
M.D.	So do I. Those designs of yours could be crucial for his grand opening of the new division. We have got to pull out all the stops. You know we were second choice?	Proposals are going to be compared with at least one competitive tender.
Head of Design	No. That's news to me. Where did you hear that?	
M.D.	Oh, yes. He had a deal with Veniti's of Rome, but they let him down at the last moment. I have my sources. Anyway is that all? Are you all right?	Wise not to assume that competitor is out of the race.
Head of Design	I'm not ill. But you see, it's not . . .	MD should have continued listening.
M.D.	You're a good designer and I don't pay you enough. Don't say it. I know that you could probably do better elsewhere, but don't worry. I'm thinking of a really bumper bonus for you on this job.	

	The discussion	**Notes**
Head of Design	Great. But the important thing for me . . .	
M.D.	. . . is what's important to us all. I know, you want money in the bank. I'll be honest. I need you and if this Stoker business takes off you can name your own price.	Don't assume that other people's needs are the same as yours.
Head of Design	Mr Dixon that's not important. You just don't understand, do you?	
M.D.	Since when was money not important? Listen Mary. All I understand right now is that a deal with Paul Stoker is going to mean a huge step forward for 'Own Label Garments' and if we blow it, well – we could be a second-division player in the fashion business for ever.	

Paul Stoker – customer – and his assistant driving to Own Label Garments meeting

Assistant	Are you sure 'Own Label' are up to the job?	
Customer	Yes, positive. They are not only good, they're dependable. Dixon's people won't let us down like those Italians.	Preferences for one of competitors indicated
Assistant	Does Dixon know that?	
Customer	I sincerely hope not. There are some things it's better for him not to know. If he is going to save our bacon for the Stylarama opening, I'd rather that he's kept in blissful ignorance.	Customer not wanting to give one potential supplier a clue that he has the edge over competitive offerings.
Assistant	And what about the three extra outlets you've been given? Does he know about them?	
Customer	Good heavens, no! If Des Dixon knew that at this stage, he'd know how much stock I need.	
Assistant	So, what's wrong with him knowing that?	
Customer	It'd cost me. On the other hand, if he puts pressure on me to take more than he thinks I need, well I might reluctantly have to cave in, mightn't I! But at a reduced price of course. Now listen, when I ask you at the meeting – you're not going to be happy with designs, understand?	Customer avoids danger of compromising his business objectives. Prepares respective roles of him and his assistant.
Assistant	Okay. But it may be that I really might not like them. What then?	

	The discussion	**Notes**
Customer	I think you will. Their head of design is a cracker. Her designs could be very helpful to us when we're up and running, not to mention getting us started.	
Assistant	Word has it in the trade that she is unhappy and might be on the move.	
Customer	I have heard that too. I just hope Dixon can keep her, that's all. It'd be a bad day for 'Own Label' if she left and I'd hate to see Des Dixon in trouble. Or me for that matter.	This could be an important point in the negotiation, more important than price considerations.

A telephone conversation between 'Own Label's' buyer, Frank Charnock, and a clerk in their travel agent's office

Buyer	Frank Charnock, 'Own Label Garments' speaking. The man whose buying trip to Germany you fouled up.	Buyer adopts a hostile initial stance.
Jumpjet Clerk	Oh, yes Mr Charnock. There was some mix-up over the dates of your flight, I believe.	Seller avoids starting an argument over buyer's barbed criticism.
Buyer	Not from my end there wasn't, as you well know. Your 'mix-up' as you call it, and I would emphasize your, has lost my company a great deal of money in lost orders. Yet in your letter to me, you refuse point-blank to make any sort of reparation.	Buyer's remarks indicate his annoyance rather than desire to deliberately disconcert seller.
Jumpjet Clerk	As I explained in my letter, Mr Charnock, it's not company policy for us to pay compensation.	
Buyer	Are you saying that you don't have the authority to offer it?	Buyer testing negotiating authority of seller.
Jumpjet Clerk	Well, yes.	
Buyer	Then you had better put me on to someone who has.	
Jumpjet Clerk	I'm quite sure I can handle this matter for you myself Mr Charnock.	
Buyer	I see. And you can handle your bosses when you have to explain how you've lost them my company's business?	Buyer puts seller on the spot.
Jumpjet Clerk	Mr Charnock could you wait just a moment.	
Jumpjet Manager	Hello, Mr Charnock. Jeremy Saunders here, customer liaison manager. I know about the problem of your German flight and you have my sincere apologies.	Seller reacts calmly.

	The discussion	**Notes**
Buyer	Well the question is: What are you going to do about it?	
Jumpjet Manager	What are you suggesting we do?	Good approach to ask open-ended question.
Buyer	I'm suggesting that if you want to keep my company's travel business which last year was over £285 000 ($498 750), you're going to have to offset our losses over this. It has cost us a great deal of money in lost orders.	Buyer spells out his initial negotiating position, which has probably been slightly exaggerated.
Jumpjet Manager	Yes, it's all very regrettable, Mr Charnock, but you have my firm's assurance that it won't happen again.	
Buyer	That is hardly relevant is it, if I take my company's business elsewhere. I've got half-a-dozen buying trips in the pipeline, and before I decide who to book them with, I want to know what you are going to do to compensate us over this Germany fiasco.	Buyer indicates the loss the seller could face; unless valued concessions are offered to him.
Jumpjet Manager	Well, I'm afraid a cash payment is genuinely out of the question. But I am going to stick my neck out and offer you something which I think you will find equally attractive.	Seller trades up value of a possible concession that will cost less than cash compensation.
Buyer	Such as?	
Jumpjet Manager	Well, these trips you are planning. If you were to book them all with us, I think I could offer you a discount of say, 5 per cent on the air fares.	Seller makes an offer to test buyer's reaction.
Buyer	You are giving me nothing. I can get that at Retfords Travel. And in any case, the air fares are not going to add up to much because the trips in question are mainly in Europe. You are not at first base yet.	Buyer minimizes value of concession, putting seller under pressure to improve offer.
Jumpjet Manager	Well we might also be able to offer you a discount on hotel bills.	
Buyer	That begins to sound a bit more like it. If you were to offer, say, a 10 per cent discount on air fares and hotel bills, I might be tempted to guarantee you my next six bookings.	Buyer asks for high level of discount.
Jumpjet Manager	We couldn't offer that sort of discount on hotels, I'm afraid.	
Buyer	But you could on air fares?	
Jumpjet Manager	Possibly	
Buyer	And what sort of discount *could* you offer on hotels?	
Jumpjet Manager	Certainly no more than 5 per cent.	

The discussion		Notes
Buyer	That might be acceptable. Let's see. To save our business you'd be able to knock 10 per cent off air travel, and 5 per cent off hotel bills *for all our future bookings?*	It should have been seller who summarized deal at this stage not the buyer.
Jumpjet Manager	No. Just off the next six provided you gave us guarantees that *all six* were booked through us.	Seller avoids being forced to concede on future business.
Buyer	And what about any future business I might put your way?	
Jumpjet Manager	Well, we'd have to see what we could do for you then.	Again seller avoids being forced to concede future business.
Buyer	Very well then, if you will confirm those discounts on both air fares and hotels in writing, I'll send you provisional details of the six trips.	Should be seller not buyer who summarizes what has been agreed.
Jumpjet Manager	Good, I will do that today. Now tell me Mr Charnock, are you married?	
Buyer	Yes, I am. Why?	
Jumpjet Manager	Well, if Mrs Charnock cared to accompany you on one of your trips, we'd be more than happy to provide an air ticket for her, with our compliments.	Excellent way of cementing good relations for future business.
Buyer	That's very civil of you.	
Jumpjet Manager	And we'd be only too happy to extend our discount on hotel bills to her as well.	
Buyer	Thank you very much	
Jumpjet Manager	Not at all. Just a little gesture of appreciation to a valued customer. Please let me know when your wife would like to travel with you and I will see to it personally. Goodbye Mr Charnock.	Seller's perceived high-value concession that probably does not cost much means that this, rather than the mistake over the original flight, is remembered by buyer.
Buyer	(Putting the phone down) says to himself: Well, well, well. That was a much better outcome than I could have hoped for. Let's hope our managing director can do as well out of Paul Stoker today.	

Meeting in managing director's office, present MD, customer and his assistant. Designs of Own Label are being studied

Customer	Hmm . . . Mary seems to be losing her touch a bit.	A series of rather exaggerated initial stances by customer and MD to pull each other out of position.
MD	And yet just a moment ago you were telling me that I'd be a fool to let her go.	

	The discussion	**Notes**
Customer	Well, we all have our off-days, I suppose, but these colours! I've never liked blue much.	
MD	It looks alright on Caroline (customer's assistant).	
Customer	Ah, but *royal* blue's different isn't it. Now these designs, what other colours are you offering?	
MD	For your grand opening – none. It's only eight weeks away, remember. And of course we're having that cloth *specially* for those designs.	MD stresses that designs are special to enhance value to customer.
Customer	So for the time being, what you are saying is that it's this colour or nothing. That could be quite a problem. What do you make of these, Caroline?	Customer tries to diminish value and introduces a tactic planned before the meeting.
Customer's assistant	Frankly, not a lot. I don't think they're up to the standard we want for Stylarama. I think that we may be wasting our time here.	
Customer	Well, I don't think that I'd go that far. But I've a number of reservations.	
MD	Fine. Then why don't you spell them out. You're among friends.	MD keeps calm and seeks to have the customer's shopping list spelt out.
Customer	Well, colour for a start. If you are saying it's this or nothing for the grand opening, then I suppose I have to accept or not. But there would have to be colour variations afterwards.	
MD	We can talk about that. Now what other problems have you got?	MD continues probing to make sure total shopping list is out in open.
Customer	Well, there is Caroline's view that we are wasting our time here. She has to be persuaded that I am making the right decision, that is if we make any decisions today.	
MD	Well, you are the boss so that should not be too difficult should it?	A comment that could put the customer's back up.
Customer	You don't know Caroline, I don't want my right-hand man or should I say woman feeling that we would be wrong. Still, supposing, and I mean just supposing, that we *did* decide to take these or some of the designs. What sort of figure did you have in mind?	Buying signal.
MD	Well, obviously that would depend on the quantity.	
Customer	Which would depend on how many I could afford on my very tight budget. So let's talk price.	Customer indicates that he is looking for some price bargaining.

The discussion	Notes
MD Let's talk *price* and *quantity*. There are six designs, right? Two dresses, two tops, the trousers and the skirt. Now if you were to take 2 000 of each design – that's 12 000 garments in all, I could let you have the dresses for £35 ($61.25) a piece, and the separates at £22 ($38.50).	MD links quantity and price and aims high on both.
Customer Please do me a favour, £35 and £22? It's not silk we are talking about you know.	Customer attempts to rubbish these prices by ridiculing them.
MD It is a lovely fabric, you have to agree and specifically printed for you for those designs.	
Customer Pity about the colour. Our deal could founder on that.	
MD At that price, I should think that we could offer one alternative colour.	MD keeps *basis* of the negotiations going with an offer.
Customer At that price, you should be able to offer me the whole 'Dulux' range. Still, I might be willing to accept just the one colour alternative at £28 ($49) for the dresses and £17 ($29.75) the separates. But only for 9 000 garments.	Customer reveals his counter-offer on prices and the gap between two sides is out in open for a point-of-balance to be agreed – but not yet.
MD You know that 9 000 hardly constitutes a production run, does it? Certainly not over six different garments. The only way that I could justify it would be to knock it down to, say, four designs. And even then it would be an expensive business for me. Maybe one that we don't want either.	MD tests situation by seeking a concession to get away from reducing production run.
Customer But just think, it would be moving you up market though, wouldn't it and there would be the spin off from other customers. Do you want to stay in the second division all your life?	Customer ignores this concession requires and dangles better price margins from higher quality market.
MD We do all right in our existing markets. It beats going bankrupt, giving stuff away to you.	
Customer I could always find you a job with us as a floor-walker. But listen – let's say for the sake of argument that I took the 12 000.	Customer appears to be moving towards MD's position
MD In four styles or six?	
Customer Let's say six, or better still, let's say five, losing one of the tops. That way saves you a production run and makes things a lot easier for you. So I would	Seller now has a picture of production and financial implications of customer's statement and where a point-of-agreement might be.

	The discussion	**Notes**
	take the 12 000 but I wouldn't pay more than £28 ($49) and £17 ($52.50).	
MD	That's much, much too low. I might be able to get it down to £30 ($52.50) and £20 ($35), but the only way I could do that for you would be on 15 000 garments.	MD makes counter-proposals – a clue to his settling price.
Customer	15 000? How many outlets do you think I've got? We're not Marks & Spencer.	
MD	Well then, the alternative would be cutting down on the quality that distinguishes these designs. The velvet trims would have to go for a start and that would spoil the whole balance.	MD proposes a change that would not be attractive to sell.
Customer	What do you think, Caroline?	
Customer's assistant	Well, you know that I'm not crazy about the designs as they are now. Any cutback on the quality, and I think I'd like them even less. But 15 000 garments! That's an awful lot to shift.	Customer uses assistant's arranged response as a foil to reduce perceived value of Own Label's offerings.
Customer	And on top of that then there's delivery costs. I take it you would deliver that amount *free*?	
MD	You have to remember, it's not as if Stylarama is even a regular customer of ours.	Don't give a concession like this without something back in return.
Customer	Take it from me. If we can reach a sensible deal here, I'll be putting lots more work your way. We'll be regular all right.	
MD	Well, if that were the case, then I might be able to offer you free delivery but it would still depend on how quickly you wanted the items.	Free delivery now being tied to commitment from customer.
Customer	I would want 9 000 for the grand opening in eight weeks.	
MD	Let's make a few notes. Fabric here in four weeks. That's 2 000 week plus. Yes? If we are talking about five designs – no problem.	MD starts to write down shape of deal that is now coming together.
Customer	And the rest two weeks later.	
MD	That might be pushing it.	
Customer	It's you, remember, who's trying to push us into taking 15 000. I'd be happy with just 9 000.	
MD	If we pull out all the stops for you it will mean overtime putting the cost back up for us.	MD highlights cost to him of what he is offering to do.
Customer	Alright then: 9 000 for the grand open-	

	The discussion	**Notes**
	ing, another 3 000 within two weeks and the remaining 3 000 – say, two weeks after that.	
MD	Yes, that sounds better. Now on that basis I would be prepared to write off delivery charges just this once.	
Customer	Let me just see how this looks in black and white. I'm prepared to take five of these designs – 3 000 of each design at £30 ($52.50) each dress and £20 ($35) for separates. No economies on trimmings and one alternative colour.	Customer spells out the package thus far as he sees it.
MD	Right. And I am prepared to deliver them free on the basis of 9 000 inside eight weeks, 3 000 two weeks after that and the rest two weeks after that.	MD confirms agreement of package noted down by customer.
Customer	I think that we're getting there wouldn't you say. Oh, except for just a couple of minor points that should not present any difficulty.	MD beware! What's coming now?
MD	Oh, yes. What are they?	
Customer	Don't worry nothing contentious. For each design I want 40 per cent medium, 30 per cent in small and 30 per cent large.	
MD	Of course. That's one point. What was the second minor point?	MD makes sure other point is brought out.
Customer	Oh, its just repeat orders although I don't expect that there'll be any, since you are snowing me under with the damned things. But we might as well cover ourselves. Shall we say, seeing it's you a 10 per cent discount?	'Carrot' of possible repeat orders a signal that customer is almost ready to do deal.
MD	Come on! Let's say the usual 4 per cent.	
Customer	Split the difference then, 7 per cent on the off-chance of there being any repeat orders – though how I'm going to shift what I've got is beyond me.	Customer tries to reduce value to him of 4 per cent and makes counter-proposal.
MD	If the past is any judge you usually manage. Alright, 7 per cent.	Hope MD has calculated cost of 7 per cent discount?
Customer	Then I think we are in business. That's a deal apart from one last thing. You hold on to Mary that design genius of yours.	
MD	I'll do my best. Right I will get my secretary to type up the contract on the basis of the terms we have agreed today and you should have it in the next	The deal is concluded and decision on discarding one design beginning of business – a commitment.

294

The discussion	Notes

couple of days. Now if you first decide which top design you want to lose, then I think we have achieved what we set out to do today.

The customer and his assistant walk back to their car with a final comment from:

Customer Caroline, it looks as if we might have some cheap stock for the follow-on business for our new outlets with those 7 per cent discounts. A very satisfying deal I think.

Customer feels that he has done a good deal.

A telephone call from the management trainee to the buyer.

Management Trainee Ah, Mr Charnock. Some good news. The fabric for the Stoker designs has arrived. It is just being unloaded.

Buyer Excellent. They said that they could do it in four weeks, and that's bang on schedule. Let the managing director know, will you please.

Management Trainee I've left a message with his secretary. The MD is tied up in another meeting with Paul Stoker. More good news. I gather he's planning to put some more work our way.

Buyer That sounds good. Now can you meet me in five minutes at the warehouse to have a look at this fabric.

In the managing director's office: meeting between customer Paul Stoker and MD

Customer So do you think you could get me some new designs together based on these lines?

MD Of course. I'll get Mary working on some ideas straight away. By the way she decided to stay with us.

Customer You're a lucky man. So all this was just a nine-day wonder, eh? Just a little ploy to put up her salary.

MD No, far from it. I tried to put up her money, and her bonuses – but would you believe it – she wasn't really interested. Do you know what she wanted?

MD learned a lesson about people's emotions and needs. Don't assume – get the facts.

The discussion   **Notes**

	Time off. A holiday. A bit of extra help in the office. She was just shattered, that's all. Over-worked.
Customer	And she never said anything to you?
MD	No. Mind you – I have to admit I never asked. Anyway, the problem is solved. She's had her break and I am going to sort out some extra staff for her. Let's go and have some lunch.
MD's Secretary	Before you go Mr Dixon, Mr Charnock is on the phone and wants to speak to you.
Buyer	We've got a disaster on our hands. I think you'd better come down to the warehouse right away.
MD	But, I can't do that, I've got Paul Stoker with me.
Buyer	Well, this concerns him so don't let him go. And I'm not exaggerating, it's big trouble.
MD	Right I'm on my way. (to Mr Stoker) Could I leave you here for a few minutes Mr Stoker. There's a little matter I've just got to resolve. Shouldn't take long.

At the warehouse: MD, buyer and management trainee

Buyer	I'm glad you've got here. Look that's the fabric Bellard's have sent us for the new Stoker designs. It's not the stuff we ordered.	All negotiations should have a contingency plan – 'What if . . . happens?' What would we do?
MD	It certainly is not, so get on to them and tell them to print the right stuff and in double quick time.	
Buyer	I have already done that. They admit it's their cock-up, but they can't print what we ordered in time for the grand opening.	
MD	So it boils down to this. If Paul Stoker is going to have those garments for the opening this is the fabric he's got to have.	
Buyer	It's worse than that. It is not only the wrong colour, it's the wrong pattern and the fabric is a different weight! But this is a better quality than the other stuff we ordered.	Any possible areas where concessions could be offered?
MD	Never mind about that. If Stoker finds	

The discussion		**Notes**
	out he'll crucify me. What am I saying – it's 'When?' not 'If!' Even if I could persuade Stoker to take it, there's no guarantee that this fabric will work with Mary's designs.	
Management Trainee	Mr Dixon, I don't think that would be too much of a problem. Remember I did study design in my degree course. Slightly fuller skirts, a few minor changes to the trimmings, these few minor changes should work alright with our original designs.	
MD	They had better otherwise we can say goodbye to Paul Stoker's business. Now listen. Tell our head of design to get down here straight away. Then collect Paul Stoker from my office and take him to Gino's where we have a table booked for lunch and I'll join you as soon as I can.	When you need time to think out a new approach, – MD took one approach; another is to use telephone.
Buyer	If Stoker does take this fabric, the time we'll lose on the cutting, we should make up on the machine and pressing. It's good stuff to work with.	
MD	But it must be a lot more expensive than the other fabric.	
Buyer	It won't be after I've finished with Bellard's. They will be begging us to take it off their hands at a knock down sale price – if they want to keep our business.	Reduced price on higher quality fabric provides ingredients for negotiation to get back on track.

In the managing director's office with MD and head of design and joined by Paul Stoker

Customer	What happened to *you*, then? We did not wait but had lunch.	
MD	Sorry about that, something cropped up that had to be sorted out at once. I hope young Dudley looked after you all right?	
Customer	Yes, bright young man. A bit loose with his mouth though. What's all this I hear about some super-grade fabric you've been keeping from me. I don't call that very friendly at all. You might at least have shown it to me.	
MD	Well, eh … oh, you mean this. It's only just arrived. I would have men-	

The discussion		Notes
	tioned it to you seeing that you weren't too happy with the blue material. But we weren't really expecting it so soon.	
Customer	It's alright this, who's it for?	
MD	Well, I could possibly let you have it. But as I said I wasn't really expecting it in. But if you are really interested we would ask Mary if it might be possible to amend her designs a bit.	MD does not appear *too* eager which might upset the delicate and weak position he is in.
Customer	Do you mean for the grand opening?	
MD	Well, just to offer you an alternative if you might want one, especially as your assistant, whose opinion you value so highly, was so definite.	
Customer	Hmm . . . I might well be interested. What sort of changes would it mean, Mary?	
Head of Design	Nothing too horrendous. Just a couple of the trims and a bit of a change to the skirts.	
Customer	It's much better stuff than the other.	
MD	So it should be, its more expensive certainly.	MD enhances the value to the customer of this new fabric.
Customer	Oh yes? Remember we've agreed a deal already.	
MD	Yes. I just thought you might be interested, that's all.	
Customer	How much?	
MD	Well, if we kept all the other details as per – I could probably do the dresses at . . . £32 ($56) and the separates at £22 ($38.50).	MD aims high on prices at just below his original offer made at start of negotiations.
Customer	Not interested. Now if you could do it for the same price as the other . . .	
MD	Then I'd be losing money. It's much better material, as you've said.	
Customer	Easier to work though. That would save you a bit on production costs.	
MD	Not that much I'm afraid. Mind you, if you could manage without a colour variation.	MD looking for a variable.
Customer	I might at £30 ($52.50) and £20 ($35).	
MD	Alright £30 and £20. So, exactly the same deal as the other but no colour variation.	This is a good deal for MD. He will save on costs twice.
Customer	15 000 garments in five designs. 9 000 for the opening, 3 000 two weeks after that, and the last 3 000 a fortnight later – delivery free. And I'll want to see	Deal is once again concluded; satisfactorily from customer's viewpoint.

The discussion   **Notes**

	exactly what design changes Mary's made before I finally agree.
MD	Of course. When could you be finished by, Mary?
Head of Design	I could have them by tomorrow and we could send Dudley over to you with them.
Customer	Right. It will give me a chance to thank that young man when I see him. But for him . . . oh I must get a move on I've got a train to catch. And we'll talk about those future plans at some other time. Goodbye.
MD	I must have words with Dudley too. Mary how would you fancy him working in the design office, doing some of the donkey-work?
Head of Design	All right by me. He's a bright kid and some of his design ideas are all right too.
MD	Good. I will get my secretary to find him and get it all tied up today.

. . . ends

Recommended reading and viewing

Communication

Braysich, J. (1979), *Body Language: A Handbook*, Australia: Braysich Enterprises.

Lidstone, J. (1985), *Making Effective Presentations* (Audio manual), Aldershot: Gower.

Pease, A. (1981), *Body Language*, London: Sheldon Press.

Negotiation

Fisher, R. and Ury, W. (1986), *Getting to Yes: Negotiating Agreement Without Giving In*: Business Books.

Hawver, D.A. (1984), *How to Improve your Negotiation Skills*, USA: Alexander Hamilton Institute Inc.

March, R. (1989), *The Japanese Negotiator*: Kodansha International.

Finance

International Labour Office, Geneva — *How to Read a Balance Sheet.*

Jay, A. (1977), *The Balance Sheet Barrier*: Video Arts.

Film

Video Arts — *Negotiating Profitable Sales*, (Part I, 'The Preparation' Part II 'The Negotiation') film based on John Lidstone's book of same title: Gower 1977; also booklet of same title written for film by John Lidstone: 1979.

The Open College — *Reaching Agreement*: Comprising Workbook, Assignment booklet and Video of 'Own Label': Negotiation Technical Adviser John Lidstone.

Index

Accounts, 11–17
Achievers, 121
Action programmes, 154–5, 156, 160, 171
Administration, costs of, 27–8
Advertising, 4, 136
Agendas, 89
Agreement(s)
  assessment of likely point of, 84–5
  on price levels, 97
  recording of, 75–6, 89, 131
  types of 61–2
Agricultural industry, 30–31
Allocation of costs, 40–41
Alternative closes, 71
Appropriation accounts, 16
Argyle, Michael, 180
Assessment and evaluation of negotiation, 245–7
Assets
  in balance sheet, 12
  reduction of, 28
Attention, physical and psychological, 179–83
'Attractive extras' in negotiation, 81
Audience see Listening
Autocracy, 122

Background questions, 68
Balance sheets, 11, 12–15
Barriers to communication, 177–9, 219–22
Belonging and learning, 223
Benefit analysis sheets, 69
Benevolent autocracy, 122
Body language, 181, 185–7, 214
  eye contact, 180, 191–3, 227
  hand movements, 194–8
  head movements, 199–200
  by posture, 207–13
  to show concern for time, 187–9
  while seated, 200–4
  with spectacles, 207
  while standing, 205–6
  while telephone answering, 189–91
Bottom-up style of management, 122
Breakdown and deadlock, avoidance of, 88, 129
Break-even charts, 41–8
Brewing industry, 3–4
Business cycle, 13
Buyers see Customers
Buying process, 64–5, 70

Capital equipment, 31
  negotiation case study in, 253–65, 267–81
Capitulation, 61
Car industry, 2, 3
Case studies in negotiation
  in fashion business, 283–99
  in plant and plant hire business, 253–65, 267–81
Cash flow, 23–4
Cathartic communication, 181
Celebrations, post-negotiation, premature, 89
Checklist opening technique, 231
Chemical industry, 42
'Closed' questions, 66–7
Closing
  of a presentation, 236–7
  techniques for, 70, 71, 89
Clothes, personal, 227
Collaborative agreements, 61–2
Commitment, asking for, 236–7
Committee style of management, 122
Communication
  barriers to, 177–9, 219–22
  improvements in, 179–83, 222–4
  see also Body language; Listening; Presentations
Competition and competitors, 1–3, 4
  awareness of, 35–6
  in negotiation, 81, 147, 148, 167–8
Compliments, 231
Concessions
  costs and value of, 82–3
  'enhancing' of, 73, 128–9, 130–1
  trading of, 86–7, 129, 130
Concluding see Closing
Conduct
  of negotiation, 127–40
  preparation for, 86–9
  of a presentation, 229–39
Contribution system, 41
Cooperative advertising, 136
'Cost plus' pricing, 44
Costs, 1, 10–11
  allocation of, 40–41
  and break-even charts, 41–8
  of concessions, 73, 82–3, 91–117, 128–31
  customers', reduction of, 27–8
  definition of, 39–40
Courses and workshops in negotiation, 241–7
Credit periods, 103–6, 133

Curiosity, 230–1
Current assets, 11
Current liabilities, 13
Customers and buyers
    behaviour of, 119–26
    decision-making by, 2, 4, 9, 31
    financial knowledge about, use of, 27–37
    in large companies, 3–4
    and 'marketing concept', 1, 5
    see also Negotiation; Presentation

'Dead-end' questions, 66–7
Deadlock and breakdown, avoidance of, 88, 129
Decision groups, 123
Delivery, negotiation about, 106–7, 134, 135
Democratic leadership, 122
Demonstrations, physical, 233
Design of mass-produced goods, 2
Dictatorship leadership style, 122
Direct request closes, 71
Disagreement, 88
Distractions, 178, 179
Distribution
    costs of, 1, 27, 42, 106
    example of profitability ratios in, 20–21
    takovers of outlets for, 4
Distributive agreement, 61
Divisive agreements, 61
Dramatic openings, 230

Economic changes, effects of, 36
Eden, Anthony, 178
Effect, learning, 223
Electrical goods industry, 2
Emerson, Ralph Waldo, 178–9
Environment summary, 144, 146–7, 166–7
'Essential' elements in negotiation, 81
European Economic Community, 3
Evaluation and assessment of negotiation, 245–7
Expert power, 123–4
External courses in negotiation, 241–3
Eye contact, 180, 191–3, 227

Failure avoiders, 121
Fall-back position, 74, 81, 83
Fashion business, 283–99
Finance of a business, 9
    and costing, 39–48
    customers', analysis of, 27–37
    measurement of, 17–24
    operation of, 10–11
    recording of, 11–17
Financial item gaps, 72
'Financial merchandising, 31–4
Fixed assets, 12
Fixed costs, 39–40, 41
Forward association, 223

Gestures, 227, 233
    see also Body Language
Government legislation, 36
Grocery industry, 28–9, 30
Group presentations see Presentations

Hand body language, 194–8
Harvey-Jones, Sir John, 55, 61
Head body language, 199–200
Historical trading analysis, 144, 145, 165–6
Honesty in negotiation, 88
Hotel industry, 3
Howlett, William, 9

Imitation of products and services, 1–3, 9
In-company workshops in negotiation, 243–6
Industrial buying process, 64–5, 70
Industrial machinery, 31
    negotiation case study in, 253–65, 267–81
Inflexibility, 129
Informative communication, 181
Initial stances, 127–8
Integrative agreement, 61–2
Integrity in negotiation, 88
Inter-active listening, 182–3
Interest payments, 10, 102–3, 104
Inventory see Stocks

Jargon, 221

Leadership styles, 122
Learning process, 222–4
Legislation, awareness of effects of, 36
Levitt, Theodore, 217
Liabilities in balance sheet, 12–13
Liquidity, 15
Listening
    effective, 177–84
    at a presentation, 225–8
Long-term liabilities, 13

Management accounts, 11–17
Management styles, 122
Mannerisms, 227
    see also Body Language
Manufacturers
    example of profitability ratios of, 20–21
    marketing environment of, 1–3, 4
'Marginal costing', 46
Margins, 4, 10, 92, 93
'Market' approach to pricing, 45
Marketing environment, 1–3, 4, 35
Marks and Spencer plc, 4
Maslow, A. H., 120
Meetings for negotiation, 74–5
    see also Presentations
Merchandising, 135–6
    financial, 31–4

Mergers and takeovers, 1, 3–4, 9
Mix of products, 99–100
Motivation, theory of, 120
Multinational companies, 2, 3

Needs
    hierarchy of, 120–21
    identification and awareness of, 68, 73, 78, 79–80,
        225–6, 231–2
Negotiation
    case studies of
        in fashion business, 283–99
        in plant and plant hire business, 253–65, 267–81
    conduct of, 127–40
    preparation for, 73, 77–89, 141–60
    principles of, 62, 72–6, 116–17
    relation of, to selling, 57–63, 75
    and selling skills, 65, 67–8, 69
    training in, 241–7
    worked example of, 163–71
    see also Concessions; Presentations
Negotiators, 73–4, 88, 119–20
'Net asset' format of balance sheets, 15
New technology, 36
Non-verbal communication see Body language
Note-taking, 75–6, 89, 131

Objections, dealing with, 70, 235–6
Objectives
    in negotiation, 77–9, 157
    in presentations, 229–36
    of sales volume, 151–2, 169
Observer role, 88
'Open' questions, 66
Opening techniques
    in negotiations, 84–5, 87, 127–8
    in presentations, 229–32
    in sales meeting, 65–6
Operational item gaps, 72
Organizational profiles, 122, 124–5
Output and productivity, 10–11
'Overheads', 39–40
'Own label' products, 2

Packaging, 2, 134, 136
Participative autocracy, 122
Pay negotiations, 128
Performance of a business, 9–10
    and costing, 39–48
    customers', assessment of, 27–37
    measurement of, 17–24
    recording of, 11–17
Persuasive communication, 181
Phased price increases, 97
Planning and Preparation
    for negotiation, 73, 77–89
    format for, 141–60

worked example of, 163–71
    for a presentation, 215–18, 228–9
Plant and Plant Hire business, 253–65, 267–81
Position power, 123
Posture and body language, 207–13
Power in companies, 123–4
Preconceptions and prejudice, 178, 221
Preparation see Planning
Presentations
    conduct of, 229–39
    planning for, 215–18, 228–9
    of products and services, 2, 4, 69–70
Prices and Pricing, 2
    'cost plus' and 'market' approaches to, 44–5
    costs of concessions in, 91–5
    as negotiating gap, 72, 132, 135
    timing of increases in, 96–7
Priorities and Problems, questioning for, 68
Productivity, 10–11
Production, costs of, 1, 10–11, 27
Products
    allocation of costs to, 40–41
    range and mix of, 98–100, 136
    similarities of, 1–2
Profit and Profitability
    and break-even charts, 41–8
    and cash flow, 23–4
    and concessions, 92, 93, 95, 99, 101–2
    importance of, 4
    margins of, 4, 10, 92, 93
    ratios of, 18–22, 27–9
Profit and Loss Account, 11, 15–17

Quality, 132
Quantifiable elements in negotiation, 72, 80–81
Questioning techniques, 66–8
Quotation closes, 71

Range of products, 98, 136
Rapport, development of, 231
Ratios of profitability, 18–22
    use of, 27–9
Rehearsal of negotiation, 88
Repetition and learning, 223
Return on Capital employed ratio, 18, 19–22
Return on Sales ratio, 18–19, 20–22
    customers', use of, 27–8
Role-playing, 244–6
Roosevelt, Franklin D., 223

Sales
    cost of, 27
    see also Sales Force; Selling
Sales on Capital employed ratio, 19–22
    customers', use of, 28–9
Sales Force
    changing nature and role of, 3–4, 5
    competitive quality and, 2

new skills for, 5–6
use of financial knowledge by, 22, 27–37, 39, 48
checklist for, 49–51
see also Negotiation; Presentations
Seated body language, 200–4
Selling process, 65–71, 83
relation of, to negotiation, 57–63, 75
Service companies, marketing environment of, 1–3
Services
allocation of costs to, 40–41
similarities of, 1–2
Shareholders' funds, 12–13
Silence, 182
Situation analysis, 141–8
Situational questions, 68
Size of companies, 3–4, 9
Soames, Christopher, 178
Soft drinks business, 132–7
Solvency, 14–15
Specifications for products, 2, 133
Spectacles and body language, 207
Stability period for prices, 97
Stances in negotiation, 84–6, 127–8, 129–30
Standards
of performance measurement, 9
worldwide parity of, 2
Standing body language, 205–6
Stocks, 133–4, 135
costs of, 95, 101–3
reduction of, 10, 28
turnover of, 29, 30
valuation of, 15
Stories and anecdotes, 231
Strategies
for negotiation, 127–8, 158–9
for sales, 153, 170
Summary closes, 71
Supplies, reliability of, 132–3

Support, negotiation about, 107–8
SWOT analysis, 149–50, 168

Tactics in negotiation, 128–40
Takeovers, 1, 3–4, 9
Taxation, 31
Technological developments, 36
Telephones, answering, and body language, 189–91
Thinking sequence, 225–6
'Three day week' (1973), 10
Time
commitments to, as concession, 96–8
concern for, and body language, 187–9
use of, 75, 88
Trade Unions, 128
Trading account, 16
Trading of concessions, 129
preparation for, 86–7
Training and education
of buyers, 4
in negotiation, 241–7
Trial closes, 70, 71, 89

'Unimportant' elements in negotiation, 81
Unquantifiable elements in negotiation, 72, 80–81

Variable costs, 40, 41
Visual aids, 233–4
Voice control, 227
Volume of sales
customer concessions in, 95–6
and price concessions, 91–4

Warehousing, 42, 136
Warnings about tactics, 139–40
Weston, Dame Agnes, 230
'Working capital', 15
Workshops and courses in negotiation, 241–7